M000240230

Macroeconomics

Political Economy and Development

Published in association with the
International Initiative for Promoting Political Economy (IIPPE)

Edited by
Ben Fine (SOAS, University of London)
Dimitris Milonakis (University of Crete)

Political economy and the theory of economic and social development have long been fellow travellers, sharing an interdisciplinary and multidimensional character. Over the last 50 years, mainstream economics has become totally formalistic, attaching itself to increasingly narrow methods and techniques at the expense of other approaches. Despite this narrowness, neoclassical economics has expanded its domain of application to other social sciences, but has shown itself incapable of addressing social phenomena and coming to terms with current developments in the world economy.

With world financial crises no longer a distant memory, and neoliberal scholarship and postmodernism in retreat, prospects for political economy have strengthened. It allows constructive liaison between the dismal and other social sciences and rich potential in charting and explaining combined and uneven development.

The objective of this series is to support the revival and renewal of political economy, both in itself and in dialogue with other social sciences. Drawing on rich traditions, we invite contributions that constructively engage with heterodox economics, critically assess mainstream economics, address contemporary developments and offer alternative policy prescriptions.

Also available

Theories of Social Capital:
Researchers Behaving Badly
Ben Fine

The Political Economy of Development:
The World Bank, Neoliberalism and Development Research
Edited by Kate Bayliss, Ben Fine and Elisa Van Waeyenberge

Dot.compradors:
Crisis and Corruption in the Indian Software Industry
Jyoti Saraswati

Beyond the Developmental State:
Industrial Policy into the Twenty-First Century
Edited by Ben Fine, Jyoti Saraswati and Daniela Tavasci

Microeconomics:
A Critical Companion
Ben Fine

Macroeconomics
A Critical Companion

Ben Fine and Ourania Dimakou

PlutoPress
www.plutobooks.com

First published 2016 by Pluto Press
345 Archway Road, London N6 5AA

www.plutobooks.com

Copyright © Ben Fine and Ourania Dimakou 2016

The right of Ben Fine and Ourania Dimakou to be identified as the authors of
this work has been asserted by them in accordance with the Copyright, Designs
and Patents Act 1988.

British Library Cataloguing in Publication Data
A catalogue record for this book is available from the British Library

ISBN   978 0 7453 3687 9   Hardback
ISBN   978 0 7453 3682 4   Paperback
ISBN   978 1 7837 1806 1   PDF ebook
ISBN   978 1 7837 1808 5   Kindle ebook
ISBN   978 1 7837 1807 8   EPUB ebook

This book is printed on paper suitable for recycling and made from fully managed
and sustained forest sources. Logging, pulping and manufacturing processes are
expected to conform to the environmental standards of the country of origin.

Typeset by Stanford DTP Services, Northampton, England

Simultaneously printed in the European Union and United States of America

Contents

List of Boxes   viii
List of Diagrams   ix
List of Abbreviations   x
Preface, Preliminaries and Acknowledgements   xi

1   Macroeconomy versus Macroeconomics?   1
   1.1   Overview   1
   1.2   The Short-Run and Long-Run Syndrome and Beyond   4
   1.3   From What to How   11
   1.4   Further Thoughts and Readings   18

2   Accelerator-Multiplier: Stabbing the Knife-Edge in the Back?   20
   2.1   Overview   20
   2.2   The Model   21
   2.3   The Greater Realism of Eliminating Instability?   28
   2.4   Further Thoughts and Readings   29

3   Classical Dichotomies   31
   3.1   Overview   31
   3.2   Dissecting the Classical Dichotomy   32
   3.3   The Short- and Long-Run and Micro and Macro Dichotomies   41
   3.4   Further Thoughts and Readings   44

4   Growth Theories: Old, New or More of the Same?   46
   4.1   Overview   46
   4.2   Old Growth Theory   47
   4.3   New Growth Theory for Old?   54
   4.4   Growth Econometrics   59
   4.5   Further Thoughts and Readings   64

5   The Keynesian Revolutions   67
   5.1   Overview   67
   5.2   IS/LM as Neoclassical Synthesis   67
   5.3   Reappraising or Reducing Keynes?   74
   5.4   Further Thoughts and Readings   83

6   Post-Keynesian Dilemmas   86
    6.1   Overview   86
    6.2   Post-Keynesianisms?   87
    6.3   Kaldor–Pasinetti Savings   90
    6.4   Post-Keynesianism as Mainstream?   95
    6.5   Further Thoughts and Readings   99

7   Keynesian Revolution: What Keynes, What Revolution?   101
    7.1   Overview   101
    7.2   The Revolution Portrayed or Betrayed?   102
    7.3   Further Thoughts and Readings   107

8   From Monetarist Counter-Revolution to Fundamentalism   108
    8.1   Overview   108
    8.2   From Vertical Phillips Curve ...   109
    8.3   ... to New Classical Economics   112
    8.4   From the Not so Sublime to the Even More Ridiculous   121
    8.5   Further Thoughts and Readings   122

9   Forging the Consensus: Monetary Policy and Real Business
    Cycle Theory   125
    9.1   Overview   125
    9.2   Monetary Policy under the NCE   126
    9.3   Real Business Cycle Theory   132
    9.4   Further Thoughts and Readings   139
    Appendix A: Solution and Calibration of a DSGE Model   141

10 From New Classical Fundamentalism to New Nonsensus
    Macroeconomics   144
    10.1 Overview   144
    10.2 Consensus is Borne ...   146
    10.3 ... and Shattered?   152
    10.4 Further Thoughts and Readings   153
    Appendix B: Surveying the Fundamentals in the
        Three-Equation NCM   155

11 International Macro?   159
    11.1 Overview   159
    11.2 Monetarism and Keynesianism Go International   159
    11.3 Phase Diagrams and Stability Analysis   166
    11.4 Further Thoughts and Readings   170

12 The Enigmas of Overshooting   172
   12.1 Overview   172
   12.2 Inflexible Output and Overshooting   172
   12.3 Overshooting with Keynesian Features   179
   12.4 Further Thoughts and Readings   182
   Appendix C: Does the Dornbusch Overshooting Model Have
       Rational Expectations?   183

13 Whither Macroeconomics?   186
   13.1 Overview   186
   13.2 Further Thoughts and Readings   188

References   189
Index   193

List of Boxes

1.1 Efficient market hypotheses 3
2.1 Adaptive expectations 24
2.2 Difference equations 25
2.3 Difference and differential equations 27
5.1 Ricardian equivalence theorem 85
8.1 Adaptive expectations are behavioural and non-theoretical: the Koyck transformation 114
8.2 From adaptive through rational expectations to econometrics 123
10.1 Models typology: how many new Keynesians are there? 145

List of Diagrams

4.1	Steady-state balanced growth for the Solow–Swan model	49
4.2	Changes in the steady-state balanced growth path from saving ratio increases	50
4.3	Differences in growth paths and adjustments to growth paths	62
5.1	IS/LM curves	69
5.2	Keynesian liquidity trappings	70
5.3	Household pseudo-indifference curves	75
5.4	Households constrained on goods	76
5.5	Households constrained on labour	77
5.6	The constrained household	78
5.7	The constrained firm	79
5.8	Quantity-constrained regimes	80
6.1	Labour supply and demand	96
6.2	Monopoly supply of goods	97
6.3	Monopoly supply of labour	98
6.4	Monopolies of goods and labour	99
8.1	Phillips curve	110
8.2	Friedman's vertical Phillips curve	111
8.3	Adjustment to money supply increase for adaptive and rational expectations	118
11.1	The J-curve	164
11.2	BP curve	165
11.3	IS/LM/BP curves	165
11.4	Trade and employment equilibrium	167
11.5	Labour market adjustment	168
11.6	Trade balance adjustment	169
11.7	Phase diagram and stability	169
11.8	Adjusted and enhanced stability	170
12.1	Phase diagram	177
12.2	Adjustment	177
12.3	Overshooting	178
12.4	Keynesian adjustment	180
12.5	Keynesian overshooting?	181

List of Abbreviations

CD   Classical Dichotomy
DSGE   dynamic stochastic general equilibrium
EMH   Efficient Market Hypothesis
HP   Homogeneity Postulate
IRS   increasing returns to scale
MEC   marginal efficiency of capital
MMEC   monetary marginal efficiency of capital
NCE   New Classical Economics
NCM   New Consensus Macroeconomics
NGT   new growth theory
OGT   old growth theory
PMEC   physical marginal efficiency of capital
RBC   Real Business Cycle
RBE   real balance effects
RWE   real wealth effects
SL   Say's Law
SSBG   steady-state balanced growth
TA^2 technical apparatus and architecture
TFP   total factor productivity
WL   Walras' Law

Preface, Preliminaries
and Acknowledgements

One of the two authors of this book has taught macroeconomics at graduate level for more than 40 years, the other is relatively new to the game, although recently trained. Such a clash of experiences has been fruitful in deciding what to include in this text and how to include it. We have been presented with a number of problems in light of our objectives. First, our readership is liable to be mixed in abilities and knowledge. In general, we expect most of the basics from an undergraduate degree in economics. Even so, we have occasionally reviewed elementary material, partly because it is often improperly understood, and partly because it can look different when presented within a critical and more rounded perspective. For this and other reasons, we have provided a number of boxes dedicated to particular topics to supplement the text. Some are technical, some are not.

Second, economics is (increasingly) technically demanding in terms of mathematical requirements. It is necessary to deploy and command technical material, both as skill acquisition in and of itself and to gain a sense of the nature of economics on the technical terms on which it is so dependent. As a result, many economics textbooks are disproportionately mathematical in content, difficult to follow and negligent of the motivation for, and significance of, one damn model after another. So the difficulty here is to offer some select technical material without it being at the expense of substantive content and serving purely as a goal in its own right. Exactly the same comment has been made regarding the counterpart volume *Microeconomics: A Critical Companion*, where it is probably even more applicable, although macroeconomics is certainly catching up (or even overtaking) given its rapprochement with microeconomics.

Third, macroeconomics in principle covers a vast range of subject matter, although it has fashions of becoming more or less narrow in its scope and preoccupations – ranging over dealing with long-term growth, short-run deviations, crises, the national, the international, and so on. As such, a judicious choice has to be made concerning the breadth and depth of material to be presented.

Fourth, unlike most other texts on macroeconomics, the critical stance adopted here reflects the goal of introducing students to alternative ways of thinking – often ways that were the orthodoxy but have now been discouraged and excluded from students' previous training, often rendering the idea of alternatives and alternative thinking both counterintuitive and subject to resistance if not incomprehension. The approach to this is uneven across the chapters, with greater or lesser attention to the mainstream, the technical material, the critique and what might be alternatives.

Finally, one of the problems in teaching economics in general, and macroeconomics in particular, is that the technical demands can be so heavy upon students that they take up an undue weight of care and attention, in complete disproportion to the significance of what is being communicated. It takes a moment to say that maybe the financial system cannot be reduced to the supply and demand for money but much, much longer to explain how, upon that assumption and others, that New Classical Economics suggests state intervention is ineffective at best (see Chapter 8). But which of these is the more important? Of course, ease of expression and learning is far from the only or main criteria concerning what it is important to cover and how, but there are clearly some trade-offs. It is essential that students of economics are accomplished in the techniques they have been taught, but surely not without simultaneously having developed conceptual understandings and a keen sense of what is important or not, in terms of both what is within the material and what is not.

Essentially, what follows represents a lecture course of 30 hours or more with an almost exclusive focus upon theory as opposed to applied macroeconomics, whether empirically or policy oriented (although we do offer some theoretical coverage of these topics). We would not describe what follows as an alternative or heterodox macroeconomics textbook. We are far from convinced that such a volume is possible or even desirable, reasons for which are given in Chapter 13. In some respects, our goals are both more modest and more ambitious than writing an alternative textbook of macroeconomics, received wisdom or set of models. Rather, by taking the presentation of macroeconomics as it is, or has been, as a critical point of departure, we hope to elaborate its content, reveal its deficiencies and point to the sorts of considerations that need to be incorporated into our understandings of the macroeconomy.

We want to thank, if not in name, those who commented on the text at various stages in its preparation. Thanks also to the team at Pluto, and especially Dan Harding for his meticulous copy-editing. Most of all, though, thanks to the students who have borne the burden of teaching us what to teach them and how best to attempt to do so.

For a slightly fuller prefacing account of the difficulties of teaching economics critically, see the preface to the counterpart *Microeconomics* volume.

Ben Fine is Professor of Economics at the School of Oriental and African Studies, University of London, and holds honorary positions at the Universities of Johannesburg (Senior Research Fellow attached to the South African Research Chair in Social Change), Rhodes University (Visiting Professor, Institute of Social and Economic Research), and Witswatersrand (Associate Researcher, Corporate Strategy and Industrial Development).

Ourania Dimakou is a Lecturer in Economics at School of Oriental and African Studies, University of London.

1
Macroeconomy versus Macroeconomics?

1.1 Overview

The purpose of this chapter is to highlight the nature of mainstream macroeconomics both in terms of substantive content, conceptualisations and methods. Prior to the global financial crisis, it was argued that a wide consensus had been reached in macroeconomics over the passage of the previous 30 years or so, with compromise and convergence between monetarism and Keynesianism. Effectively, what was a consolidation around what is to constitute the prime subject matter of the field and how it should be explored, found a presence not only in academic research, but also across policymaking circles (particularly central banks) and undoubtedly teaching.

What should be acknowledged in this evolution of macroeconomics into the current consensus is a manifold reduction in the scope and method of the study of the macroeconomy, not only relative to previous theorising in classical political economy, but also at the expense of what has been excluded from other approaches at the time that macroeconomics emerged. These include, for example, structural characteristics and processes of the capitalist economy such as monopolisation, distribution of income, role of institutions, sources of productivity change and an integrated view of cycles and growth. This reductionism can be traced at a number of levels, not least through the prominence and division between macroeconomics and microeconomics; the subordination of the former to the latter, particularly, but not exclusively through convergence on general equilibrium; the division and narrow conceptualisation of the short and long runs; and all of this through the corresponding methods of inquiry.

In short, today's New Consensus Macroeconomics (NCM) views its primary object as the study of short-run deviations of macroeconomic aggregates from a given long-run equilibrium. The latter is fixed, whilst the deviations are presumed to be the outcome of exogenous disturbances to an otherwise stable system. Under particular conditions, there may be room for (primarily) monetary policy to stabilise the system. This framing is undertaken by employing a very specific method, noticeably through deductive mathematical and quantitative modelling.

To understand the current state of macroeconomics, the following sections offer a brief overview of the evolution of some important aspects of mainstream theorising in (macro)economics. Whilst macroeconomic theory has offered, occasionally token, differences at particular times, and certainly has done so over time, there are common themes regarding how it has developed in conceiving the workings of the economy as a whole. These include how it should be disaggregated into its constituent parts (its structure), how markets are linked and rendered consistent with one another (an aspect of general equilibrium) and, related but distinct from the last theme, how the macroeconomy is aggregated back up to form a totality. In all these respects, microeconomics has been an increasingly essential influence, notably through the convergence of macroeconomics on general equilibrium and aggregation from optimising individual behaviour, as well as through the ethos of reliance upon formal models and mathematical, deductive reasoning.

Further, how time is treated in macroeconomics, specifically in distinguishing between the short and the long runs, has been conceptualised on many different levels, whilst these have been applied confusedly and interchangeably according to the question at hand. More specifically, short-run factors are narrowly understood, at least in part in order to maintain the distinction between it and the long run, with the latter an umbrella for a broader, but still narrow, range of other factors. This is illustrated, with considerable contemporary relevance, in how money and finance have been conceived within mainstream macroeconomics, with finance assigned predominantly to the domain of microeconomics and lying outside of the short/long-run dichotomy for macroeconomics.

Such neglect of finance in NCM theorising has been dramatically exposed by the financial crisis of the 2000s. It has demonstrated that money and finance cannot be treated as if separate – as if belonging, respectively, to macro and micro – and finance in particular straddles equally questionable dichotomies between short and long runs. Tensions involved between the micro and macro spheres and the role of money and finance are also reproduced in the various versions and concepts of the efficient market hypothesis (discussed in Box 1.1). In short, the crisis has exposed limitations of mainstream macroeconomics that cannot be rectified by simply improving the model, as it is the very methods and framing of the macroeconomy that are at issue. Despite this (and the same point does not apply to money and finance alone but to other great determinants of the macroeconomy that are subject to neglect within macroeconomics), the reaction to these omissions by the mainstream has been business as usual and to set aside the crisis as a cascade of inconvenient truths. This is a habitual vice of the discipline, as will be seen, which is far from uncommon across the history of mainstream economics more generally, and one that is cumulative both intellectually and institutionally in its adoption in both breadth and depth, if not thereby verging on addiction. This is one way, at least, to understand why macroeconomics has (been) driven to such extremes with limited capacity to change let alone reverse direction.

Box 1.1
Efficient market hypotheses

Financial economics in the sphere of microeconomics has been heavily oriented around the efficient market hypothesis (EMH) since the early 1970s, especially under the influence of Eugene Fama's contributions. Significantly, the EMH has been subject to a number of different definitions and interpretations and can be difficult to pin down beyond saying that if markets work efficiently, then they work efficiently. But whatever the conundrums around operational definitions, behind the EMH lies the proposition that stock prices efficiently incorporate and reflect all available relevant information. Consequently, stock markets are impossible to predict (and hence beat), with speculators' profits, if any, being only temporary as any opportunities to make excessive profits will be competed away by other traders with comparable information to those doing better. More specifically, the EMH has been interpreted and tested in at least three different forms. In its weakest form, prices reflect all past (historical) information, while the semi-strong version conjectures that all new information is quickly absorbed and signalled through asset prices. Finally, in its strongest form, asset prices simply follow a random walk, and so are entirely unpredictable, merely reflecting, at any point in time, not only past but all public *and* private information (that is, not even insiders' private information can systematically beat the market – since other traders can follow the lead of those doing well even though we might reasonably believe this to be the source of speculative busts and booms rather than efficiency).

At the heart of the EMH rest neoclassical presumptions about rational expectations and calculable risk as well as perfect and complete information dissemination. More importantly, with financial markets viewed as the means of mobilising and allocating resources in the real economy, the EMH further postulates that asset prices are correctly valued, in the sense that they reflect the model's (the real economy's?) equilibrium prices (i.e. fundamental values). Hence, any deviations from the equilibrium prices will be random (rather than systematic). Despite these propositions having been open to dispute on their own terms, the vast financial deregulation that was witnessed from the 1970s helped to support the case for the supposed efficiency of financial markets. Inevitably, the EMH consolidated the reduction of macroeconomics to microeconomics, of finance to money (supply) within macroeconomics, and the presence of econometric estimation in place of theory.

1.2 The Short-Run and Long-Run Syndrome and Beyond

The division within economics between macroeconomics and microeconomics is well established and dominates the discipline in such a way that everything else, with the exception of the increasingly prominent econometrics, is a special subject or an option in teaching and, to some extent, research. Everyone does macro and micro, and econometrics, but no other field is compulsory in the same way and to the same extent. Even so, this conventional division, and form of hegemony and privilege, within the discipline is relatively new. It derives from the rise of Keynesianism in the 1930s, partly in response to the Great Depression. This gave us macroeconomics: an explicitly constructed concern with the workings of the economy as a whole, with a focus on the causes, cures and, if more occasionally, the consequences of massive unemployment.

Such a specification of macroeconomics left open a considerable space for other fields of study on which to focus. These can be loosely divided into two categories. One is equally concerned with the functioning of the economy as a whole but with issues overlapping with, but distinct from, the determinants of (un)employment and other, what would now be thought of as, Keynesian macroeconomic aggregates such as prices and output. Thus, economics can, and no doubt should, concern itself with the role of institutions, the distribution of income and wealth, the sources of technological change, monopolisation and formation of large-scale corporations, and trade unions, quite apart from problems of development and change around the world. The second, apparently much more mundane, category is the study of parts of the economy in isolation from the bigger picture, whether it be a household, an industry or a firm.

The second category is what has given us microeconomics. Not entirely by chance, it was in the process of being established, if with somewhat earlier origins than Keynesianism, in the 1930s, having gained a huge impetus from the marginalist revolution of the 1870s which gave birth to methods and concepts that are now familiar, such as marginal utility, marginal product and marginal cost, individual optimisation, and efficiency and equilibrium, and much more besides. The consolidation of microeconomics, alongside macroeconomics, as constituting the core of the discipline (with econometrics barely on the scene at this time) was completed in the second decade after the Second World War, not least with advances in general equilibrium theory.

With these three categories, macroeconomics, microeconomics and everything else, it is important to acknowledge that their weight within the discipline and the boundaries between them have not remained fixed. For boundaries there has been a double shift, with an uneven pace and incidence since the 1950s. One has been the increasing subordination of macroeconomics to microeconomics. The other has been the marginalisation of the 'everything else' category in terms of its methods, theories and conceptualisations except where it has been incorporated into microeconomics (or possibly an increasingly, micro-like macro). Development economics, for example, has been declared by some, indeed an increasing number, as not requiring separate methods to those applied to developed economies. After all, effective demand is effective demand wherever it prevails, as is the optimising behaviour of individuals. The (initial) conditions might be different but the principles remain the same. Much the same applies to one 'optional' field after another within the curriculum.

There is, however, a bit of a paradox across this outcome. As observed, the emergence of, and division between, macro and micro arose out of particular focuses on particular problems (unemployment for macro, optimising behaviour in supply and demand for micro) and could do so only by neglecting other considerations, the concern of the other fields. Having established themselves, however, micro and macro have increasingly turned their attention to incorporating those other concerns that they had studiously avoided in order to get themselves up and running in the first place.

Of course, it may well be that by some hugely fortunate, intellectual accident the principles discovered by micro and macro via this route do, indeed, have a much broader and legitimate scope of application, specifically to subject matter beyond their original intent. This is, however, more than questionable. At the very least, it has to be acknowledged that the micro/macro divide, far from being a dynamic duo, only broadens its scope of application by excluding, and even precluding, other methods, theories, concepts and factors from consideration.

This is going far beyond the subject matter of this text, which is concerned with macroeconomics alone. But the point can be illustrated by considering what is or should be the subject matter of macroeconomics. On the one hand, especially for the uninitiated, it might be thought that the subject of macroeconomics would be the analysis of the workings of the economy as a whole. On the other hand, there is macroeconomics as it is constituted as an academic discipline which is seen to be considerably narrower than the previous definition. Following the Keynesian revolution, macroeconomics primarily became the study of short-run deviations in employment and output, together with other macroeconomic aggregates such as the general price level, around what has been generally taken to be a given trend, or even an equilibrium. More than occasionally, macroeconomics may stray into wider domains, such as growth, but these have become and remained far from central to the vast bulk of macroeconomics. Indeed, in many respects growth theory has stronger affinities to microeconomics than even to a narrowly defined macroeconomics.

This point can be made in a different way. Macroeconomics as the study of the workings of the economy as a whole long predates, if not in name, macroeconomics as currently constituted. The classical political economy of Smith, Ricardo and Marx, for example, certainly addressed the issue. But they did so with very different methods, concepts and objects of study, not least with a preoccupation with classes, distribution, the pace of accumulation and technical change and, indeed, whether capitalist growth could be sustained indefinitely. So, paradoxically, the emergence of macroeconomics as a commanding field within economics had the perverse effect of narrowing down what has been considered to be the workings of the economy as a whole, and not only in relation to what came before in the nineteenth century but also in relation to the 'other' economics that was present at the birth of macroeconomics itself, concerned with business cycles, institutions, distribution, technical change, monopolisation and so on.

Further, the process of narrowing the scope of macroeconomics, whilst marked by a distinct leap with the initial emergence of Keynesianism, has strengthened subsequently. It has done so through three processes that will be highlighted throughout the rest of this text. First has been the increasing attachment of macroeconomics to general equilibrium. This does itself have two distinct elements. On the one hand, there is the issue of consistency in the treatments of markets and market behaviour in the aggregate. Specifically, every (intended) sale must correspond to an (intended) purchase or, if interest is paid, someone else must receive it. Such reliance upon what is known as Walras' Law (or Say's Law in the absence of money, see Chapter 3), ties macroeconomics to general equilibrium. The contrast is with partial equilibrium in which, for example, the use of inputs by a producer, through which revenue accrues to the supplier, is examined no further.

Significantly, if not necessarily logically as a separate step, the consistency across all markets attached to Walras' Law, understood as the balance between supplies and demands in aggregate, is readily envisaged to lead to the presumption that all markets are linked through prices as a matter of adjustment, nominally over time, if out of equilibrium. Walrasian adjustment is one in which prices increase where there is excess demand and fall where there is excess supply. As is well known, as a consequence of developments within general equilibrium theory itself, it cannot be assumed except under stringent conditions that Walrasian adjustment will lead to equilibrium (let alone that it exists, and is unique and efficient). There is also the issue of whether production and trading take place before or after prices have had a chance to adjust to their equilibrium values (raising what is known as Hicksian false trading). The model of such Walrasian adjustment is explicitly seen as relying upon a Walrasian 'fictional' auctioneer, one who calls prices, assesses supplies and demands, and adjusts prices until they are correct. The problem is that we need the fiction, as so-called perfect competition depends upon everyone being a price-taker so there is no one to make the prices. James Meade, a Nobel Prize winner like John Hicks, who also invented the Keynesian IS/LM framework (see Chapter 5) wondered what the price of coffee would be, whilst traders were waiting for the auctioneer to decide their true equilibrium values.

So there is plenty of prestige behind the questioning of the validity of Walrasian adjustment for understanding the workings of the macroeconomy. As with many other such conundrums, despite increasing reliance upon general equilibrium, macroeconomics has tended to ignore whatever mathematical or technical results derived from it that are unpalatable for its model building. But the Walrasian architecture of equilibrium and adjustment has increasingly become part and parcel of macroeconomics, focusing on how supply and demand are formed and adjust around quantities and prices, on the basis of given preferences, resources and technologies, in conditions of greater or lesser competitiveness or market (im)perfections. Other issues profoundly affecting the macroeconomy tend to be excluded by a Walrasian framing drawn from general equilibrium.

To a large extent, then, whilst it is more or less taken for granted in principle, if not always in practice, that macroeconomics needs to incorporate Walras' Law, it is a moot point whether such corresponding consistency in the analysis of markets as a whole dominates much that has been excluded from macroeconomic analysis. Be this as it may, it is important to recognise that commitment to Walras' Law is entirely independent of the underlying theories of supply and demand over which it exerts its command. For, on the other hand, in the convergence of macroeconomics on general equilibrium there is the separate increasing reliance upon aggregating over optimising individuals as the foundation for macroeconomics. In short, and as a second overall feature of macroeconomics, it has increasingly become subordinated to microeconomics (with general equilibrium in the lead in this respect but not exclusively so).

These different aspects of the second theme (the convergence upon general equilibrium) is all related to the third theme running through the evolution of macroeconomics – how it relates the short run to the long run. Here, it is important to be careful over three different ways in which the distinction between the short and the long run are made. One, and the most obvious and common in popular parlance, is to refer simply to the passage of time. Clearly the short happens before the long run, although the two are ultimately connected to one another with the passage of time itself.

Second distinguishing short and long runs is also related to the passage of time but, in addition, includes in part an empirical and in part a theoretical content. After all, it is traditional within economics to place variables in a hierarchy of the speeds with which they are presumed to adjust. For a firm, for example, it is considered relatively easier and quicker to vary the level of output, although this might create strains until more employment is taken on. This is itself easier and quicker to vary than installing new capital equipment in order to be able to respond more fully and easily to increased demand. Accordingly, output is deemed to respond in the very short run, employment in the short run, and capital in the long run. Other variables, such as institutions, might be taken to change even more slowly. However, this hierarchy of variables by speed of adjustment is not merely an empirical matter of how quickly things change in practice, as this can itself vary by time and circumstance. Rather, the relative speed of adjustment of variables also reflects theoretical choices, with one of the biggest differences in this respect being between Keynesianism and monetarism: the former considers that outputs can adjust very quickly (to demand), whereas the latter considers that prices will adjust quickly to equate supply and demand at full employment.

The third notion of the long run as opposed to the short run has nothing to do with time as such. It is simply the definition of equilibrium where all variables are assumed to have had the opportunity to change, whereas not all can change for the short run. There can be no presumption that movement to such an equilibrium takes place through time. And, indeed, the parameters that define this long-run equilibrium, or even the structure of the economy itself, however defined, might change faster than any passage to the equilibrium itself.

It is characteristic of mainstream macroeconomics to use these very different notions of short and long runs interchangeably. This is precisely what allows for the short run to be understood as deviations around a long-run equilibrium which is both unchanging and unaffected by what happens in the short run. This is so even though, for example, the short run involves variability in levels of investment that surely have an impact on 'long-run' productive capacity and productivity.

But this incoherence around the short and long runs are of much deeper consequence because of the associated narrowness with which short-run factors are themselves understood in part in order to sustain its putative relationship with the long run. Of necessity, those factors that are incorporated into such macroeconomics, and how they are incorporated, conform to how the short and long runs are conceived and related to one another. The point can be illustrated by reference to how money and finance are treated in mainstream macro-economics. Money is predominantly seen as a simple asset that also serves to transmit income into demand through serving as a means of payment. Typically, the demand for and (fixed) supply of money are set to be equal with one another. Finance, on the other hand, in terms of the mobilisation and allocation of resources for investment, is primarily seen as residing (with efficiency taken for granted) at the microeconomic level and is set aside in examining short and long runs (see Box 1.1).

Such a perspective has been cruelly exposed by the global crisis of the 2000s (as admitted to some extent by economists). As analysed by a variety of approaches across heterodox economics, deploying the term financialisation, the global crisis has been closely related to the excessive expansion of financial markets for speculative purposes at the expense of what might be termed both real investment and its effectiveness. In short, financialisation has witnessed a disproportionate expansion of finance relative to GDP (this ratio has roughly grown three times over the last 30 years) and has a number of features, such as: involving a proliferation of different types of speculative assets increasingly removed from real economic activity; witnessing the penetration of finance into ever more areas of economic and social life; and having a profound effect on the distribution of income and wealth, with a corresponding strengthening of the economic, political, ideological and institutionalised power of finance (usually denoted by the term neoliberalism).

Of course, this is far from offering a full account of what financialisation is and what has been its impact and significance for contemporary capitalism. But it suffices to expose the limitations of a mainstream macroeconomics organised around independent short and long runs and general equilibrium. And, whilst this has been forcibly exposed by the global crisis through the unavoidable example of the treatment of money and finance within mainstream macroeconomics, this is only the tip of the iceberg as far as other topics are concerned, which make the same point either because they are ill-treated or absent from the mainstream, such as distribution, monopoly, technical change, conflict and the exercise of power, and the role of institutions, especially the state.

However, if these issues are brought to bear, and are highlighted by the global crisis, the huge divide between what macroeconomics is and what it ought to be is readily emphasised. Just before the crisis, or even after it had begun to break, macroeconomics was congratulating itself on having learned how to deal with what were taken primarily to be the consequences of random shocks on the stability and prosperity of the economy. In its wake, little has changed in the theory other than to have lost its self-confidence and complacency whilst policy measures, such as quantitative easing taken to the extreme of minimal interest rates, have proven powerless to restore sustained growth, not least as austerity measures have also been relied upon after a brief flirtation with some Keynesian stimulus.

This is all particularly striking and even paradoxical given that the 'fundamentals' underpinning the economy have been so favourable. Fundamentals might be thought to refer to levels of deficits and the like, but at a more fundamental level – the fundamental 'fundamentals' as it were, related to underlying material conditions – the prospects for the global economy have been extraordinarily strong both over the last 30 years of relatively slow growth compared to the post-war boom and into the current crisis. To be specific, if simply listing and unduly overgeneralising for brevity, the following features have been most favourable for capitalist growth: the capacity for productivity increase arising out of a huge diversity and range of application of new technologies; the decline in the strength and organisation of working class and progressive movements, especially across trade unions, political parties and anti-imperial struggles; huge increases in the global labour force through migration, the Chinese road to capitalism and increasing female labour market participation; high levels of advanced country cooperation under the hegemony of the USA, not least with the collapse of the Soviet bloc; and the triumph of neoliberalism, not least in the form of containment of the social as well as the monetary wage.

The point to emphasise, then, is two-fold: that the short and long runs are inseparable and that the factors that underpin them tend to be absent from mainstream macroeconomics. This point is further reinforced once account is taken of broader institutional considerations. There can be little doubt that the neoliberal ideology of targeting minimal state intervention and leaving as much as possible, especially finance, to the free market has taken something of a battering in the wake of the global crisis, if only possibly token and temporary. For the policy responses in practice have remained extraordinarily timid and limited in scope. If, for example, the state is making a comeback, it certainly is not along the lines experienced during the post-war boom when Keynesian macroeconomic policies were complemented by a whole, arguably more important, sheaf of interventionist policies around health, education, welfare, and industrial and regional development.

Rather, as symbolised by 'quantitative easing', the top priority is to restore the viability of the financial system. This is accompanied at most by weakening and token deference to reregulation and the clawing back of disproportionate rewards to those in the financial sector. Stimulus to effective demand has primarily been adopted in the mildest forms of Keynesianism through monetary policy whilst directed fiscal stimuli take a back seat (or are thrown off the transport altogether, as the deficits that have accompanied support to finance dictate austerity measures to cover interest payments to the very financial system that has created the problem and had, accordingly, to be rescued). This is all despite what is a unique characteristic of the current crisis: the common acceptance that it is in general, if with notable exceptions, in no way due to excessive wage demands or state expenditure to furnish a social wage. Nonetheless, the blameless in working and social conditions are being hit very hard by recession and austerity.

One reason for this has already been identified, in terms of the favourability of conditions for macroeconomic performance – the weakness of progressive movements that are, in turn, more aligned to state intervention. In addition and equally, though, the last 30 years has witnessed the emergence, growth, strengthening and institutionalisation within governance and beyond of financial elites at domestic and international levels. This implies not only particular sets of policies towards promoting private capital both directly, through privatisation for example, and indirectly through fiscal austerity, but also the transformation of the capacity to conceive and formulate alternative policies themselves.

Are such factors no less important than the more conventionally conceived 'fundamentals'?

The nature and significance of these factors has been heavily debated across the social sciences, not least under the rubric of what is perceived to have been a shift towards neoliberalism (although some deny that this is a useful way to understand our current predicament). What stands out, other than the acknowledged shift in balance from Keynesian to monetarist perspectives, is that neoliberalism might just as well not exist as far as macroeconomics is concerned – other than as a shift towards more austere policies and in suggesting policymaking itself is being made independently of political pressures through an independent central bank (itself something of a myth). That neoliberalism might be something more and deeper than shifts in policy and policymaking, incorporating financialisation and its direct and indirect effects, for example, is simply unconsidered. Once again, this is indicative of the reduced way in which the macroeconomy is conceived both in terms of what it is and why it is that way. Thus, there clearly is a close relationship between financialisation and neoliberalism and, without specifying it exactly, the implication is that macroeconomic performance does, and macroeconomic analysis should, both specify that relationship and its implications over short and long runs and how they interact with one another. But it is precisely such issues that are precluded by the mainstream.

1.3 From What to How

The developments in the subject matter of macroeconomics and the divide and prevalence of the micro/macro duo are heavily intertwined with developments in the methods (and underlying methodological stances) deployed in the study of the (macro)economy. This is so not least because the methods and specific techniques adopted ended up, to some large extent, defining the subject matter of (macro)economics and, even more so, the basis of economic scientific endeavour.

By methods in economic enquiry we refer to particular systematic ways and techniques through which the subject under study is analysed. Although different methods can be viewed and employed independently from the overall research agenda, they inevitably reflect a particular stance on how the nature of the realm under study, and the nature of the knowledge that can be generated, are perceived. Although the aim of this section is not to provide a thorough analysis on such profound and controversial philosophical issues, it is essential to examine the main characteristics of the theoretical and organising concepts and the methods that underpin the evolution in the scope and the overall research programme of macroeconomics.

Ever since the marginalist revolution at the end of the nineteenth century and the break from classical political economy, economics began to deploy different methods for the study of its subject matter. The particular conceptualisation of how the economic system can be understood and studied brought forth theoretical concepts and methods that are all too familiar today, as epitomised by the (rational) optimising individual as the basic unit of analysis in an economy viewed as feeding into a series of market relations, organised around the concepts of rationality, equilibrium and efficiency.

Such a perception of the nature of the world (reality) and its analysis led to the establishment of economics as a distinct discipline relative to the other social sciences, and to the first in a series of steps narrowing its subject matter and method. On the one hand, the focus on the self-interested, transhistorical individual (be it a household, a firm, a state or a nation) that expresses itself through a series of concrete, calculable optimising actions in market transactions took the historical, political and social realms out of the picture. Such a methodological perspective removed consideration of bigger issues dominant in classical political economy, such as wealth and capital accumulation or distribution of income among classes, and established the study of the economy from the prism of its individual components, themselves defined narrowly as maximising (utility, profits and so on) agents with given preferences, endowments and technologies. On the other hand, and as a second dimension of reductionism, such an understanding led to theories and concepts being examined through more and more deductive and axiomatic modes of reasoning. That is, making a set of assumptions (for example, rational optimising individuals) and reaching a set of conclusions through mathematical reasoning, and moving away from inductive and historical methods based on close empirical observation and correspondingly open and contextually generated theory. Such a shift in method raises profound issues with the realism (however understood) of theories, as it privileges deductive reasoning (on the basis of questionable assumptions) and internal logical consistency above all else, and thereby narrows the boundaries of economic questions to be explored and the methods by which to explore them.

During the interwar period, and along this process of establishing the marginalist principles and methods, there were other distinct approaches to economics. Old institutional and applied economics were more grounded on empirical and inductive methods and focused on broader issues of monopolisation, distribution of income, labour relations and so on. In the wake of the Great Depression, Keynes' work came to offer both a response to the phenomenon of massive unemployment and an (at least implicit) attack on the prevailing marginalist theories that were unable to address let alone explain it. With optimising individuals and firms, however constrained, an equilibrium is always obtained in principle, and unemployment, if it exists, can only be voluntary if not deliberately obstructed. That is, the organising concept of equilibrium (as market clearing) among optimising units precludes, by construction, such phenomena as unemployment and the need to explain them other than as market inefficiencies.

With Keynes, the emergence of macroeconomics as a distinct field did not stop the parallel development of microeconomics along the lines discussed above with an increasing implosion upon its own concepts and methods. It was at that same time in the early 1930s that economics came to be defined as the science of the allocation of scarce resources across competing ends, although it would take a couple of decades before this was readily accepted as such. Keynes' call for a separate distinct field of enquiry did entail a change in both the focus of study and in methods. Keynes, in particular, adopted a more inductive reasoning driven by empirical observation of mass unemployment, and viewed the economy as a holistic entity that could not be decomposed into, nor derived from, its highly disaggregated constituent parts. Given such a methodological stance, new theoretical (effective demand, fundamental uncertainty, liquidity preference, marginal efficiency of capital, etc.) and organising (equilibrium as a state of rest, rather than market clearing) concepts reflect a methodological break with marginalist theory. Whilst retaining (or even exacerbating) the division between short and long runs, with the former treated as deviations around a fixed long run, Keynes' holistic approach emphasised the role of effective aggregate demand for macroeconomic activity. Rejecting Say's Law, he focused on the role of speculative finance in bringing about inadequate levels of investment, output and employment. An equally important contribution was the conceptualisation of expectations based on the notion of fundamental uncertainty rather than (probabilistically) calculable risk. Keynes himself was also opposed to two of the analytical techniques that have, nonetheless, become standard tools: mathematical modelling (except for clarifying explanation) and the use of econometrics for policy predictions. The inadequacy of such methods is directly related to his stance on the notion of the future state of the world and its systemic uncertainty.

Despite the distinctive features of Keynesian economics (and especially of Keynes' thought itself), the deductive/mathematical methods associated with microeconomics made a leap forward immediately after the Second World War with macroeconomics as well, through what has been termed the formalist revolution. During the post-war boom, such macro and micro levels evolved separately, allowing for compromise across continuing methodological dissonances. Intellectually, though, this conceded methodological ground to microeconomics as set out in general equilibrium theory, and paved the way in principle for macroeconomics to become subordinated to microeconomics, as eventually occurred after the collapse of the post-war boom and the monetarist counter-revolution of the 1970s.

In particular, first economics did become more technical, not least in the form of a disassociation (or eclectic association) between theory and application/evidence. Theory was to be thought of, and constructed in, the form of models, which were then to be 'confronted with the data' in very particular, if not narrow, ways. The terminological shift from theories to models and from empirical observation to data is not accidental. For theory became synonymous with model building, with a set of assumptions more or less loosely based on marginalist principles and logical (mathematical) reasoning leading to corresponding outcomes. The shift from evidence to data pertains to both the way empirical observation is conceptualised and constructed (as solely quantifiable measures) and the way it is related to theory, in verifying (or not) the predictions of the models.

Second, and putting aside the degree of axiomatisation, mathematical model building was increasingly removed from representing reality to become preoccupied with its own internal needs, answering in very particular ways its own questions. Indicative of this is the proof of existence of general equilibrium, which was achieved on the basis of a set of very restrictive (or unrealistic) assumptions, such as no increasing returns to scale, a high degree of gross substitutability across all goods and services, existence of forward markets for all goods and services, and many more. Nonetheless, the realism of such conditions necessary to guarantee the existence of a general equilibrium occupied a position of secondary importance in the search for a tractable solution. What is even more striking is that preoccupation with general equilibrium has entailed two further internal problems that have been tackled with limited success, if not set aside altogether – notably uniqueness and stability of the discovered equilibrium. Particularly for the latter, considerations of the dynamics of the modelled system have been muted. In other words, answering the question 'Does there exist a general equilibrium in the model economy so constructed? superseded another: 'How is the equilibrium coming about?' It is along these lines that the disassociation from real economic issues widened. Not only does the existence proof not directly translate into any sort of equilibrium existing in reality, but it also ignores analysis of how the equilibrium could materialise (and how likely this is), or the conditions (assumptions) under which this could possibly happen. This became a common feature in most subsequent model building, whereby arbitrary assumptions are considered unimportant relative to meeting the internal needs of the model itself, this method being perceived as 'rigorous' because of its mathematical form and reasoning, and not because of the (ignored) validity of its premises nor its representation of reality.

Third, parallel to such mathematical modelling were the emergence of statistical/econometric methods, together with the increasing availability of statistical data. Driven by the same eagerness for more 'rigorous' quantitative work, the economic system (both for each variable and for relationships among variables) became increasingly viewed as a set of random (probabilistic) distributions. Under this approach, new econometrics methods were developed for the study of the economy and its supposed statistical properties, and as the means for testing the predictions of theories. Statistical analysis was not only confined to the study of macroeconomic aggregates or the estimation of an empirical relationship, but also served to provide testing techniques for the verification of models through a hypothetic-deductive mode of confirmation. Theoretical models became considered useful only to the extent that they could lead to testable hypotheses and predictions, and econometric techniques were deemed to accomplish this. Therefore econometrics became increasingly prominent, whilst this parallel development strengthened the relationship between mainstream economics and econometric analysis more generally. And economics became wedded to instrumental positivism. Models are viewed purely as instruments and, consequently, their assumptions – as merely raw materials for deductive reasoning – are not relevant for testing. Rather, it is only the predictions of the models that should be liable to ex post testing and empirical refutation.

This is a short exposition of the building blocks of the form taken by the deductive and empirical testing methods that were developing from the 1950s onwards, until being established at the core of modern 'scientifically rigorous' macroeconomics. Soon after the Keynesian revolution, attempts to mould Keynes's work into this frame of analysing the macroeconomy arose. Starting from the IS/LM framework (or neoclassical synthesis, see Chapter 5) Keynesian economics increasingly diverged from its original inspiration, particularly in terms of methods but also content. Models with (more or less) Keynesian insights were developed both theoretically and empirically along these lines.

With the demise of Keynesianism and the rise of monetarism and New Classical Economics (NCE), these methods and techniques were rendered both more universal and systematic by their own criteria, as an orthodoxy was consolidated with general equilibrium to the fore and added theoretical elements, notably rational expectations. With the 1980s came Real Business Cycle (RBC) theory (see Chapter 9), as the extreme complement of NCE, consolidating mathematical and statistical modelling under the sparsest application of microeconomic principles. Formalism was further enhanced, and the aim and content of the research programme became more explicit and more quantitative. The ultimate goal was to fit the stylised facts, themselves defined as observed statistical properties of macroeconomic aggregates. And in the consensus that came about after the 1990s, whereby the RBC paradigm is selectively tempered by the addition of one or other new Keynesian (market imperfection) elements (see Chapter 10), the methods were reinforced and routinised. Advanced mathematical and quantitative techniques formed the core of economics teaching. Macroeconomics, as the study of short-run deviations, themselves caused by exogenous shocks around a given long-run trend, are analysed under the rubric of the dynamic stochastic general equilibrium (DSGE) paradigm. This is an umbrella of mathematical models that command full convergence on general equilibrium from microfoundations in a 'dynamic' context. The long-run equilibrium is static and fixed whilst the dynamic element focuses predominantly and narrowly on individual optimisation over time. The DSGE framework can be viewed as an extension of the static analysis of the general equilibrium first fully forged in the 1950s. However, it itself remains static in nature, in the sense that the dynamics of the equilibrium (how the equilibrium is caused in the first place and why it cannot change) are left unaddressed. Dynamics is solely understood as the study of short-run deviations around a long-run static equilibrium.

Leaving aside a detailed debate on methodological issues and methods, it still follows that the methods increasingly being adopted led to two paradoxical implications. The same progressively narrow methods that elevated economics to supposed 'scientific' status, and thereby distinguished it from the other social sciences, also led to the narrowing of its subject matter and substantive content.

But it is important to acknowledge that the second implication is not a consequence exclusively of formalism, although it certainly eased the way. For whilst there is nothing wrong with mathematics per se, which can indeed clarify exposition, there are limits on what can be analysed through mathematical models, and this applies equally to concepts, analytical categorisations and relationships among concepts. There is an innate difficulty in modelling systemic factors and processes, and mathematical functions entail a universality and stability of relationships that are unacceptable in terms of applicability to social phenomena and relations, let alone processes and social change. However, with the theoretical premise of social (or macro) phenomena being solely derived from the individual optimising behaviour that brought them about, it made sense to analyse them through mathematical representations. To look at it the other way around, commitment to a particular form of mathematical modelling implies a particular form of theoretical and conceptual content.

As mentioned already, the increasing formalism of macroeconomics, and mainstream economics more generally, insulates its theory from reality by universally applicable and self-serving mathematical models. However, the basis of empirical evidence by which theories can be tested needs to presume that evidence (data) is independent from theory. And such a presumption is invalid. Evidence cannot be collected in a theoretical or conceptual vacuum. However consciously, measurement constructs are derived from the analytical categories of theories, themselves underpinned by ontological stances. This applies both to quantitative variables (for instance, GDP being defined and measured only over goods and services that have a market price, reflecting the theory's focus on the exchange sphere, or the delineation between consumption, production and investment in national accounts), and to qualitative variables (such as corruption, trust and rule of law, as such unquantifiable phenomena enter into the theoretical sphere). Beyond the measurement problem, with the advance and prominence of statistics/econometrics, statistical methods applied to reveal the properties of the data are also contingent on the theories that generate the need for them to be examined in those terms; be it on how we distinguish among the cyclical, secular and stochastic components of aggregate time series, how we extract the long-run trend, how we deal with endogeneity/ simultaneity or how we estimate expectations. So, for instance, extracting the long-run trend for a data series (say GDP) is driven by the theoretical presupposition of the distinction between short and long runs, or the simultaneity problem is an econometric concern derived from general (as opposed to partial) equilibrium theory. Simply put, data are not objective nor exogenously given. Thus, testing for a theory's conformity with observable reality, whilst the latter is itself a by-product of the former, is unavoidably problematic.

This is not to set aside the usefulness of empirical work, only to emphasise how it is positioned with, and serves, the mainstream within its own orbit or self-serving terms of reference. Lack of realism of assumptions as a matter of principle (although assumptions are also occasionally sought to be justified) is not a promising starting point. Paradoxically, if not perversely, the fact that there is necessarily so much unrecognised ambiguity, and even incoherence, in the relationship between theory and evidence in the mainstream has even allowed it to disregard evidence of its own theoretical deficiencies, as the procedure of testing and rejecting theories is rarely followed through in practice. This is so because it is more or less impossible to refute theories (models) by empirical testing methods, not least because theoretical assumptions can be modified and empirical evidence reformulated.

The inefficacy of the testing techniques could not have been more exposed with the financial crisis of the 2000s, whereby the events since 2007 have shown the deficiencies of orthodox macroeconomics on the grounds of its own methods of testing theories (DSGE models were predicting anything other than a crisis, and data were verifying this up until it happened). Such a 'grand' refutation of the predominant theory should have surely led to some paradigm shift (as, for instance, occurred with the demise of Keynesianism and its displacement by monetarism in the 1970s). Nonetheless, and despite some lively discussion and critical reflections within the academic profession, a closer look demonstrates at most a mild reconsideration, particularly in the role of finance and the need to include the financial sector into an otherwise unchanged DSGE form of modelling. That is, refinements at the technical level were considered without sufficient critical reflection on the methods, techniques and aims of the research programme as a whole as opposed to minor modifications to its individual parts (not least by throwing in market and behavioural imperfections). In short, mainstream macroeconomics has been casual in its theoretical and empirical methods, and these even seem to be mutually supportive as such – at least in practice if not in principle.

1.4 Further Thoughts and Readings

To reiterate, the point here is not to give a detailed analysis of methods and their appropriateness – itself a subject of profound debate on philosophical, ontological and epistemological levels. Rather, the point is to highlight that the methods that have been adopted in mainstream macroeconomics are instrumental to both the implications and the conclusions per se in (macro) economic theory, and to the scope and nature of the recommendations that can be derived from such an approach to analysing the economy. The specific methods increasingly and uncritically adopted in macroeconomics (and indeed microeconomics) are implied by and condition the substantive content of the economic theories put forward, and consequently the problems and solutions that can and cannot be proposed. In short, at every level of method, theory and concept, it is necessary to be at least as mindful of what macroeconomics leaves out as what it includes, with the latter totally dominating the former.

As will be seen in the chapters that follow, the narrowness of the methodological stance of mainstream (macro)economics and its theoretical and organising concepts can to some extent explain the equally narrow understanding of the economic system, its systemic processes and its main agencies. This can be seen, for example, in terms of policy recommendations and the insistence on at most the regulatory role of the state since, as a science of choice, all that is needed is to change (individual) incentives appropriately – evident in pretty much all spheres of the system (markets) – with high minimum wages and generous unemployment benefits presumed to distort incentives in labour supply; with high (capital) taxation distorting incentives to invest; with patents improving incentives to innovate, and so on, bringing us to the crisis of the 2000s with some recognition of needing to tame financial markets incentives from excessive risk taking.

The extent of preoccupation with instrumentalism and commitment to the predictive power and accuracy of the theory accounts for a reduction in explanatory power, since models and whichever (causal?) mechanisms they lay down are treated as mere instruments for the purposes of fitting stylised facts (or event regularities). To the extent of insistence on formalism (of a specific mathematical type), social phenomena and concepts are reduced to fit a rigid theoretical premise and a method which requires concrete, universal and measureable definitions, whilst other concepts are excluded (until rendered in the required form).

By the same token, questions of the type 'If not this model, then which one?' that have indeed been increasingly raised in the aftermath of the crisis, and are continually raised by students, are themselves misplaced, not least as macroeconomics itself is being misconceived. Certainly, judging models by their predictive power is limited if not fallacious not only as it ignores explanatory power and substantive understanding of the object under study, but also as the empirical evidence to be tested against cannot be theoretically empty. Evaluating among different theories (that have distinct ontological positions) inevitably means looking at varieties of alternatives with distinct conceptualisations, distinct understandings of the nature of the social, economic and historical, and essentially different explanations that themselves need not be thought of as being the same across time and space. So, the aim of this book is not to discover the best united or universal theory, but rather to acknowledge the limitations of mainstream macroeconomic thinking both from within its own narrow terms, but also from the point of view of other approaches and their relevance to differences in place and time, in deference to the 'macroeconomic' context.

On the relationship between short and long runs, see Sanfilippo (2011) and Schmid (2010). On economics in the wake of the crisis, see Spaventa (2009), Krugman (2009), Buiter (2009), Besley (2011), Blanchard et al. (2010), Blanchard et al. (eds) (2012) and McCombie and Pike (2013). For some account of the history of macroeconomics, see Fine (1998, chapter 2) and de Vroey and Malgrange (2011). On financialisation, see Fine (2012). See Ball (2009) for a defence of the efficient market hypothesis post-crisis, but Guerrien and Gun (2011) and Crotty (2011) for criticisms and alternatives. On discussion of methods in economics, see Blaug (2003) and chapter 3 in Backhouse and Fontaine (eds) (2010). For a discussion on the main characteristics of neoclassical economics see Arnsperger and Varoufakis (2006), and Lawson (2013) and Fine (2016) for a critique.

For much on the evolution of microeconomics and its influence on macroeconomics, see counterpart volume *Microeconomics: A Critical Companion*.

2
Accelerator-Multiplier: Stabbing the Knife-Edge in the Back?

2.1 Overview

The first, simple contribution to what was to become Keynesian economics was developed in the early 1930s by Richard Kahn, a colleague of Keynes. It is the simple multiplier. As generations of students have learned, $Y = I/s$, where Y is income, I investment and s the propensity to save, with $1/s$ being the simple multiplier of impact of autonomous or exogenous expenditure, in this case I, on effective demand (and, by implication, on income, output and employment). I might even be replaced by more general autonomous expenditure, A. Such a model is presumed to give a static, short-run equilibrium in which, especially in the context of unemployment, effective demand is generated by autonomous expenditure at the level I initially, then cI when that income is partially spent (at rate $c = 1 - s$) and partially saved (at rate s), then c^2I and so on, c^3I, ..., c^rI, ..., etc. Total increased demand, $I(1 + c + c^2 + c^3 + ... + c^r + ...)$ sums to $I/(1 - c)$ which equals I/s.

From the point of view of effective demand, the saving, sY, is a leakage out of the system as the multiplier effect on demand is less the greater it is. This is in contrast to non-Keynesian macroeconomics in which, at the extreme, increased saving would automatically lead to a corresponding increase in investment that would exactly match the loss of demand due to reduced consumption expenditure. For Keynesians, though, leakages into savings do not automatically lead to such an increase in investment (and there is no necessary signal from savers through the market that they intend to consume in the future, motivating producers to make the necessary investments). So, within the Keynesian multiplier, increased saving is a loss of effective demand (and potentially output and employment) unless it is translated into investment (to provide for future consumption), something that cannot be assumed to occur automatically. Indeed, in what is termed the paradox of thrift, the *more* we save the *less* we might invest. This is because increased saving reduces demand and discourages producers from making investments and potentially puts the economy into a downward spiral of recession. Such a possibility is modelled in Section 2.2. In addition, it should be observed that leakages can also occur through imports (at the expense of demand for domestic production even if boosting production elsewhere) and through using the extra income to save in the special form of holding money (or other assets) rather than spending it on consumption.

Taking account of holding money became a standard part of Keynesian economics, not least through the LM curve (see Chapter 5). And the level of investment was determined through the IS curve, making it negatively dependent upon the interest rate or the cost of borrowing capital to make investments. This chapter, though, concerns an issue that came to the fore prior to these considerations. What is the 'dynamic' relationship between investment and output (as opposed to an equilibrium outcome), in the sense of how will they mutually evolve over time? It proceeds by offering a simple account of the level of investment, the so-called accelerator. This is put together with the simple multiplier as laid out in Section 2.2, together with an account of its somewhat surprising implications.

2.2 The Model

The accelerator-multiplier model of the macroeconomy is remarkable in a number of respects. First, it dates from the end of the interwar period. Second, it continued to be taught until around the end of the post-war boom. Third, it attempts to address the interaction between growth and cycles, if somewhat unsuccessfully, but does as a result analyse the short and long runs simultaneously. Fourth, the lack of success in generating growth and cycles is a result of the mathematical properties of the model. For the mathematics of the models is such that the models necessarily lead over time, somewhat exceptionally, to regular cycles around a static equilibrium or, more likely, either to explosive instability or to convergence to a static equilibrium. Where steady growth is the equilibrium, it is unable to give rise to regular cycles as well. Fifth, through its simple form the model offers a framework through which to view later developments within macroeconomics, ones which both reject its simple assumptions but, by doing so, tend to undermine the unpalatable results of the model concerning the inability of the capitalist economy to generate short-run stability around a steady growth path.

As indicated by its name, the accelerator-multiplier model has two components. Consider first the simple multiplier. From Keynesian economics, it follows that:

$$Y_t = I_t/s.$$

Where Y is income, I is investment and s is the rate of saving out of income, with t representing the time subscript. This means that the investment generates income through the multiplier in the same time period in which it is itself spent.

If it took time for the multiplier to take effect, with a one period lag for example, then the equation above would become $Y_t = I_{t-1}/s$.

In order to determine output in any period, then, it is necessary to know the level of investment. This is given by the accelerator. Here, the idea is that the level of investment will be made to meet anticipated increase in demand over previous output. Suppose anticipated demand is Y_t^*, then anticipated increase in output is $Y_t^* - Y_{t-1}$. If the capital–output ratio (how much capital is needed to produce a unit of output) is constant and equals v, the amount of investment needed to produce the anticipated increase in output is $v(Y_t^* - Y_{t-1})$, so that this equals I_t, and:

$$Y_t = I_t/s = v(Y_t^* - Y_{t-1})/s \tag{2.1}$$

For long-run equilibrium, expectations will turn out to be correct, so that:

$$Y_t = v(Y_t - Y_{t-1})/s$$

and, by rearrangement, g, the rate of growth of the economy, equals:

$$g = (Y_t - Y_{t-1})/Y_t = s/v.$$

So, over time, the economy can grow at the equilibrium rate of s/v. This is what is known as the Harrod–Domar warranted rate of growth. Basically, as the formula suggests, it derives from s and v: s is the rate at which output is turned into saving and hence investment, and v is the inverse of the rate at which output is produced by that investment. So, if s is bigger and/or v smaller, the warranted rate of growth, g, is bigger as more output gets put into investment and/or that investment creates more output. Just to be clear, a bigger s does make the (equilibrium) warranted rate of growth larger. However, as will become clear as the model is laid out, increasing s may lead to lower growth in the short run, since effective demand will be depressed – this is the Keynesian insight laid out above.

In the Harrod–Domar model of growth, account is also taken of labour as an input. It is assumed to combine with capital in fixed proportions to produce output. It is also presumed that the supply of labour is determined by the rate of growth of population, the so-called natural rate of growth, n, say. This involves a thicket of assumptions, not least that it is constant and that population and the labour force grow at the same rate (or that there is a constant participation rate and/or unchanging age composition of the workforce). Given this, the economy can only be in long-run equilibrium if s/v = n, that is, the natural equals the warranted rate of growth. Otherwise if s/v > n, there will eventually be a growing shortage of labour and surplus of capital, and vice versa if s/v < n.

It has been possible to find the long-run equilibrium of steady-state (or constant), balanced (or fixed ratios of capital, labour and output all growing at the same rate) growth because expectations can be specified for the long run as equal to the equilibrium values. This has allowed the model to be closed, at least in the long run, as an extra, third equation is needed apart from the accelerator and the multiplier to determine, Y, I and Y^* (that extra equation being $Y^* = Y$, for long-run equilibrium). This will not, however, work for the short run for which a process of expectations formation is needed for when the economy is not in equilibrium, and expectations are not equal to their equilibrium values. Before specifying this, consider what happens in the short run in the following way. From use of equation (2.1):

$$Y_t/Y_t^* = v(Y_t^* - Y_{t-1})/sY_t^*.$$

Since $s/v = g$ and $(Y_t^* - Y_{t-1})/Y_t^* = g^*$, the expected rate of growth, it follows that:

$$Y_t/Y_t^* = g^*/g.$$

Suppose that $g^* > g$ – that is, that the anticipated rate of growth is greater than the equilibrium level. Then it will turn out, as can be seen from the equation, that $Y_t > Y_t^*$ – that is, the actual output level achieved will be even greater than the output anticipated from the growth rate (even though this is already higher than the equilibrium growth rate). As mentioned already, to take this any further it is necessary to specify how expectations will be determined in these circumstances.

Recall that output growth was expected to be higher than warranted by the equilibrium rate of growth, with the result that output turns out to be even higher than was expected. In other words, the apparently unduly optimistic expectations (relative to the warranted, equilibrium growth rate) turn out to be unduly pessimistic (relative to outcome, i.e. $Y_t^* < Y_t$). As the expectations undershoot outcome, it might be considered natural to revise them upwards and invest more, in order to close the gap between those expectations and outcome. But if so, $g^* > g$ once more (with an even bigger gap than previously), and the cycle will repeat itself time and time again. The result is that the economy takes off into explosive growth.

Should growth expectations be pessimistic, $g^* < g$, then more or less exactly the opposite occurs. Actual output will turn out to be even lower than pessimistic expectations. If expectations are revised downwards as a result of expectations above outcome, then output will subsequently be that much lower and so on, leading to explosive decline. Accordingly, Harrod saw the accelerator-multiplier model in terms of what he termed a 'knife-edge'. Everything is okay as long as the economy is on the steady-state, balanced growth path. But any disturbance will send it into explosive instability, either side of the equilibrium.

This proves a considerable setback for a model that is intended to integrate the short and long runs in a way that mirrors, at least to some degree, the conventionally conceived empirical properties of the economy, taken to be, at least as a first approximation, regular cyclical short-run variations around a long-term trend. Such an outcome for this model raises the issue of whether growth and cycles could be generated by amending it in some way, not least for example the lag structure. The answer is no. To see this, it will be necessary first to specify the expectations formally. They are what are known as adaptive expectations, to be covered more fully in Chapter 8 (see Box 2.1).

Box 2.1
Adaptive expectations

Essentially, expectations are revised in the direction of reducing the error that was made. In other words: $Y_t^* = Y_{t-1}^* + \lambda(Y_{t-1} - Y_{t-1}^*)$ where $0 \le \lambda \le 1$ is a parameter of adjustment.

So, if $Y_{t-1} > Y_{t-1}^*$ expectations are adjusted up by the difference, weighted by λ. This equation can be rewritten as:

$$Y_t^* = \lambda Y_{t-1} + (1 - \lambda)Y_{t-1}^*.$$

This shows that this year's expectations are a weighted average of last year's and the actual outcome. If λ is large, we weight towards what last happened (and for $\lambda = 1$, expectations are simply last year's outcome); and if λ is small, the weight is towards retaining our expectations as they are (and for $\lambda = 0$, we stick to whatever our expectations were previously no matter how wrong they may have been).

From there:

$$Y_t^* = \lambda Y_{t-1} + (1 - \lambda)Y_{t-1}^* \tag{2.2}$$

But, from a rearranged 2.1:

$$Y_t^* = (s/v)Y_t + Y_{t-1} \text{ and similarly } Y_{t-1}^* = (s/v)Y_{t-1} + Y_{t-2}.$$

Substituting these into (2.2) gives, after simplification (the details are unimportant):

$$Y_t(s/v) + Y_{t-1}(1 - \lambda)(1 - s/v) - Y_{t-2}(1 - \lambda) = 0.$$

This is a difference equation of order 2. It cannot generate both growth and cycles (see Box 2.2). The same remains true if the lag structure is altered. The difference equation may become of a different order but it will still be dominated by its single dominant root of largest absolute value.

Box 2.2
Difference equations

The simplest difference equation is of the sort $Y_t - aY_{t-1} = 0$. This just means that Y_t increases (or decreases if a < 0) by a multiple of a in each period. If the process starts off at $Y_0 = b$ say, the so-called initial conditions, then Y_t is readily seen to equal ba^t. In this case, as long as some value of the process is given at some time, it is possible to work out the value of Y_t by multiplying by a for each period forward in time and dividing by a for each earlier period. As such, just some initial value is needed. It does not have to be at time zero, although this might be taken as such for measuring the beginning of the process. This difference equation is said to be of order 1 because the difference between the earliest and latest time for the variable Y in the equation is just one period of time. This is also a linear difference equation, as there are only linear terms in the Y_t – that is, no squares or other functions. If it were of order zero, Y would simply be a constant and never change. The most general linear difference equation takes the form:

$$a_0Y_t + a_1Y_{t-1} + a_2Y_{t-2} + \dots + a_nY_{t-n} = 0.$$

This is of degree n since that is the time period spanned by Y_t and Y_{t-n}. How is a solution obtained for this? First note that if n initial conditions are given, say the values for $Y_0, Y_1, Y_2, \dots Y_{n-1}$, then it is possible to find Y_n, as it equals $-1/a_0\{a_1Y_{n-1} + a_2Y_{n-2} + \dots + a_nY_0\}$. And, having got Y_n, it is possible to get Y_{n+1} by the same procedure across the previous n values from n to 1, and so on for all other values. So, in principle, it has been shown that n initial values suffice to solve the difference equation (and the same holds true if not given a sequence of initial values, only the algebra is slightly more complicated).

To find a solution through algebra, form what is called the auxiliary (polynomial) equation for the difference equation. This is as follows with a simple enough logic:

$$a_0x^n + a_1x^{n-1} + a_2x^{n-2} + \dots + a_{n-1}x + a_n = 0.$$

This polynomial has n solutions, or roots as they are called for x. Let one of them be α say. Then try $Y_t = A\alpha^t$ as a solution to the difference equation. It works by clever construction since: $a_0\alpha^n + a_1\alpha^{n-1} + a_2\alpha^{n-2} + \dots + a_{n-1}\alpha + a_n = 0$.

The same must be true of all of the other roots. As a result, the following is a solution if the $\alpha_1, \alpha_2, \dots \alpha_n$ are the roots of the auxiliary equation:

$$Y_t = A_1\alpha_1^t + A_2\alpha_2^t + A_3\alpha_3^t + \dots + A_n\alpha_n^t.$$

▶

Is this the most general solution? The answer is yes because there are n unknowns, the A_i, and with n initial conditions (or different values of t for which Y is given), there will be n simultaneous equations to find the A_i. In other words, since these n solutions are linearly independent, there is no room for any other solution to be added. What happens to Y over time? Well, it will be dominated by whichever of the αs has the highest absolute value as it will grow faster than anything else. If negative, Y will fluctuate. If the absolute value is greater than one, it will grow indefinitely. And if the biggest value equals one, Y will remain constant (if fluctuating for -1). This means that in the long run, the most complicated linear difference equations of whatever higher order eventually come to behave like, or be dominated by, the same sort of solution as the simplest one-order equation that was the starting point above. There is, though, one thing – a very special case – that can go wrong with this account. What if one or more of the αs are equal to one another? Then, in case of two coinciding for example, it can be shown that the solution for those two is, say, $A_1\alpha^t + A_2 t\alpha^t$. In this case, Y will in part grow (at the rate t) over time. But, once again, despite this growth it will ultimately be dominated by α^t (which is more powerful than any power of t as can be seen by taking logs). And the same is true in case other roots of the auxiliary equation coincide in pairs, or even greater multiple coincidences mean a solution of the same sort with higher powers of α, but these will always be dominated by the largest α^t.

As suggested, linear difference equations cannot generate growth and cycles. To do this, the model must be rendered non-linear. This was done at the time the model was put forward by the simple expedient of relying upon what were literally called floors and ceilings. Here the idea, in a phase of explosive growth, is that the growth will hit a constraint of some sort, capacity for example, so that the demand-induced expansion will come to a halt and, as a result, be thrown into reverse. Ultimately, the decline will also hit some sort of lower bound (some level of fixed expenditure on consumption goods or export orders for example) and then the economy will be thrown back into a phase of expansion. The more or less arbitrary appeal to floors and ceilings demonstrates a commitment both to the accelerator-multiplier model itself and the need to accommodate both growth and cycles. Of course, in principle non-linear difference equations of a less arbitrary type might be used (use also might have been made of differential instead of difference equations, see Box 2.3 with the added bonus of an explanation of the eponymous e). Unfortunately these are not subject to ready solutions. In addition, non-linear equations suffer not only from less tractability from a mathematical point of view but are also liable to generate multiple equilibria – another source of inconvenience unless wishing to offer some rationale for high- and low-level equilibria or the possibility of poverty traps. These, though, are merely marginal points in the evolution of macroeconomics, where the much simpler solution to the short-run/long-run syndrome has primarily been to treat them as if they were independent of each other. In this way, the long run is set aside as a trend and stability is merely considered as short-run deviations around a given equilibrium.

Box 2.3
Difference and differential equations

As may already be familiar, there are two different ways of doing macroeconomic models with dynamics (i.e. change over time). One is to use difference equations, or what is called discrete modelling, as the model divides time into separate periods. Typically, with output denoted by y_t at time t, increase in output from the period is $y_t - y_{t-1}$, and the growth rate from the previous period will be $(y_t - y_{t-1})/y_{t-1}$. If y_t grows at the rate g, then y_t will be compounded at this rate and equal $y_0(1 + g)^t$.

The other way of looking at dynamic economic models is through continuous time, with $y(t)$ representing y at time t, with this often reduced to just y and the time understood as implicit. In this case, if the rate of growth is g, then $(dy/dt)/y = g$, or $dy/y = gdt$. By integrating both sides, it follows that $\ln y = A + gt$. This means, taking anti-logarithms, that $y = Ae^{gt}$.

It follows that compound growth in discrete models corresponds to exponential growth in continuous models. More generally, each model in discrete time has a corresponding analogue in continuous time, and vice versa.

The relationship between compound and exponential growth can be seen as follows. Suppose that instead of paying interest once a year at the rate r, it is paid n times a year at equal intervals at the same rate. This is more advantageous because of interest paid on the interest earned during the year. Indeed, the unit growth by the end of the year is $(1 + r/n)^n$. What happens to this expression as n goes to infinity? The expression in the bracket seems to push it to 1 as r/n goes to zero. But the exponent outside the bracket seems to push it to be infinitely large, since this is so for a^n as n goes to infinity for any $a > 1$. What can be shown is that this expression tends towards the number e^r. So e forges the link between compound and exponential growth as letting n go to infinity is equivalent to allowing for continuous growth.

Just for the record, e can be shown to equal $1/0! + 1/1! + 1/2! + ... + 1/i! + ...$ where, by convention, 0! is taken to be equal to 1, e is an irrational number and approximately equals 2.718, and $e^x = 1 + x + x^2/2! + x^3/3! + ... + x^i/i! + ...$

This is why, when e^x is differentiated, it equals itself.

What is the choice between using difference equations and differential equations for economics modelling? In principle there would appear to be none, as there is a strict correspondence between the two. In practice, it is better to work with continuous models theoretically as the mathematics is easier and more developed – it is hard to solve discrete models unless they are linear, which is highly restrictive. On the other hand, data tend to come discretely rather than continuously so there are liable to be some errors in treating discrete data as if they were continuous.

2.3 The Greater Realism of Eliminating Instability?

The accelerator-multiplier model is remarkable because of its capacity to demonstrate, with disarming simplicity, how the macroeconomy, if left to itself, can be extraordinarily dysfunctional in generating extreme instability. But that very simplicity necessarily depends upon a thicket of special assumptions. Relax these assumptions, and the model both becomes more complicated and is liable to temper if not eliminate the possibility of instability.

First is the assumption of adaptive expectations (to be addressed in more detail in Chapter 8). It is these that lead to such instability since, as shown, optimism leads to the undershooting of expectations relative to outcome, which then repeats itself indefinitely. This carries the implication that expectations are not only wrong in one period but that they permanently undershoot if in a phase of expansion (and overshoot if in decline). Does it make sense for agents to get their expectations wrong indefinitely without revising how they make them? This provides the space for the introduction of rational expectations.

Second, by merely focusing on meeting the increase in expected demand, the investment function, leaving aside how the expectations are formed, takes no account of a number of factors. What about the cost of investment, not only in terms of the rate of interest on capital used, but also how quickly the investment is put in place? It would surely become costlier to invest huge amounts all at once as explosive growth takes off (and possibly to wind down and break contracts if in decline). Such actions would dampen the momentum underpinning the cycle.

Third, use is made of a very simple saving function, with the implication that consumption is a fixed proportion of current income. But, in a boom, consumers are liable to assume that their greater income is liable to be temporary and, if optimising over their lifetime of utility, higher consumption will be spread over their remaining years of life, reducing the multiplier to tenths of what its value would have been otherwise. This is to appeal to the permanent income hypothesis in which cyclical movements through the multiplier will be dampened by reacting to changes in current income as if they were only considerably smaller changes in permanent income – note this is not current income that is permanently higher but simply the way in which a temporary increase in current income is treated as shared across the rest of a lifetime.

Fourth, the model is notable for not including any price mechanism whatsoever. Surely, during the boom, the prices of both investment and consumption goods would begin to rise, thereby choking off demand and the multiplier. The opposite would hold in a period of decline.

Last, the model is even more notable, if not surprising in view of the previous point, for a total absence of money. During the boom, it might be expected that the demand for money would rise, to be able to make the extra consumption and investment purchases, and this would in turn lead to a rise in the rate of interest. This too would choke off demand (not least as the cost of investment), tempering a phase of expansion (and similarly for decline).

Significantly, these five considerations have all become incorporated as part of the standard toolkit of macroeconomics. They might be thought of as elements of non-linearity, if less abrupt and arbitrary than ceilings and floors. But it is more appropriate to see them as having, almost certainly unwittingly, allowed for the accelerator-multiplier to be put aside, together with both its preoccupation with addressing short and long runs simultaneously and allowing for extreme instability (as opposed to short-run deviations alone around a given equilibrium).

2.4 Further Thoughts and Readings

The presentation offered here follows that in the introduction to Sen (1970) which, interestingly, was published as an edited collection on growth not macroeconomics. As will be seen, this was just the point in time when macroeconomics was about to consolidate its character as short-run deviations around a long-run equilibrium as well as incorporating other extremes of narrowness such as reliance upon representative individuals, rational expectations, microeconomic foundations and more or less perfectly clearing markets. It was also the point at which what is now known as the old growth theory had more or less reached its limits (apart from the ubiquity of calculating total factor productivity, see Chapter 4 here, and chapter 5 in the counterpart *Microeconomics* volume). A little extra life was breathed into it through adding the extra twist of growth with exhaustible resources (the mainstream's response to the oil crises of the 1970s) and through the use of fancier mathematics (optimal dynamic processes rather than simply steady-state analyses). This was insufficient to keep growth theory going until new growth theory (see Chapter 4) burst on to the scene in the mid-1980s, with growth and cycles having been reduced to the theory of real business cycles that emerged as the long-run counterpart to the NCE (see Chapters 9 and 10).

Although Harrod developed the accelerator-multiplier model, the growth model that provides the knife-edge's equilibrium, $s/v = n$, goes by the name of Harrod–Domar. Domar's contribution is interesting, modifying the warranted growth rate to $\sigma s/v$, where $0 < \sigma < 1$ and is supposed to signify a lower growth rate due to a reduction in capacity utilisation. Domar argues that the growth process requires input resources to be moved from productive capacity that might not be technologically obsolescent – the capital can still be used – but which is economically obsolescent because new investments are more productive. This might be because they embody more advanced technology, but even this is not necessary. Machines may have a lifetime over which they become less productive until they are scrapped even though they could still go on producing. For growth to be sustained at the appropriate level, machines will have to be routinely scrapped as they come to the end of their economic as opposed to their technological life. This is so that the resources they use as inputs can be shifted over to the new, more productive machines. In other words, each machine has a life in which, when it is a new investment, it receives inputs from other machines being retired, and then carries on producing until its own time for retirement comes.

But Domar identified a potential problem. No capitalist willingly gives up producing whilst there is still both life in their machinery and a profit to be made. If the price of inputs can be forced down below their perfectly competitive level, the old machines can continue to produce at a profit, and will retain inputs at the expense of the new, more highly productive machines which will be unable to work at full capacity (and might even be compensated for this to some degree by the impact on profits of lower level of input prices, albeit at less than full capacity). In other words, forcing wages down in particular may allow for old machines to continue in use at the expense of full capacity on new investments.

What is significant in this stylised account is the way in which the short-run adjustment mechanism (shifting resources from old to new machinery as part of the investment process) has an effect on the long-run rate of growth. It does connect the short to the long run! Nor does the mechanism apply solely to inputs. The new machines also need to take markets for output away from the old. Domar, in a sense, proxies the impact of all of these short-run mechanisms by consolidating them into a single measure of reduction in capacity utilisation and hence growth rate to $\sigma s/v$. But there is no reason why such mechanisms should be even across the different effects and time. And, in addition, there may be further repercussions on how much is invested – what's the point if you cannot get the inputs or the markets to warrant use of your more efficient machinery. This begins to open up a much more complex understanding of the relationships between the short and long runs and how they cannot be taken as independent of one another. But it is not in general an opportunity taken up by mainstream macroeconomics.

3
Classical Dichotomies

3.1 Overview

It is a conventional wisdom that Keynes was keen to avoid addressing issues of microeconomics in putting forward what was to become Keynesian economics in order judiciously to set aside unnecessarily controversial issues in pursuit of persuading his fellow economists. For his purposes, it was irrelevant whether relative marginal productivities or utilities equalled relative prices or not. Consider, for example, what would be the effect of a small decrease of the money wage in the context of high unemployment. Presumably, from mainstream microeconomic principles, this would lift the marginal product of labour above the real wage, and increase the demand for, and so the level of, employment. For Keynes, the immediate, or most important, effect of reducing money wages is not to make employing more labour more attractive but to reduce the level of demand for consumption goods out of wage revenue. This could even have the perverse effect of increasing unemployment. So, for Keynes, it was more a matter of whether the level of overall effective demand would be sufficient to guarantee full employment irrespective of optimisation or not at the microeconomic level. Without sufficient investment, there would be insufficient demand and, in addition, insufficient investment was liable to occur from time to time because of excessive speculation within a financial system more attuned to immediate returns on stocks and shares than on longer-term prospects for returns from real investments that would only accrue in the more distant future and on the basis of the aggregate demand having been generated in the present.

This is to anticipate Chapters 5–7. What it does raise now, however (as it did then, only to be avoided by Keynes), is the relationship between macroeconomics and microeconomics. In recent times, this has been interpreted as the relationship between individuals (usually optimising) and the economy, and how in mainstream macroeconomics to aggregate from one to the other, as opposed to heterodox economics in which attention is paid to the systemic properties of the economy as an object in its own right and as the basis on which to address the functioning of the disaggregated elements of the economy. Either way, the relationship between the microeconomic and the macroeconomic depends upon how the economy is disaggregated and how the individual components fit together (see also Chapter 7). This is not simply the relationship between agents taken as a whole, for example whether representative individuals as households or firms (see Chapter 5), or representative classes (see Chapter 6). But it also involves the relationship between different sectors of the economy.

For mainstream macroeconomics, its relationship with microeconomics has always been tense, problematic and generally fudged. As covered in Section 3.2, one tension that arose relatively early, as the compatibility between microeconomic principles and the newly emerged Keynesianism was being investigated, was the validity of the so-called classical dichotomy in which the real and money economies are perceived to be independent of one another. As is shown, this was a tension that could be resolved but only at the expense of two factors: first, money was shown not to be neutral in the short run, so the classical dichotomy does not prevail; second, the classical dichotomy remains valid in the long run. This is because real balances – the ratio of money to the price level – can be out of equilibrium in the short run with impact upon demand, for example, whereas prices can adjust in the long run to restore the economy, and real balances, to equilibrium.

There are, however, a number of startling implications of this resolution of the problem of the classical dichotomy from a wider perspective, as discussed in Section 3.3. One is the extent to which it does not address other tensions across the micro/macro divide that cannot be readily incorporated into the framework of microeconomics because they are systemic in character. These include issues such as distribution of income, monopolisation and the role of trade unions and other institutions in macroeconomic functioning quite apart from the dynamics of technological change. Whilst they were the subject of much analysis in the interwar period as a reflection of changes going on at the time, especially within the US economy, these issues became excised from mainstream macroeconomics, which was the simplest method of avoiding their incompatibility with microeconomic principles.

By the same token, the classical dichotomy between the real and money economies is readily shown to be a close companion of two other dichotomies, not only between micro and macro but also between the short and long runs. Paradoxically, whilst money is shown to affect the short run, it has no impact upon the long run even though the long run is the outcome of the disturbed short run. This is itself the consequence of the running together of both the passage of time and given equilibrium in defining the long run (see Chapter 1). As a result of this, it is hardly surprising that the three dichotomies cannot be satisfactorily reconciled without reducing their respective contents.

3.2 Dissecting the Classical Dichotomy

The classical dichotomy, so named because it was taken to be representative of a longstanding approach within economics (including classical political economy), is based upon the idea that there is a division within the economy between the so-called real economy (comprised of inputs and outputs, supply and demand, production and consumption, etc.) and the money (or financial) economy. Further, the presumption is that the real economy is determined by fundamentals such as production and utility functions and available resources independently of the money economy. However, in the real economy only relative prices will be determined. As a result, the money economy has the role of determining the absolute price level. Sometimes, as a result, money is perceived as a veil, lubricant or catalyst for the real economy, facilitating but not determining the outcome of market relations.

At a simple level, suppose the economy is represented by a representative firm that employs labour alone to produce output. It maximises profit by setting the marginal product of labour equal to the real wage. By the same token, the representative employee maximises utility by setting ratios of marginal disutility of work and marginal utility of consumption equal to the real wage. From this, the supply of, and demand for, both goods and labour can be derived, together with equilibrium quantities where they cross. There might appear to be two equations here, one for goods and one for labour so that both p, the price of goods, and w, the wage, can be found. But the two sets of equations are effectively equivalent to one another because of Walras'/Say's Law, see below, and the identity imposed by budget constraints so that whatever is spent on consumption goods must be earned by wages (and the profits from the firm). As a result, it is impossible to find the absolute values of p and w, but the real wage, w/p, will be able to be found, see for example the simple model of general equilibrium and Diagram 3.4 in the counterpart *Microeconomics* volume.

This is where the money economy does its work. Suppose that the bigger the output, the bigger in proportion is the amount of money needed to ease processes of buying and selling on the market, and now representing the overall price level by p (aggregated in some way out of the vector of individual prices), the level of real output by Y (similarly for aggregation across goods), and k by the inverse of how quickly money circulates in facilitating sales and purchases (either at the same rate across all goods and types of money or as a rough aggregation), then:

$$M = kpY.$$

This is the standard formula for the quantity theory of money. M is supposed to be the supply of money, assumed fixed, and kpY is the demand for money (how much is needed to undertake transactions, with more in demand the slower money circulates, the higher the price level, and the more the amount of output to be circulated). As Y is given by the real economy, it follows that p is determined as M/kY. Note, though, as already indicated, that p and Y are only being used as aggregates for convenience here. For the simple model, labour inputs and goods as outputs could be designated as separate from one another with different velocities of circulation. Then, with L labour and G goods with prices, w and p:

$$M = k_1 Lw + k_2 Gp.$$

Together with the real economy, which gives the value of w/p, this one allows the absolute price level to be found. Much the same holds true in case there are any number of goods and corresponding prices. The real economy determines only relative prices and the money economy gives supply of money as fixed to be set equal to the demand for money that will depend upon output and price (and wage) levels and speeds of circulation of goods (and labour), thereby providing an extra equation for finding the absolute price level, possibly:

$$M = k_1 p_1 y_1 + k_2 p_2 y_2 + \ldots + k_n p_n y_n, \text{ as the expanded form of } M = kpY.$$

In this light, there is a clear connection between the classical dichotomy as such and another dichotomy of much more recent, if longstanding, vintage between microeconomics and macroeconomics, as the top equation, immediately above, disaggregates the economy into n sectors, whilst the bottom one reaggregates to the economy as a whole. It is this relationship, as formulated, between micro and macro that will prove troublesome.

Along with the classical dichotomy, denoted by CD say, there are a number of other properties of the model. One is the homogeneity postulate, HP. This is at most implicit in what has been described so far. But, for the real economy, generalised to a number of sectors and agents, there will be supply and demand curves for each agent. These can be aggregated over agents to give supply and demand curves for each of the n sectors, $S^i(p_1, p_2, \ldots, p_n)$ and $D^i(p_1, p_2, \ldots, p_n)$, respectively. Excess demand for any good, i, can be denoted by:

$$E^i(p_1, p_2, \ldots, p_n) = D^i(p_1, p_2, \ldots, p_n) - S^i(p_1, p_2, \ldots, p_n).$$

This is the system of supply and demand curves that derive from underlying fundamentals. From this it follows that each of these curves is homogeneous of degree 0 in the price vector, $p = (p_1, p_2, \ldots, p_n)$. This is equivalent to presuming that all that matters for supply and demand are relative prices (and if these were declared in pence rather than pounds, or whatever monetary unit, the outcome would be exactly the same). Further, what matters for equilibrium is that there be some price vector p^* such that $E^i(p_1^*, p_2^*, \ldots, p_n^*) = 0$ for all i, since then each market is in equilibrium.

Of course, the price vector prevailing might not be p˙. But, because this is a system of supplies and demands aggregated up from optimising individuals, each of these individuals will have an aggregate level (in value terms) over all individual goods demands and supplies that equals zero – no individual can intend to demand without intending to supply something in return of equal value. Adding over all individuals, this means that the overall value of excess demands across all sectors and individuals must be zero. Or, to put it another way, if the economy is out of equilibrium there will be some excess demands and some excess supplies. The sum of these in total must be equal to zero. This is known as Say's Law, after a French economist working at the turn of the nineteenth century, who suggested in a sort of one-sided way that supply creates its own demand (rather than vice versa). Say's Law, denoted here by SL, most famously through Keynes as a critical point of departure, became associated with the idea that it is impossible for there to be a general glut in market economies or excess supply in all markets at the same time. This is because if the sum of excess demands is equal to zero, they cannot all be negative. There might not be equilibrium, but at least one market must be in excess demand if there is at least one in excess supply. So within this frame of reference, SL is not just an equilibrium condition, but an identity, something that must always hold in all circumstances.

Returning to the money market, this can also be characterised by excess demand, in simplest form of aggregated supply and demand for money, as:

$$EDM = kpY - M.$$

Again, this might not be in equilibrium. But surely the argument for Say's Law must apply not just for the real sector but for all markets? If an individual intends to buy more than is sold, the difference must be made up by an intended reduction in demand for (or holdings of) money (in order to pay for the excess, and vice versa, with an excess supply of goods and a corresponding excess demand for money). Although, it should be emphasised, this is not a uniformly standardised terminology, here Say's Law will be used to apply across the real economy alone, and what will be termed Walras' Law (WL), will apply across all markets taken together, that is, both the real and the money economies.

Now it seems that there is more to the classical dichotomy than a simple division and independence between real and money sectors. The dichotomy is comprised of CD, HP, SL and WL. On this basis, in the 1950s, Patinkin demonstrated the simple but devastating result that the classical dichotomy is invalid, as the four properties cannot all hold simultaneously. The proof is elementary. Consider any set of prices. Double these as a hypothetical exercise to see what would happen to the system of supplies and demands. This is a hypothetical exercise in the sense that the properties of the model (or its various equations and functions) are being interrogated as opposed to suggesting this is the way the economy would actually behave according to the model. From the doubling of the prices, it follows from the HP that the real economy (i.e. the individual supply and demand functions) will remain the same. As a result, all excess demands will remain the same and sum to zero (this is true in any case from SL and so the HP is not needed for what follows). On the other hand, the excess demand for money will change since, as it is at the moment, doubling all prices will double the demand for money. But the supply of money remains fixed. As a result WL will be violated if it were holding already since excess demand for money has shifted in the money market whilst excess demand for goods has remained at zero. This means that, contrary to WL, the sum of excess demands across all markets cannot always be zero since it cannot hold both before and after the hypothetical shift in prices (given that overall excess demand has shifted between them).

The need to reject the CD is often perceived to be puzzling but the reasons for the rejection are not hard to follow as such. For a system of excess demands within a pure real economy, the hypothetical exercise of doubling all prices leaves the system of excess demands unchanged (from HP and SL, although the latter is all that is needed for zero excess demand in the real economy). But the doubling of prices does create an excess demand for money, thereby creating overall excess demand for the economy as a whole in violation of WL. All that is needed for this outcome is that the supply of money be fixed and the excess demand for money not remain constant for changing prices. This is surely reasonable on its own terms and it might be expected that the doubling of all prices, for example, would lead to a doubling of the demand for money irrespective of what else the demand for money depends upon (not just a fixed velocity of circulation and the level of output but also expectations of inflation, the interest rate, and so). Whatever money you need in one set of conditions, you might expect to need twice as much for double the prices in the otherwise same set of conditions. Without this, there is some sort of money illusion, a belief of being in a different world merely because all prices have been equally inflated or deflated (even denominated in one currency as opposed to another or a different unit of the same currency). Indeed, the lack of money illusion is hard to escape in most macroeconomics, since it would otherwise mean that lots of banknotes instead of a few of the same value make you seem better off, more productive or something similar. This may well be true to some minor degree for those who do suffer from money illusion but it would be hard to base systematic economic analysis upon it.

To some degree, this discussion suggests how the rejection of the classical dichotomy might be resolved, and this was how Patinkin himself proceeded. Formally, it requires that one or more of CD, HP, SL and WL should be rejected. First, observe that WL, like the lack of money illusion, is somewhat sacrosanct since every sale is a purchase so that all purchases and sales (and intentions as such) should add up to zero for each individual and so remain so if aggregated across *all* markets. The problem with SL is that it only aggregates across the real economy and does not include the money market. As a result SL should be rejected, and WL retained since, for example, there could indeed be a general glut across all goods markets (each and every one in excess supply) if there is a corresponding, equal and opposite, excess demand for money.

Otherwise, what is easily recognised is that with the hypothetical doubling of prices, the real economy remains the same because of HP but there is a need for more money to facilitate buying and selling at these higher prices. With such a shortage of money for making transactions, there is liable to be a reduction in those transactions. This means there can be a shortage of money with an impact on the real economy (or there has to be some mechanism of money or credit creation that allows the money supply to increase with prices, but most mainstream macroeconomics does not allow this, unlike post-Keynesianism that does emphasise the endogeneity of the money supply, see Chapter 6).

This is essentially arguing for a rejection not only of CD (a shortage of money can restrict demand) but also of HP, since doubling prices, whilst leaving relative prices unchanged, will affect supply and demand because of the shortage of money needed to undertake transactions or serve other purposes. The question is how and by how much should money affect the real economy. There is at least a partial common sense answer in view of avoiding money illusion. As money is needed for transactions, the amount needed is in proportion to the price level. Accordingly, the excess demand for goods should be written as $E^i(p_1, p_2, ..., p_n, M)$ where the E^i, and each of the constituents of S^i and D^i, are homogeneous of degree 0 in the $(p_1, p_2, ..., p_n)$ *and* M taken together. In other words, doubling all prices and M ought to leave supply and demand untouched, a sort of revised HP, HP' say. Otherwise, as for HP, doubling all prices will leave the economy short of money and restrict, or at least amend, overall economic activity. More usually, this excess demand function gets written in a form such as:

$$E^i(p_1, p_2, ..., p_n, M/p), \text{ or even } E^i(p, M/p),$$

where p is the vector of prices and divides M in the second argument to indicate the E^i is homogeneous of degree 0 in M and prices. But this is a clumsy if convenient notation given that it is not possible to divide by a vector, p, although p might be taken to be a composite aggregate price as in $M = kpY$ (although this glosses over microfoundations and aggregation).

In short, the economy becomes specified by $E(p, M/p)$, with E a vector of the excess demands, E^i, and by $M/p = f(Y, ...)$. Here, somewhat clumsily again, given p is a vector, M/p represents the supply of money in real terms, homogeneous of degree 0 in M and p, since doubling the price level means twice as much money is needed in nominal terms to be able to undertake whatever transactions are to take place; and f(Y, ...) incorporates the other factors that might affect the demand for money (other than the price level) with, of course, f(Y) = kY being the simple case of the quantity theory of money. For equilibrium:

$E(p^*, M/p^*) = 0$ and $M/p^* = f(Y^*, ...)$.

This is the market clearing Walrasian equilibrium. Given that E is a vector, it is defined as each market being in equilibrium and hence clearing.

As a result, in summary, the CD is rejected since, as could not be more explicit, the money supply appears in the real economy (the system of excess demands, E). So HP is rejected; doubling all prices does not leave E unchanged unless M is doubled as well. SL is rejected, as any overall excess demands in goods market can be equal and opposite to those in the money market. But at least WL is retained!

The rejection of the CD means that money does matter to the real economy. But how much does money matter? Suppose, for example, there was a positive shift in resources and so an increase in activity in the real economy. There would presumably be insufficient money to undertake the extra level of transactions. Prices would fall but, subject to stability and the existence and uniqueness of a new equilibrium (not considered here at all), a new equilibrium would be found with a lower level of p^*.

On the other hand, suppose that the real economy remained the same but that the money supply, M, were simply doubled. It follows immediately that there will be some short-run disequilibrium, presumably excess demand (as everyone thinks they have more money than before – $2M/p^*$ as opposed to just M/p^*), but the new equilibrium will be $2p^*$ (which can easily be checked as satisfying the equations for equilibrium with the real economy unaffected). Indeed, the equations for equilibrium depend upon the variable M/p, and this is what matters for the model rather than the absolute value of M itself. This is so whether the economy is in equilibrium or not, as M/p appears as such in the system of supply and demand for goods and for money.

From all of this, it follows that money is not what is termed neutral in the short run. The dynamics of this model, connecting its own conception of the short run to the long run, have not been specified, only the system of supply and demand for goods and money. But in the short run, before prices adjust in absolute terms, even if they are correct in relative terms (that is, at their equilibrium values), the quantity of money affects whether the economy is in equilibrium, according to what are termed the real balances, M/p (with presumption of excess demand, for example, and prospective price increases if the absolute value of prices is too low).

On the other hand, in the long run, after prices have had an opportunity to adjust, subject to stability, the outcome for the real economy will be unaffected by the quantity of money as the absolute price level will adjust in proportion to the quantity of money. In other words, money is neutral in the long run or the classical dichotomy does hold for the long but not the short run. Note, though, that another dichotomy has been introduced between short and long runs (see Chapter 1 and what follows in this chapter for discussion of the confusion around these issues).

The result of long-run neutrality of money (or classical dichotomy) is hardly surprising given the way the model has been constructed. If there is only a single equilibrium for the real economy, and if there is no money illusion, the only possible outcome for a stable economy is to have long-run neutrality of money. The most money can do is to affect the adjustment process and not the equilibrium outcome.

This will be discussed further in Section 3.3. For the moment, let us return to the issue of the extent to which money matters, but from a different point of view than short- and long-run neutrality. How much do real balances that appear in the real economy affect its working in the short run? This depends upon how M/p affects the vector of excess demand functions, E. From a theoretical perspective, this implies asking why agents hold money and with what effects. Mainstream economics has great difficulty answering this question for the simple reason that it does not have a satisfactory account of why money (continues to) exist and how it got to exist in the first place, generally relying unsatisfactorily on some sort of mechanism by which barter became more efficient and money a way of economising on transactions costs. The problem is, though, once you get into a set of well-established equilibrium trades, you would no longer need money as these trades become routinised. And, if you need money to tide over uncertainty, then you are not going to be in equilibrium. Either you are in equilibrium and you do not need money or you are out of equilibrium and you need a theory (of money) that acknowledges this.

Not surprisingly, this simple conundrum tends to be overlooked, either by excluding money from economics or by just assuming there are reasons for holding it. For the latter, this can be because it is deemed to contribute to utility or to production in some way. So, the best way to acknowledge the rejection of the classical dichotomy is to include real balances, M/p, in the utility function, or even in the production functions. Perhaps agents feel, and/or are, better off if they have more real balances, the better to be able to handle uncertainties, whether unfortunate emergencies or golden opportunities.

Even putting this aside and allowing for some rationale for holding money as real balances in a long-run equilibrium in which you might be better off just spending it, what is the short-run impact of these real balances? Are they liable to be large or small? One way to address this issue is to seek to measure such real balances. This raises certain problems, since the use of many different measures of the money supply, as more or less liquid, are well known. But there is a further problem concerning the nature of money and how real balances affect the workings of the economy in the short run.

This can be shown by an oblique route. Forget money for the moment and just consider assets in general in order to discuss real wealth (and real wealth effects, RWEs, as opposed to real balance effects, RBEs, when consideration of assets is confined to money). Suppose the prices of those (non-money) assets go up for whatever reason. Does that mean that the (closed) economy has more real wealth? Clearly not, as exactly the same assets exist as did before. I am better off if I sell my house, but whoever buys it has to pay more and there is an equal and opposite wealth effect. If I stay in my house, I have in a sense gained nothing other than to sell and buy house services to myself at a higher price. Much the same is true of all assets. If they go up in price, that is great for those who own them but there is an equal and opposite effect on those who do not and who might wish to purchase the services they provide. So, changing asset prices does not change real wealth and the only real wealth effect seems to be distributional. This is far from negligible as is evidenced by those who gain and lose on capital gains in housing markets, but macroeconomics has been studiously negligent of distributional issues altogether, let alone through wealth effects.

Does exactly the same argument apply to money and, therefore, eliminate the real balance effect just as it seemed to rescue macroeconomics from the deficiencies of the classical dichotomy? Well, the answer is, and is not (the paradox will become clear), to be found in the distinction between inside and outside money. The point about the zero RWE is that, subject to distributional effects, every asset has a corresponding liability and so the net effect of the RWE is zero. Does the same apply to the RBE? The answer depends upon finding a money that, as an asset, does not have a corresponding liability. This is called outside as opposed to inside money. It is easy enough to specify inside money. If one person allows another to buy something on credit, some money as means of purchase has been created but the seller has gained an asset (the IOU) equal and opposite to the buyer's liability.

But what of outside money? In particular, cash seems to be an asset against which there is no corresponding liability. And if the state increases the money supply, does this not increase the amount of outside money and real balances as no one has to pay back the money created? Well, not necessarily. Suppose that as a result of the increase in the money supply, inflation is anticipated in proportion. Then agents will perceive that they have become worse off in proportion to the increase in the money supply and so have suffered the equivalent to a reduction in their assets equivalent to the increase in the money supply. By the same token, this must have been true of increases in the money supply in the past. So there is no outside money after all. Similar arguments can be made about other ways in which the state might appear to increase outside wealth, with fiscal deficits presumed to lead to inflation or compensating taxation in the future (the so-called Ricardian equivalence theorem of action of, and reaction to, the state with regard to taxation in particular, see Box 5.1). This, however, makes it clear that the definition and impact of RBEs are inseparable from one another and from how the macroeconomy is perceived to behave (for example, in response to increases in the money supply or the role of the state more generally). The more you are inclined towards monetarism, the more you will reduce both the definition and impact of the real balance effect, in contrast to Keynesianism. Either way, within this frame of analysis, a macroeconomic model needs to be specified for which the RBE is more of a consequence than a defining moment. In this respect, it is hardly surprising that the RBE serves more as a theoretical device for uniting and making consistent the relations between the real and money economies rather than as a target of empirical investigation in its own right.

3.3 The Short- and Long-Run and Micro and Macro Dichotomies

As indicated, the classical dichotomy does itself generate two further dichotomies – between the short and long runs and between the microeconomic and the macroeconomic – although these might be better described as 'tensions'. The resolution of the classical dichotomy, through the simple if ingenious device of introducing the real balance effect in the real economy, has the effect of rejecting Say's Law, the homogeneity postulate (unless including money holdings), and the classical dichotomy itself, at least in the short as opposed to the long run, given that money remains neutral in the long if not the short run. But where does this response to the classical dichotomy leave the other two dichotomies?

First, for the short-/long-run dichotomy, as indicated, money matters for one but not the other. The reason for this is transparent. The long run is a fixed equilibrium and cannot be affected by anything, including the short run and whether its deviations from the equilibrium are due to monetary or other disturbances. After all, the long run is given by the solution to the two equations (although one is a vector of equations, one for each sector) for excess demands and money market equilibrium:

$$E(p, M/p) = 0 \text{ and } M/p = f(Y, ...).$$

Only if there are multiple equilibria, which creates problems of its own which tend to be set aside unless useful for other purposes, can the short run affect the long run at all, although it is important to be mindful that the idea of the long run combines two ideas – of equilibrium and of the passage of time, see Chapter 1.

Second, for the micro/macro dichotomy, it is apparent that given that the model is a general equilibrium with money incorporating the RBE, then the short run is affected through the adjustment process, as real balances adjust to their equilibrium values alongside everything else. The reason for this is that the long-run equilibrium is determined by the so-called fundamentals of preferences, technologies and endowments. But, surely, during the short-run adjustment these will themselves be affected, not least as a short-run depression, for example, would reduce levels of investment and corresponding resources available for production? To put the point polemically, it is estimated that the current global crisis may take ten years or more to make up for lost production – is this long enough to count as affecting the long run? More generally, it is stretching credibility not to allow the microeconomics of a given equilibrium (the long run) to be affected by the macroeconomics of short-run adjustment.

Third, dovetailing both of these extra dichotomies, is consideration of what is taken as given. The most striking example is the money supply. The connections between short and long runs and between micro and macro are forged by the role of the supply of, and demand for, money – or, more exactly, the stability or fixity of the equation $M/p = f(Y, ...)$. Even if this takes the form of $M/p = Yf(...)$ or, simpler still, $M/p = kY$, there is the option of the money supply becoming endogenous (credit more readily available in a boom and restricted in a recession), or of transactions being undertaken more or less efficiently in light of economic conditions. In other words, does the velocity of circulation remain constant irrespective of prevailing conditions, or at least is it only dependent upon variables determined within the model? Recent experience suggests otherwise, with quantitative easing doing little to decrease the demand for money (at least by banks that might lend it) and stimulating demand.

Fourth, this is indicative of a much more general problem across the two dichotomies – the impoverished treatment of money within the model itself. At the micro/macro and short/long-run levels, it plays two roles only. On the one hand, it is an asset that is held in the form of real balances, M/p, for the services that they might provide. On the other hand, within this simple model, the services provided are apparently confined to being able to make transactions whenever necessary (although $f(Y, ...)$ in principle contains a host of other variables that might justify holding money for other purposes: for speculation, to guard against inflation, etc.). But again (drawing upon the experience of the current crisis), at the micro level, financial markets, as opposed to money as such, are supposedly the means by which financial resources are both mobilised and allocated efficiently for the purposes of investment. As discussed in Chapter 1, in the context of financialisation, as has even been acknowledged by orthodoxy in the wake of the crisis, the dichotomy between the microeconomics of financial markets and the macroeconomics of the supply of and demand for money is not sustainable, especially when financial institutions are recognised to be able to go bust and have profound knock-on effects to other financial institutions and the real economy.

Fifth, some commentary has already been made on the conflation of two of the ways in which short and long runs are distinguished, as passage of time and as defined by equilibrium. What of the third, the relative speed of adjustment of different variables? Implicit in Patinkin's resolution of the dichotomy is the presumption that money, or changes in money markets, has immediate effects that are faster than any other variable, since individuals choose to change how much they hold (or demand) of a fixed supply once it is itself changed. These changes may be small or large, into speculation or real markets and, for the latter, into quantities (if Keynesian in leaning) or prices (if monetarist), but they do occur faster than anything else.

More generally, the role of the financial sector in mediating the two, or three, dichotomies is significant in less dramatic, if still important, circumstances. How much and how well the financial institutions mobilise and allocate investment, as opposed to engaging in speculative ventures, affects the levels and productivities of investment. And, as already seen, such short-term influences on the economy can hardly be disassociated from putative long-run outcomes whether tied to equilibrium or not.

Resolving the classical dichotomy in the way covered here is inextricably attached to the contribution of Don Patinkin in the 1950s when he was working with the US Cowles Commission. This was concerned with building macroeconomic models of the US economy, drawing upon the intellectual traditions of its time. These included the newly emerging, or by then evolving, Keynesian economics as well as the microeconomics associated with what has been dubbed TA^2, the technical apparatus of utility and production functions and the optimisation, efficiency and equilibrium of general equilibrium theory. This was also embedded in the formalist revolution of the 1950s that increasingly rendered economics axiomatic and mathematical. In this light, Patinkin's discovery of the conundrum posed by the classical dichotomy, and his proposed solution to it, is hardly surprising.

But there were other intellectual influences of the time that are easily overlooked in retrospect because they were not, and could not be, addressed within this increasingly formalistic framework. Economists at the time, and in Cowles, were conscious of other issues bridging the short and long runs and microeconomics and macroeconomics. One was covered in Chapter 2 (how to integrate short and long runs in terms of growth with cycles). In addition, the institutionalist traditions of American economics from the interwar years, and the influence of economic historians with their traditions of empirical investigation, also offered topics for investigation across the dichotomies identified. Specifically, what are the implications of corporate structure, and monopolisation, for macroeconomic performance? How does technical change come about and how is this incorporated into long-run growth? What are the implications of the distribution of income for macroeconomic performance? And what role do other institutions play in macroeconomic outcomes, most notably trade unions and bargaining over wages and conditions in some sectors but not in others?

As suggested, whilst these issues were to some degree prompted for the same reasons as the classical dichotomy, they were inevitably addressed in an entirely different way. They were at most acknowledged and then simply set aside, either being left to fields other than macroeconomics or ignored altogether. This reflected, on the one hand, an increasing separation between the short and long runs for the purposes of macroeconomics and, on the other, a continual tension between microeconomics and macroeconomics that has persisted until the present day, albeit with shifting balances and content. What is inescapable is that macroeconomics was being steadily reduced in its scope of what was to be explained and how it was to be explained.

3.4 Further Thoughts and Readings

As suggested in Chapter 1, macroeconomics has increasingly converged on two different aspects of general equilibrium theory: one is the optimising behaviour of individuals and reliance upon corresponding microeconomics; and the other is consistency across markets. These are, of course, both elements of TA², but it is important to recognise that they are different from one another. In particular, in the context of the classical dichotomy and its resolution by Patinkin, what is at stake is the second aspect alone, or Walras' Law. What is not at stake is how the real economy as such functions since, as is apparent from its general nature, the equation for excess demand functions $E(p, M/p)$ may be derived from any sort of underlying understanding of the derivation of supply and demand (although there is a presumption of satisfying homogeneity in M and p). For this reason, more radical versions of the real economy (allowing for monopoly for example) can be consistent with Patinkin's resolution of the classical dichotomy. As a result, despite this potential radicalism, and subject to retaining a unique long-run equilibrium – however radically conceived is the real economy, with whatever implications for short-run adjustments – it will necessarily always be tied to the long-run solution determined by fundamentals (although these might not be derived from TA²).

In short, the coincidence of Walras' Law and a unique long-run equilibrium are by themselves sufficient to place considerable constraints on what can be achieved by macroeconomics. Abandoning the idea of a unique long-run equilibrium is probably not too challenging, not least since, as already argued, there is every reason to believe that short-run adjustments can have considerable effects on the long run (whether conceived as lack of unique equilibrium or the passage of time and not equilibrium at all). But macroeconomics without

Walras' Law seems to be more or less inconceivable, since every (intended) sale is a purchase and vice versa.

This, however, depends upon treating the macroeconomy as if it is a set of accounts rather than something that evolves through time. Just to compile those accounts, it is necessary artificially to bring time to a halt, even though exchanges are sequenced and the quantities and values of what is produced are never at rest. It follows that how Walras' Law is constructed and construed inevitably reflects particular views on how the economy moves through time. And for the vast majority of macroeconomics that movement is understood as a sequence of equilibria (and as such, as points at which Walras' Law holds). As a result (as will be seen in Chapter 8-10 for example), relying upon Walras' Law as a touchstone of rigour can have the effect of reducing the qualitative content of the consequential macroeconomic theory. Indeed, to some extent it has already been seen that Walras' Law is not a precondition for macroeconomic insight, as illustrated by the accelerator-multiplier model and knife-edge of Chapter 2, where no account is taken of the Law at all.

The real balance effect was first highlighted by Arthur Pigou in the 1930s, leading to and reflecting a dispute with Cambridge colleague, Keynes. Pigou argued that the RBE would tend to stabilise the economy since, in a recession, as prices fell, the RBE would rise together with expenditure. As seen, the RBE takes on a different role in Patinkin's resolution of the classical dichotomy but, somewhat perversely, it retrieved its original role within the IS/LM framework of Keynesian economics (see Chapter 5).

For a discussion of Patinkin and the classical dichotomy, see Bridel (2002) and Hahn (2002). For a discussion of the origins of money from a Marxist perspective, and a critique of alternatives, see Lapavitsas (2005). For more radical versions of the real economy that incorporate money, etc., see Godley and Lavoie (2007).

4
Growth Theories:
Old, New or More of the Same?

4.1 Overview

Growth theory fits uncomfortably around macroeconomics. On the one hand, no one can deny that it has to do with the workings of the economy as a whole. On the other hand, it is primarily concerned with the long run as opposed to the short run that preoccupies the bulk of macroeconomics, with the long run and growth taken as given for the purposes of investigating deviations around them. Symbolically, many macroeconomic textbooks have excluded growth theory altogether, or otherwise treat it as an item separate from the rest of the content. This has begun to change, with the increasing reduction of macroeconomics to microeconomics, not least through RBC theory (see Chapter 9).

This more recent fuller integration of growth theory with contemporary macroeconomics is not accidental in origins or content. Modern growth theory originates with the Harrod–Domar model, covered in Chapter 2, with its pre-occupation with the existence of steady-state balanced growth (or growing equilibrium over time) and the stability of such an equilibrium should it exist (Harrod's knife-edge problem). The neoclassical one-sector, or Solow–Swan, model of growth that emerged in the 1950s, now known as old or exogenous growth theory, is covered in Section 4.2. Without necessarily intending to do so, it laid much of the foundation of what was to follow in terms of new or endogenous growth theory, covered in Section 4.3, as well as the previously observed disjuncture with macroeconomics. In its technical content, and by unwitting implication in its conceptual content, it was deeply embedded within microeconomics as opposed to macroeconomics. In this respect, the central role played for the old growth theory (OGT) by the one-sector production function is salient, as it is a core component of the technical apparatus underpinning microeconomics (alongside the utility function, and the technical architecture of optimisation, equilibrium and efficiency, see the counterpart *Microeconomics* volume). Significantly, OGT, although almost contemporaneous with Patinkin's treatment of the classical dichotomies, finesses money and the short run by setting them aside and focusing exclusively and simply on the long-run real economy (although there is the potential for some attention to the short run in equally simplistic terms, which leave aside both money and unemployment). In this respect, growth theory in the 1950s can be regarded as an early and unobserved example of what has been termed economics imperialism, in which rich treatments of a topic (growth and development) is colonised by economics on the basis of the narrowest of principles and considerations – bearing in mind how, Harrod–Domar apart, growth had previously been the subject of economic historians concerned with the rise of capitalism and its continuing performance.

To be fair, the OGT also had much reduced ambitions, seeking merely to measure the sources of growth and not to explain them, as covered in Section 4.2. Even in this, it was beset by major flaws in seeking to reduce growth performance to a one-sector model, as indicated here but also covered in more detail in the counterpart *Microeconomics* volume. After all, the method of measuring technical change as a source of growth is not confined to the macroeconomy and can apply at any level of economic activity, from the individual firm upward, indicative once more of the simultaneous micro/macro nature of growth theory.

No such lack of ambition, nor departure from microeconomic foundations, is evident in the new or endogenous growth theory that emerged in the 1980s, see Section 4.3. On the basis of microeconomic principles, especially those concerning market imperfections leading to increasing returns to scale, it seeks to explain and not simply to measure the contribution of productivity increase to growth. This also gave rise to concerted efforts to estimate the sources of productivity increase through growth econometrics (see Section 4.4). This is generally recognised to have failed, with the empirical results tending to invalidate the assumptions of the theory rather than providing estimates for it. In this light, Section 4.5 revisits the relationship between the old and new growth theories and the broader relationship between growth theory and macroeconomics.

4.2 Old Growth Theory

It is understandable to take OGT as the point of departure when addressing new growth theory (NGT). In turn, OGT itself originates out of the neoclassical response to the problem of existence of steady-state balanced growth (SSBG) in the Harrod–Domar model (Chapter 2). Recall that SSBG requires that the warranted (capital stock) and 'natural' (labour force) rates of growth be equal, or $s/v = n$, where s is the savings ratio, v the capital–output (K/Y) ratio and n the rate of growth of labour. When the equilibrium condition is satisfied the economy is growing along this path, charting a trajectory in which all proportions between variables remain the same even though they expand in absolute terms. However, if the warranted rate of growth is higher than that of the labour force, there will be a growing shortage of labour, and vice versa for when $s/v < n$.

The Solow–Swan one-sector growth model deals with the existence problem by endogenising just one of the three independent forces that are brought together to form the SSBG equilibrium condition, namely the capital–output ratio. This is achieved by bringing into play the neoclassical aggregate production function (thus, allowing for substitutability between capital and labour, K and L). With s and n still taken as given, v is allowed to vary to allow $s/v = n$.

The aggregate production function, $Y = F(K, L)$, can be expressed in per capita terms given the assumption of constant returns to scale. For, if so, we can divide both sides of the production function by $1/L$, $Y/L = (1/L)F(K, L) = F(K/L, 1)$, with the second variable constant and equal to 1. In other words, output per capita, $Y/L = y$, can be produced by capital per worker, $K/L = k$, and we can collapse $y = Y/L = F(K/L, 1) = F(k, 1)$ into the representation, $y = f(k)$. With the constant savings ratio, s, and total saving translating automatically and fully into investment, then per capita saving/investment is $sy = sf(k)$. As the Harrod–Domar condition requires $s/v = n$, it follows that $sf(k) = nk$ as a condition on k for SSBG. This is simply saying that the amount of saving/investment per worker should equal the amount of new investment needed to equip each new member of labour force with the same capital (when the labour force grows at rate n, the new number of workers per year is n and they need investment per worker of nk to be provided by saving $sf(k)$). As Diagram 4.1 shows, the SSBG is achieved at $sf(k^*) = nk^*$. At this point, the growth rates of output, the capital stock and labour are equal to one another, which also implies that the ratios (Y/L, K/L, Y/K, etc.) remain constant. In other words, the growth rate of output per worker and capital per worker are zero (since both numerators and denominators grow at the same rate). Substitutability across capital and labour (from the production function) also ensures the stability of the long-run growth path. Suppose, for example, the economy is to the left of k^*, at $k < k^*$. Then, because of the shape of the per capita production function, f, reflecting the assumption of diminishing returns to capital (and labour), $sf(k) > nk$, as also follows from the diagram (as $f(k) > (n/s)k$ to the left of k^*). This automatically leads to an increase in k until it reaches k^*. Similarly for the mirror-image case where the economy stands to the right of k^*. With labour fully employed, the extra capital per worker is insufficient to produce the extra output and saving to sustain itself, so k falls until it reaches k^*.

The workings of the adjustment mechanism are the same in cases of changes in exogenous factors, such as, say, an increase in the propensity to save, s. In Diagram 4.2, the equilibrium moves from A to B, and from lower k^* to higher k^{**}. With higher savings and thus investment, there is more capital per worker available. However, whilst at the new equilibrium the capital–labour ratio (k) and output per worker (y) have increased, the steady-state growth rate remains unchanged at n. In other words, increases in savings (and, by definition, investment) have a level effect on per capita output, but no permanent effect

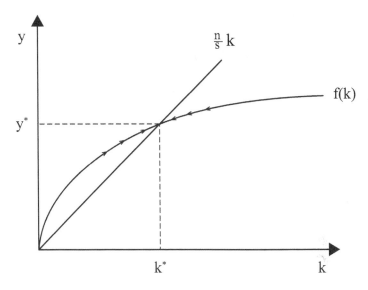

Diagram 4.1   Steady-state balanced growth for the Solow–Swan model

on the long-run growth *rate* of the economy. The same result applies to the case where population growth decreases, since again more capital per worker is available. The important point is that the SSBG rate is exogenously determined by the rate of growth of the labour force, n. At most, increasing saving, for example, boosts growth temporarily and raises per capita income but it cannot change the rate of growth itself. By the same token, per capita output remains constant along the SSBG path, and hence the growth rate of output per worker remains zero.

As is apparent, the neoclassical one-sector production function allows Harrod's existence problem for SSBG to be solved by varying v in the formula s/v = n. In principle, either s or n could have been allowed to vary (and there are models of this sort, with s varying with distribution between profits and wages, see Chapter 6, or n also varying with distribution in a Malthusian fashion if wages rise above subsistence). This is not our concern here. Rather, with the existence problem solved, we can now turn to Harrod's second problem of stability, or the knife-edge. This too has been surreptitiously resolved or, more exactly, set aside. As established in the stability analysis above, the diminishing returns production function and the fixed parameters of s and n suffice to ensure stability of the SSBG in the long run. Short-run deviations around this derive purely from having the wrong capital–labour ratio temporarily. But, as in the long run, the presumption in the short run is that all resources are fully employed, and that saving both drives the level of investment and is fully converted into investment. In short, the neoclassical growth model is purely a supply-side model that tracks the stability of the full employment path. In

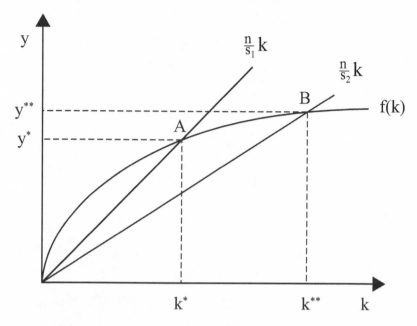

Diagram 4.2   Changes in the steady-state balanced growth path
from saving ratio increases

other words, it does not allow for deviations from the long-run trend due to demand-side considerations.

By contrast, Harrod identified the knife-edge problem by considering the demand side of investment decisions (the accelerator), particularly in the context of entrepreneurs' future expectations of output demand to be met, an issue that is totally absent from the OGT. This raises the question whether growth (let alone development) can be appropriately studied from within the organising concepts of a SSBG path and a supply-side equilibrium. Growth, in practice, is neither steady (constant and smooth over time) nor balanced (with the same composition of output). And full employment at all times along, or even alongside, the path is unreasonably presumed through the mixing and matching of all capital and labour in any necessary proportion via the neoclassical production function. To be fair, the explicit rationale of OGT was to specify the long run, especially to measure the relative contributions (of factor inputs and productivity) to growth. But it can only do so by detaching the long from the short run and, as has been seen in the stability analysis above, extrapolating the long-run to short-run analysis, thereby setting aside (Keynesian) considerations of effective demand for the short run. At this stage of analysis, and at the time, this might have seemed innocent given the goal of measuring long-run contributions to growth as opposed to short-run sources of instability. But, as will be seen, it offered the first wedge in the door of collapsing the short and long runs into one another from an analytical point of view, opening the way to presuming that effective demand could be put aside for both short- and long-run analyses, as with RBC theory (see Sections 4.5 and 9.4).

As already mentioned, technological progress was taken up in neoclassical growth theory but, as we now address, only in terms of its *exogenous* role in the SSBG path and in the measurement of its contribution to increases in output. For the first of these, technological progress, or productivity change other than from changes in k, can be added to the Solow–Swan model in the form of what is termed (exogenously imposed) labour-augmenting technical advances. The production function can be modified such that $Y = F(K, AL)$, where A is labour-augmenting technology and AL corresponds to 'effective labour'. Essentially, it is simply presumed that each unit of labour becomes more effective by the factor A. The analysis and results remain much the same as before, as can be seen by converting the system in 'per effective labour unit' terms (whenever L was present before it is now replaced by AL). The new input, effective labour (AL), has two independent and exogenous components of variation: the growth rate of the labour force (n as before) and the growth rate of its effectiveness or of A (denoted by m). Hence, with this type of technical progress, the SSBG equilibrium is given by $sf(\tilde{k}) = (n + m)\tilde{k}$, where $\tilde{k}$ is the capital per effective labour ratio, $\tilde{k} = K/AL$. The determination of the SSBG equilibrium, and the adjustment mechanism towards it, remain unchanged. But with SSBG in $\tilde{k}$, output per worker with the labour-augmenting technical progress now takes place at a constant exogenous rate, m. It is as if each worker becomes equivalent to more workers at the rate of growth m, with output per real worker correspondingly increasing. Thus, in per capita terms, the economy is growing along the SSBG path. Exogenous technological progress (of a very specific, labour-augmenting form) has an impact on the per capita growth rate (output is growing faster than labour due to increases in the latter's effectiveness).

Second, and on this basis, the neoclassical growth model has been used to measure the impact of exogenous productivity increases on increases in output. In a more general form, technological progress takes the form of exogenous changes (shifts) in the production function per se. For, the aggregate production function can be represented as $Y = F(K, L; A) = AF(K, L)$ where Y, K and L are aggregate output, capital and labour, and A, in multiplicative form, represents technological change, responsible for changes in the F function over time.

This can be shown to lead to the decomposition of output growth into three factors: growth in capital, growth in labour and what is termed total factor productivity (TFP). Taking differentials for $Y = AF(K, L)$:

$$dY = AF_K dK + AF_L dL + F dA$$

where AF_K and AF_L are the marginal products of capital and labour, respectively, and $dY/dA = F$ shows the impact that technology changes have on the production function. Diving through by $Y = AF(K, L)$ and rearranging gives:

$$(dY/Y) = (KAF_K/Y)dK/K + (LAF_L/Y)dL/L + dA/A.$$

Denoting the growth rate of variable x by g<x>:

$$g<Y> = AF_K(K/Y)g<K> + AF_L(L/Y)g<L> + g<A>$$
$$g<Y> = ag<K> + (1 - a)g<L> + g<A>$$

where $a = AF_K(K/Y)$ is capital's share in output and $(1 - a) = AF_L(L/Y)$ is labour's share, under the assumptions of full employment and perfect competition. This is because, for capital say, AF_K is the marginal product of capital and so equals the profit rate (price of capital), so $AF_K(K)$ equals total profit and $AF_K(K/Y)$ equals profit share. The same applies to labour's share. In other words, the so-called growth accounting equation decomposes the growth rate of output into the contributions stemming from increases in capital (weighted by its share in output), increases in labour (weighted by its share in output) and the unobserved speculated impact of technological progress. The final term can be seen to be just:

$$g<A> = g<Y> - ag<K> - (1 - a)g<L>.$$

The term g<A> gives the output increase that is not explained by increases in inputs and so is designated as due to technological progress and, as mentioned, dubbed total factor productivity (TFP). TFP is recognised to be a *residual* after the contribution of increases in inputs have been netted out from increases in output. It is explicitly acknowledged to be unexplained, or untheorised, and only measured. This procedure is supposedly distinguishing between movements along and shifts of the production function. In other words, it attempts to decompose changes in output growth due to adjustment to the SSBG path and changes in the SSBG path per se.

However, this interpretation is not valid except under very special circumstances. And the major blow of defining and measuring TFP in this way comes from the Cambridge Critique (see chapter 5 in the counterpart *Microeconomics* volume for a detailed analysis). Suffice to say that TFP measures not only shifts in the production function, but all deviations from the assumptions upon which TFP is constructed: notably perfection competition (and hence marginal product pricing), full employment (supply-side equilibrium) and the one-sector model economy (one homogeneous capital/consumption good).

The latter problem entails deeper debates in value theory but, simply put, with more than one good and with K entering the production function as an index as if a physical quantity of capital, it would be impossible to decompose changes in the quantity of capital goods, K, and changes in the relative prices of capital and other goods. Precisely because there is only one sector in the model, any change in the relative price of capital will have to be measured as a change in its quantity. Nothing might change except the price of capital, but this would be measured as technical progress if the price of capital went down (since it would appear as if there were less capital being used) and technical decay if the price of capital goes up (appears as if more capital is being used to produce the same output).

Despite all of the above, TFP has been extensively used in analysing economic performance, with Solow providing the first such study for the US economy for the first 50 years of the 1900s, and showing that about 7/8 of the output growth could be attributed to TFP changes, with only the remaining 1/8 to capital (per worker) accumulation. Empirically, the magnitude of TFP can be cut back, through refinements in measuring the principal inputs (capital and labour), and inclusion of others (e.g. skills, natural resources, etc.). Perversely though, the empirically derived patterns for TFP tend then to be explained by causal factors that violate the assumptions under which the patterns have been derived. For example, TFP is deemed to have been poor because of a recession, or because of the increasing power of trade unions. These violate the assumptions of full employment and perfect competition, respectively, which are essential for measuring TFP in the first place, indicating that as a measure it incorporates, within its residual, all of the changes that are due to the deviations from the assumptions that it necessarily makes to construct the measure (including that there is only one good or, equivalently, no relative price changes, especially for capital and labour).

Leaving aside all these problems, one of the presumed predictions of the OGT (from the perspective of the NGT) that has played a pivotal role in future developments is the so-called convergence hypothesis. If technology is freely available to all – everyone has the same production function F – it would be expected that per capita output would converge over time across countries, especially with free capital mobility. In particular, and due to diminishing marginal returns to capital, poor countries (with a low K/L ratio) would exhibit high productivity of capital and hence grow faster than rich countries (with a high K/L ratio). This opened the field for an outpouring of empirical works, attempting to measure differences, and convergence or not, in per capita output growth across the world, and eventually to new growth theories that allow for both endogenous and unequal growth across countries.

4.3 New Growth Theory for Old?

NGT originates from the contributions of Paul Romer and Robert Lucas from the mid-1980s, and within a decade it gained considerable momentum and prominence. In understanding its contribution it is appropriate to take OGT as a point of comparison, as well as developments within the discipline of economics more generally.

Despite a proliferation of diverse NGT models, they all share a set of common theoretical tenets. First, and contrary to OGT, NGT identifies and endogenises the sources of productivity increases, and in a variety of ways. Besides externalities from learning-by-doing (and by extension by adopting, adapting, watching, exporting, etc.), which are presumed to be by-products of accumulation per se, productivity increase has been modelled by focusing on the generation, use and diffusion of new knowledge. A separate R&D or 'ideas production' sector can be set up, and productivity increase to the economy as a whole can accrue through increases in quality and variety of intermediate inputs being invented, for example. The same methodology can be applied to the quality of labour, which can be enhanced through investment in the accumulation of human capital. Again, this can be modelled in various ways and with varying outcomes.

Second, and whatever the modelling device, a central tenet in NGT is its microeconomic basis, both in terms of the models being derived from optimising intertemporal decisions of representative individuals within a general equilibrium framework, and in drawing upon microeconomic theories for the analysis of economies of scale, product differentiation, human capital formation, etc. This parallels the broader developments within mainstream economic thought with the increasing prominence of microeconomics, and the convergence of macroeconomics upon it. As a result, in many respects NGT has stronger affinities to microeconomics than even to a narrowly defined macroeconomics, at least until the current macroeconomics consensus came to prevail (see Chapters 9 and 10). Convergence to microeconomics was achieved in two stages. On the one hand, if only slightly earlier, the Solow–Swan model was derived by applying principles of individual optimisation instead of assuming given parameter values. Specifically, the constant aggregate savings rate, s, is replaced with intertemporal utility maximisation, whilst leaving the rate of growth as exogenously determined by labour force growth, n. On the other hand, with much greater substantive impact, productivity increase was endogenised. As a result, what matters in the modelling of such endogenous technological advance is that all outcomes (including invention generation) derive from the purposeful optimising behaviour of individuals in pursuit of private profit, even if optimisers do not internalise the overall (generally social) benefits (or rare losses) of their decisions. An invention brings returns to all who can use it and not just its inventor, unless it is monopolised.

The third common aspect of endogenous growth models is their reliance on market imperfections, with increasing returns to scale (IRS) and externalities being foremost. Simply put, and even if constant returns to scale persist at the individual firm level, IRS are liable to emerge at the aggregate level given the knock-on effects that the innovation processes have on current and future aggregate production possibilities. Paradoxically, then, whilst externalities and implied Pareto inefficiencies were all familiar from long-established microeconomics, NGT manages to transform their, equally well known, static deadweight losses into engines of growth at the macroeconomic level.

To reiterate, and using the terminology of OGT, NGT continues to be organised around the SSBG path, $s/v = n + m$. However, now v (capital-output ratio), s (saving–investment ratio) and m (technological advances) are endogenised within a microfounded dynamic framework. The production function is organised around IRS. Behind the new assumption of IRS lie the limitations of the neoclassical constant returns to scale production function of OGT, and particularly diminishing returns to capital. The latter assumption is crucial for the two main perceived empirical and theoretical limitations of OGT that NGT was set to overcome. First is that, due to diminishing returns to capital, convergence in per capita output is predicted as poorer countries grow faster. Second, diminishing marginal product of capital leads to per capita growth stabilising at a zero rate. In other words, a higher saving–investment ratio is offset by a lower productivity of capital and ends up having only a level rather than a growth effect (higher Y/L but its growth rate settles back to zero).

But within NGT, by invoking IRS both problems can be overcome. Simply put, and despite rampant diversity in the modelling, if it is assumed that other factors of production can behave in a similar way to capital in the sense that, once used, they can be stored and accumulated through some equivalent 'investment' process that ensures sacrifice of current resources for future benefits, then it is very straightforward to generate IRS. Consider then the aggregate production function:

$$Y = F(K,L,A) = BK^a(L_Y A)^{1-a}$$

where L_Y denotes the amount of labour used for the production of final output Y, and A, as before, is a labour productivity factor. If A is assumed to be fixed, it can be absorbed into the constant term, B, and constant returns to scale prevail, with:

$$Y = (BA^{1-a})K^a L_Y^{1-a}.$$

If, however, A is a factor that varies and, in particular can be 'accumulable' (like capital), then IRS in K, L and A results, rewriting:

$$Y = BK^a L_Y^{1-a} A^{1-a}.$$

This has increasing returns, $2 - a$, since $a < 1$.

Apart from allowing for IRS, what is distinctive in its contribution to NGT is how the nature, accumulation and diffusion of this new input, A, is specified, together with corresponding market, incentive and institutional structures. These have been modelled in different ways with varying outcomes. A standard and common representation for the accumulation of A is given by:

$$\dot{A} = \delta L_A A^\varepsilon.$$

With $\varepsilon = 1$, this says that the change in A is given by a constant term δ and is proportional both to the volume of labour allocated to the production of A, L_A, and to the existing stock of A. For example, with A as human capital (as in the classic contribution of Lucas), this equation implies that growth of human capital is related positively to both the amount of labour, L_A (or time/effort) allocated in non-working activities (e.g. studying), and the skills level already attained, A. Similarly, as in R&D-based models (in the spirit of Romer's), A can be viewed as ideas or knowledge that generate new varieties of intermediate capital goods. Again, new varieties accrue over time, depending linearly both on the number of people working in the research sector and the extent to which past knowledge is non-rival, and hence contributes proportionally to new knowledge. There is, hence, a positive externality (external to the individual researcher/firm) in that accumulated past knowledge spills over to future research. Of course, with an endogenous process of R&D creation derived from optimising behaviour, the number of inventors (or investors in R&D) will depend on the monopoly rents (patent structure) that can be extracted from innovation, which in turn will also relate to microeconomic parameters such as those attached to preferences (discount factor and elasticity of substitution of consumption over time) and technology (labour or capital share derived from the production function). IRS and externalities can be extended in many ways, with other models incorporating the obsolescence of old intermediate goods as new inventions take place. These 'new Schumpeterian' NGT models may also generate cycles of growth and destruction, for whilst a quick spread of innovation may lead to high productivity increases, it simultaneously undermines the incentive to innovate by shrinking temporary monopoly rents.

The rich portfolio of assumptions, extensions and outcomes, with corresponding mathematical complexity, allow for a huge variety of models, the common feature of which is to deploy some market imperfection to generate increasing returns, and so to generate the growth rate endogenously according to the resources that fuel those increasing returns (although with optimising behaviour, the extent of endogeneity is limited to differences in parameter values

– save more, for example, and you get a higher growth rate, not just a higher output level from a higher capital–labour ratio for a given growth rate). Even so, such models tend to depend upon special assumptions around parameter values, as can be seen by exploring the formal properties of the previously presented NGT models.

Let us do so by putting aside any growth in labour, $n = 0$, for the purposes of simplicity. If $\varepsilon < 1$, then with a constant number of skills or ideas builders, L_A (necessary for SSBG), the productivity increase from skills or ideas declines to zero over time. This is because the rate of growth of labour productivity is given by:

$$\dot{A}/A = \delta\, L_A A^{\varepsilon-1}.$$

As a result the model converges to the OGT as the effect of A becomes proportionately negligible over time.

On the other hand, if $\varepsilon > 1$ then it can be shown that the model generates infinite levels of growth within finite time, which is surely implausible! This is because productivity keeps on enhancing the productivity creating process – a bit like a rocket that reduces mass as it burns its fuel and so keeps going faster and faster.

It follows that SSBG can only exist in the case where $\varepsilon = 1$, despite this seemingly being an arbitrary assumption. If, on the other hand, L_A (and L) is allowed to grow, the restrictions on ε have to change. For, in this case, even a value of $\varepsilon = 1$ leads to explosive paths as the natural growth of the economy fuels productivity growth through the increasing returns.

A fourth and important point to be acknowledged, then, is how NGT models rely upon potentially complex and dynamic general equilibrium frameworks. These tend to require strong assumptions and parameter restrictions, at times more arbitrary than those used to establish the existence of SSBG in the Harrod–Domar model.

Fifth, the majority of NGT models share other implications from their mutual reliance upon market imperfections, such as externalities and IRS. The endogenous sources of productivity increase, via imperfections of different sorts, serve both as engines of sustained growth and as sources of inefficiencies. On one hand, the impact of imperfections is felt on the rate of growth, rather than the level of output for a given growth rate. This is because they are deemed to have cumulative and knock-on effects over time. On the other hand, they lead to Pareto inefficiencies whereby the optimal levels of knowledge creation, human capital formation, the saving rate, etc., tend to be below the social optimum.

Other than the conversion from level to growth effects, there is not much 'new' with new endogenous growth theory, as it is simply a theory of technical change in light of the presence of market imperfections (which have long been associated with deadweight losses or gains in partial equilibrium microeconomics). It has been recognised that most of the ideas underpinning endogenous technical change are not new. Rather, they can be traced back to works by classical political economists (e.g. Smith, Ricardo and Schumpeter) and other schools of thought (such as in Kaldor), as well as other social sciences. Nonetheless, the adoption of pre-existing ideas and theories to forge a theory of endogenous growth is achieved only on a piecemeal basis and by stripping off and simplifying original concepts so that they can be accommodated in a framework of methodological individualism and mathematical formalisation. This applies, for example, to models deploying economies of scale and scope, specialisation and agglomeration, and the role of monopoly rents in generating innovation and clusters of innovation. As for market imperfections, as mentioned, these are readily recognised to be microeconomics projected on to long-run macroeconomics, whatever the form, content and motivation are given to the IRS, monopolistic competition, product differentiation, and externalities and inefficiencies that are deployed.

It is, thus, not surprising that many of the criticisms of OGT carry over. First, NGT proceeds as if the use of the one-sector production function, F, is unproblematic. This is simply not the case, as laid out in the counterpart *Microeconomics* volume, in light of what is known as the Cambridge Critique of Capital Theory. OGT was undermined by this but NGT simply overlooks the problems involved. This goes beyond reducing the economy, as if it could be represented by a single sector production function, to setting up capital-like sectors for the production of human capital and R&D, bundling up and representing technical change through the device of treating it like a new factor of production, A (understood as a stock of ideas, knowledge or techniques). This is a transparent treatment of production and productivity through the prism of the technical apparatus and architecture available, not even acknowledging that knowledge cannot be subject to quantification. How do we scale an idea and represent it by a change in A?

Second, the tendency for NGT to be organised around SSBG shares the same problems with OGT. This simply fails to recognise what we know to be the unbalanced nature of growth in practice, although some of this has been accommodated with the appearance of multiple equilibria and more complex dynamics that are possible within NGT.

Third, and related to the previous point, it is not clear what the outcomes of NGT are. Whilst it attempts to refute what it takes to be the (convergence) predictions of OGT, and thereby produces more 'realistic' models in some sense, there is a myriad of models with different assumptions, market and institutional settings, complexities and outcomes where all or nothing can be made to fit. Depending on parameter values, an economy's growth can be explosive or dissipate; government policy may or may not have lasting effects; multiple equilibria may question the uniqueness and stability of a SSBG; and mathematical intractability limits conclusions. Even the slightest generalisations or extensions suffice to allow for different – divergent but also convergent – growth rates, and hence not many testable or tested results have been drawn from NGT models. Such liberality of outcomes is not matched by the methods employed by NGT as it proceeds by narrowing its scope whilst expanding its applicability, not least through commitment to rigorous mathematical modelling of optimising representative individuals.

4.4 Growth Econometrics

Since the 'convergence debate' took off in the 1960s, a profusion of econometric works have emerged in light of NGT, driven by the increasing availability of aggregate data and computing power. This debate has also played an important role in the formation and framing of NGT, both theoretically and in terms of empirical content, not least as to whether convergence or divergence can be contested by the old/new growth theory duo.

Relatively rapidly, empirical investigation of convergence became focused on an evolving study of the evidence in the form of cross-sectional growth regressions at the country level. In what came to be known as Barro-type growth regressions, cross-country growth rates were regressed against initial (log) per capita GDP level. The simple idea was that convergence would mean that countries with a low per capita income would grow faster. As a result, a negative coefficient on regressions of growth on per capita income could be interpreted as supportive of both (absolute) convergence and exogenous growth theory:

$$g_Y = \alpha + \beta \log Y_0 \text{ with } \beta < 0.$$

Evidently such a specification does not account for other factors that affect growth and may differ across countries. Subsequently, so-called conditional convergence became the epicentre of research, with additional variables included in the right-hand side of the equation. Beyond conditional convergence, the inclusion of other variables could identify salient determinants of growth, whilst differentiating among those supported by OGT or those indicative of sources of endogenous growth (such as human capital, R&D expenditure and so on). Accordingly:

$$g_Y = \alpha + \beta \log Y_0 + \gamma X,$$

with X a vector of other exogenous variables, and γ its associated coefficients vector.

However, it is a moot point whether – even with a negative value of β – this would offer a valid test of convergence, for it is consistent with a set of different explanations, such as catching up or structural changes in developing countries. A negative β estimate could also result from solely statistical reasons, such as the phenomenon of regression to the mean. Galston's regression fallacy (which was itself the source of the name for such regression analysis more generally) refers to a situation in which, if countries' growth rates are identically and independently randomly distributed, then if one county's observation is by chance much higher (lower) than expected (than the mean) at one point in time, then it would be expected to be lower (higher) in the next instance (thus growth regressing towards the mean of the distribution). Hence, a negative β coefficient does not necessarily say much about the cross-sectional convergence across countries.

A second problem with Barro-type growth regressions is their lack of robustness and stability. Estimation results on convergence are sensitive both to sample and time frames and to the variables included in X. Add or take away some variables and the regression coefficients can change size and even sign. What is more, the statistical significance of the regressors fluctuates as others are added or omitted. Hence, inference with regard to the convergence proposition, and to the importance of other factors in explaining growth differentials, is at best inconclusive.

Third, and despite the above caveats, this did not stop the expansion of the empirical literature along similar lines, with more than a hundred variables having being tried in different combinations, ranging from education and investment to trade openness, fiscal and monetary variables, corruption and religion, and so on. But with the simple device of adding (or dropping) variables that work (or not), the connection with theory becomes less and less visible until it drops away entirely. Essentially, as previously observed, many theories of endogenous growth could be put forward, drawing upon voluminous causal empirical evidence, reduced past theories, or even invention itself in terms of how skills are derived or research and development is generated or adopted, with mathematical tractability to the fore. In the final case, it is impossible to solve the optimisation problems with more than a few considerations in place. Consequently, the X variables might at most be justified by some model in which they appear more or less individually. Ultimately, even this rationale is no longer necessary, and you simply add into the regression any variable that might be thought to affect growth.

In this way, the Barro-type regressions became theoryless, an exercise in its own right. But the motto of theoryless econometrics ('let the data speak for themselves') brings obstacles not only for its theory-testing capabilities but also because it ignores the fact that data themselves are constructed on theoretical presumptions, and that the econometric approach itself is not entirely theory free (particularly in its pursuit of universal regularities within cross-sectional settings). At the same time, there are so many degrees of freedom in terms of variable selection (and exclusion) that it is not clear what can be inferred out of these numerous exercises.

To be more specific, first many of the independent variables are highly correlated with one another, which is, to some extent, to be expected since correlates of growth are systematically connected. High co-linearity among independent variables, however, puts strains on the accuracy of individual estimates and on pinning causal (or not) indirect effects on growth. For example, it could be that there is a strong (causal) relationship between investment and the quality of government institutions, and that investment impacts growth via a strong institutional structure. Second, and of greater importance, the core issue of causality remains open. For example, education, investment and R&D expenditure, three of the staple ingredients in the X vector, can be viewed as both sources and consequences of growth. Or more generally, there could be underlying factors (in the error term) that affect both dependent and independent variables. In other words, there is an endogeneity problem that cannot be resolved by statistical tools, and certainly not by Barro-type regressions. Lesser reliance on theoretical grounds, even with advance in econometrical techniques, makes empirical results less convincing and meaningful. There is also the problem of functional form selection, with a linear relation from X to g_Y restricting considerably the understanding of the ways by which explanatory factors affect growth.

All of the above issues have been, to some extent, taken up by more sophisticated econometric approaches, particularly in the form of panel data estimation and a concerted focus on time series analyses – bear in mind, cross-section Barro-type regressions do not distinguish between whether the data represent convergence to SSBG paths or convergence of SSBG paths to one another. This point is made clear in Diagram 4.3. We could, for example, be appearing to converge in the short run across the two countries represented, whereas the convergence is towards long-run SSBG paths for the countries that diverge from one another. The Barro-type regressions would suggest convergence even though this is wrong. At least panel analysis can use cross-country data over time to distinguish between SSBG paths and the adjustments to them, that is, between equilibria or dynamics movements (although the extent to which segmenting time into five or ten year intervals is appropriate for the study of long-run growth is debatable).

Unlike cross-sectional regressions, panel data estimation with country fixed effects can control for country-level specificities, usually identified as exogenous differences in (initial levels of) technology. This is done by allowing for different country intercepts. However, such a parameter vector is more like a black box, including all unobserved factors that are deemed to vary sluggishly over time within each country, whilst also differing between countries. These influences

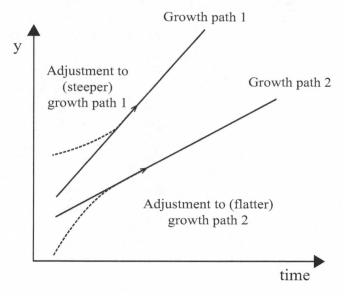

Diagram 4.3   Differences in growth paths and adjustments to growth paths

need not be just technological, but could also be institutional, political and geographical in nature. Estimates of such constant terms are, generally, found to be excessively large from one country to another – a result corroborated by new (panel or time series) TFP estimations. However, the panel estimation's main advantage is also its major drawback. Whilst accounting for unobserved country heterogeneity, it essentially gets rid of the cross-sectional variation, relying almost exclusively on within variation growth (over time within each country). And this is problematic particularly in a growth econometrics context because, first, it impedes the analysis of the effects of growth determinants (such as institutions, geography or policies) which exhibit little or no time variation. And second, unobserved country differences are treated as a nuisance – conveniently assumed rather than explicitly modelled, as in the case of cross-sectional estimations.

Either way, cross-sectional Barro-type regressions are still heavily used, not least for policy recommendation purposes. Conventionally, regressions are run log–log in the variables, and the original (prior to estimation) functional form involved is:

$$Y_t/Y_0 = a Y_0^\beta X_1^{\gamma_1} X_2^{\gamma_2} ... X_k^{\gamma_k}$$

This is a remarkable proposition, vanity even, with the growth history of the world, across all times and places, reduced to a Cobb–Douglas 'production function', incorporating any variable you consider might be relevant to growth performance. This has had two implications. One is that the parameter estimates can be readily deemed to be appropriate for handling policy trade-offs. For, given the costs of the policy – and some might be deemed to be costless, such as trade liberalisation or lifting of foreign exchange restrictions – the estimated γs give the growth elasticities of the policy parameters. Literally, in some studies, increase the number of telephone lines per population, and growth will go up by so much.

The second implication is that growth theory, which always had its origins and deep roots within the study of developed countries and within the mainstream economics forged in that context, had become universally applicable and so considered relevant, indeed imperative, for the study of developing countries. Such ambition, however, ultimately signalled its death knell, at least in principle. Probing deeper into the results of growth econometrics, first we find that whilst most economies have grown over the past 40 years, growth rates across countries have diverged to an unprecedented extent for all but the richest countries irrespective of initial conditions (thereby casting further doubt on convergence hypotheses). Second, growth across the globe has been poorer between 1980 and 2000 than in the previous two decades and with more dispersion of growth rates (although there have been 'take-offs' for China and India, incorporating two-fifths of the world's population). Third, there have been convergence clubs of nations around growth rates, roughly coinciding with East and South East Asia, South and Central America, and sub-Saharan Africa (in order of declining performance). Fourth, identifying the causes of major take-offs and slumps in growth are of importance. Fifth, policy change and reform can be of considerable significance, as can the more or less favourable response to more general 'shocks'. Sixth, there is a need for country-specific study focusing on historical and institutional context.

Stepping back from these lessons, we can draw three further general conclusions. The first is to reinforce the conclusion that models are liable to collapse the complexity and diversity of the growth experience, partly because of the nature of the beast itself and partly because of the nature of the models, whether by virtue of necessity or by design in light of how theory and modelling have evolved in practice. Second is to observe the inconsistency between the empirical results and the theories from which they derive, ones that are almost universally based upon a dynamic organised around SSBG. Third is the almost unwitting revisiting of older traditions in economics, especially the old development economics, in the sense of seeking out empirical regularities and explanations and precedents for them, even if now on the basis of considerably larger, later and more diverse data sets and more refined statistical techniques. One has to wonder what all the maths and microfoundations provides! By the same token, where is the economic theory as such, if all and sundry are simply to be thrown into the equivalent of a single equation estimate of the world? This is truly the hitchhiker's guide to the universe of growth – literally the question asked of the computer through running millions of regressions.

4.5 Further Thoughts and Readings

It is now almost 30 years since Paul Romer drafted his classic and pioneering paper on NGT. He could not have anticipated the explosion of research that would follow, not least given the modesty of his own research methods. As he confesses in retrospect on whether he was influenced by Schumpeter's notion of creative destruction:

> No, I can honestly say that it has not. Schumpeter coined some wonderful phrases like 'creative destruction' but I did not read any of Schumpeter's work when I was creating my model. As I said, I really worked that model out from a clean sheet of paper. To be honest, the times when I have gone to try to read Schumpeter I have found it tough going. It is really hard to tell what guys like Schumpeter are talking about [*laughter*]. (Snowdon and Vane, 2005: 686)

Even if we reduce the issue of development to (endogenous) growth, contingent upon productivity increase, the resulting energy devoted to explaining it in theoretical and empirical terms has been astonishing. Hundreds of variables have been deployed and millions of regressions have been run. They offered the promise of results that could be used for economic and social engineering, not least with the idea that growth is the key to poverty reduction, a central plank of World Bank perspectives policy itself best served through neoliberal nostrums.

Such ambitions have not been realised in practice. Nonetheless, the trajectory of growth theory has been part and parcel of the evolution of macroeconomics over and above its own contribution to understanding the macroeconomy, since it helped to establish technical, conceptual and empirical methods. One, generally unobserved, characteristic of the OGT is its disregard for its empirical implications where they do not suit. For example, above the SSBG path, during a boom of higher than normal growth rates because of higher than normal capital accumulation, it is anticipated that wages would be relatively higher and profits relatively lower due to diminishing marginal products and constant returns to scale. This might be thought to be the opposite of the case, as is centring analysis on SSBG more generally. And, apart from doing macro without money and finance and legitimising the detaching of the long from the short run, as observed in Section 4.1, OGT offered the earliest, although not the fullest, reliance upon microeconomics as the foundation for macroeconomics. In doing so, it also allowed for a theory of distribution (itself fundamentally flawed in light of the capital theory critique of the one-sector production function, see the counterpart *Microeconomics* volume), in which wages as the marginal product of labour and profit as the marginal product of capital complemented their use in measuring the contribution of the growth of factor inputs to the output (to allow for TFP to be calculated as the residual). Such starting points for determining distribution subsequently underpinned the use of intertemporal optimisation techniques for both saving and investment within growth theory itself, and ultimately RBC theory and dynamic stochastic general equilibrium (DSGE), although the OGT was more parametrically based for specifying saving functions and labour supply. Ultimately, though, as it went into decline whilst seeking pastures new, the OGT fully adopted intertemporal optimisation not least, for example, by responding to the oil crises of the 1970s, by doing so in the context of exhaustible resources.

Significantly, despite these continuities between old and new growth theory, and between each of them and macroeconomics as it was to become in terms of reduction to microeconomic principles and more or less perfectly working markets (see later Chapters 8–10), OGT was considerably more restrained in its claims. Robert Solow, for example, its leading proponent, is highly critical of NGT. In part, this is because it is misrepresented in being seen as failing to put forward a theory of technical change and in predicting convergence. On the contrary, the OGT considered that its framing was incapable of explaining technical change at the macroeconomic level precisely because of its dependence upon country-wide specific factors that could not be reduced to the economic. Further, there has been very little that is new in the NGT, with many of its ideas previously known to, and even presented by, old growth theorists. But these were primarily and appropriately seen as microeconomic and not to be extrapolated to the economy as a whole, quite apart from relying upon highly restrictive assumptions more driven by the requirements of the modelling than any rationale derived from realism.

As a result, Solow's OGT was deliberately self-contained in its purpose, leaving space for other methods and theories to address (short-run) macroeconomics and explanations for technical change. Despite providing the foundations for wider application of its microeconomic methods, as an old-fashioned Keynesian, Solow has been scathing about the consequences, describing the preoccupations of DSGE in the following terms:

> Suppose someone sits down where you are sitting right now and announces to me that he is Napoleon Bonaparte. The last thing I want to do with him is to get involved in a technical discussion on cavalry tactics at the Battle of Austerlitz. If I do that, I'm getting tacitly drawn into the game that he is Napoleon Bonaparte. (Klamer 1984: 146)

As for NGT itself, it is characterised by some peculiar anomalies not already covered. One is the total absence of price theory, even though the market sits in the background allocating resources and generating endogenous growth. Whilst the setting of prices might be deemed to be implicit as for OGT, this is problematic in the presence of IRS unless these are totally discounted from all of the optimising behaviour of individuals. This, then, raises a different problem – the presence of externalities, social IRS or whatever last indefinitely (the long run) and are never realised or addressed by optimising agents (despite being known by economists and with rational expectations already well on the horizon). Such inconveniences are not allowed to get in the way of modelling and estimation where rigour is presumed to reign supreme.

For an excellent review of NGT, from within its own perspective, see Aghion and Howitt (1998), where the models of Lucas, Romer and others, are also analysed. For critical overviews, see Fine (2000) and Kenny and Williams (2001). For OGT, see Sen (1970). Solow (2006) offers a sample of his views on the NGT. For the difficulties associated with increasing returns for the mainstream, see Arrow (2000). Reviews of growth econometrics can be found in Durlauf et al. (2005) and Islam (2003). For the reductionism of Barro-type regressions to a Cobb–Douglas function and the highly defective implications of ignoring non-linearities see Rodriguez (2006). Sala-i-Martin (1997) ran millions of such regressions. A rebirth of interest in growth, and yet another revival of old doctrines, is currently taking place in response to the global financial crisis, where vivid discussions about secular stagnation are taking place (and sometimes attached and combined with issues of growing inequality), and the first formal models are being produced. For a review on this, see Backhouse and Boianovski (2015).

5
The Keynesian Revolutions

5.1 Overview

In the immediate post-war period, Keynesianism rapidly came to the fore within economics, forging a significant relative supremacy over an increasingly standardised microeconomics, although both progressed in intellectual prominence in absolute terms. Equally, both were subject to representation in mathematical form. Initially, as covered in Section 5.2, the IS/LM interpretation of Keynesianism, or the neoclassical synthesis, rapidly achieved a near monopoly of macroeconomics. This is despite its considerable departures from the economics of Keynes.

To some degree, increasingly throughout the 1960s, these misinterpretations were in part the point of departure for a critical reinterpretation of Keynes in what was variously known as the reappraisal of Keynes, or fixed price, quantity-adjusting or rationing models. However, in many respects, as shown in Section 5.3, despite some correction of interpretation of Keynes over the neoclassical synthesis, the reappraisal had the effect of introducing even more anomalies in interpreting Keynes (and the macroeconomy) than it had corrected. Indeed, paradoxically it played some role in smoothing the transition from Keynesianism to extreme forms of monetarism and a subsequent Keynesian response that fell far short even of the erstwhile IS/LM framework with the emergence of new Keynesianism and the NCM (see Chapter 10).

5.2 IS/LM as Neoclassical Synthesis

Whilst it is more or less uncontroversial that there was a Keynesian revolution in the 1930s in response to the Great Depression, with a corresponding intellectual revolution and more in the post-war period, the exact nature and significance of that revolution is hard to pin down and controversial, possibly more so in the wake of the monetarist revolution and the rise of neoliberalism since the breakdown of the post-war boom into stagflation in the 1970s. The picture has been muddied even more both by what is termed the new Keynesian response to monetarism – the compromises around what is termed the New Consensus Macroeconomics (NCM) – and the bewildering disruption of conventional macroeconomic wisdoms occasioned by the current global crisis (see Chapters 8–10).

Nonetheless, as starting point, there are certain elements of the Keynesian revolution that do appear to be incontrovertible. First of all, macroeconomics came to be heavily focused on the determinants of, and interaction between, macroeconomic aggregates such as consumption, investment, output, the price level, the demand for money and so on. Second, these aggregates are attached to a preoccupation with the determinants of aggregate demand. Third, aggregate demand, as a nominal magnitude, is made up of the product of the price level and real national income, pY. Accordingly, subject to the availability of excess capacity, the differences between monetarism and Keynesianism depend upon whether increases in aggregate demand are expected to go into the price level or into the level of real national income, with the monetarist presumption that a market economy without undue state interference will tend to be at or near full (voluntary) employment as opposed to the Keynesian view that there is the possibility of (involuntary) equilibrium unemployment. Last, and by no means least, the Keynesian revolution as textbook economics was almost uniformly represented through the IS/LM framework, although it is now far from as ubiquitous, and certainly not as prominent and exclusive as it was at the height of Keynesian influence.

The IS/LM representation of Keynesianism was first introduced in the second half of the 1930s by John Hicks. It ultimately became known as the neoclassical synthesis for reasons that will become clear. Formally, the IS curve derives from the equality between saving and investment. The saving function, sY, as the basis for the simple multiplier ($sY = I$ so that $Y = I/s$) can be generalised both in functional form and by including the rate of interest as the reward or price paid in return for saving. So $S = S(r, Y)$ with $S_1 > 0$ and $S_2 > 0$ as more is presumed to be saved the higher either the level of income or the interest rate.

The LM curve is derived from the supply of money, M, assumed fixed, and the demand for money, $pL(r, Y)$, so that $M = pL(r, Y)$. The demand for money, following Keynes, is supposed to be as a result of three motives: for transactions, for speculation or as a precaution. However, whatever the reason for holding money (and there is no reason why one bit of money should not simultaneously perform all of the functions to whatever degree), the cost of doing so is represented by the rate of interest since this is given up by not letting go of the money and putting it to interest-earning use. Accordingly, whilst it is presumed that more income will lead to more money being held at least for transactions, less money will be held the more expensive it is to do so in interest foregone. So $L_1 < 0$ and $L_2 > 0$. Further, without money illusion, the demand for money should be proportional to the price level (otherwise, you demand more or less money just because of the unit in which it is denominated).

From these properties it follows that the slope of the IS curve is negative and the slope of the LM curve is positive. They will intersect at equilibrium for r and Y, see Diagram 5.1 for a fixed price level. Now, if this is not at full employment, with output too low say, then there will be excess supply of labour (and potentially goods) and the wage and price levels will fall. This will lead to a shift in the LM curve to the right. Indeed, the LM curve can be interpreted as a demand for real balances, $M/p = L(r, Y)$. With a lower price level, there are more real balances available, and for these to be held with equilibrium in the money market, either r has to be lower or Y larger than previously, equivalent to a rightward shift in the LM curve as indicated. This can continue until full employment is obtained.

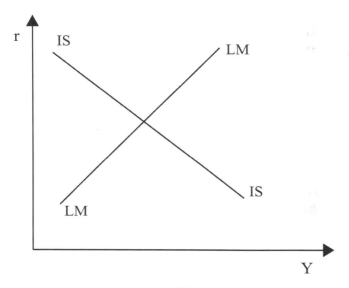

Diagram 5.1   IS/LM curves

As a result, if either prices or wages are not flexible, or are rigid downwards, there can be no movement towards full employment. What else could go wrong to prevent full employment being achieved? One possibility is that the IS curve is vertical or, in other words, reductions in the interest rate (the cost of capital) do not lead to more saving and investment. This is in effect the simple multiplier for which $Y = I/s$, where I is fixed and is independent of the interest rate. Another possibility is that the LM curve is horizontal over a section. As a result, as the LM curve shifts to the right it has no impact on the intersection with the IS curve.

This possibility is known as the liquidity trap and is usually interpreted as representing Keynes' innovation. Consider the liquidity trap in a little more detail. As can be seen from Diagram 5.2, the interest rate needs to fall in order

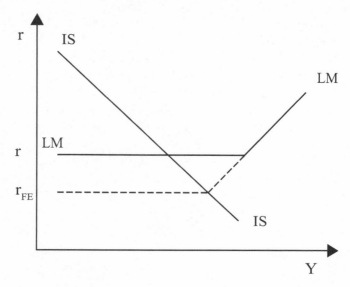

Diagram 5.2 Keynesian liquidity trappings

that investment increases. But for some reason the rate of interest does not fall, and although prices are falling and real balances are increasing, these continue to be held rather than leading to greater expenditure. In other words, there is a desire to hold on to money rather than to spend, what is known as (absolute) liquidity preference.

Why should this be so? Suppose that those releasing their money for saving purposes get the current rate of interest, r, for doing so but there is a general expectation that the rate of interest will rise (possibly because it has been higher in the past). Then there will be liquidity preference until the rate of interest rises, and the rising real balances will continue to be held. The irony is that whilst there are expectations that the rate of interest will rise, it actually needs to fall to restore full employment equilibrium but does not do so because of liquidity preference. In short, the IS/LM interpretation of the liquidity trap is one in which:

$$r_{FE} < r < r^*$$

where r_{FE} is the interest rate for full employment, r is the unemployment interest rate and r^* is the expected rate of interest. Further, because the rate of interest is too high relative to the level required to generate equilibrium, there are investments that could be made if the rate of interest were lower. Keynes used the term the marginal efficiency of capital, MEC, to denote the anticipated return to an investment. In terms of the IS/LM approach, investments can be listed in descending order of rate of return, and all will be undertaken until MEC = r, so that:

$$r_{FE} < r = MEC < r^*.$$

Significantly, the liquidity trap can be interpreted as rigidity in the money market, since the rate of interest needs to fall but will not. This is an important element in the IS/LM interpreted as the neoclassical synthesis, or incorporation of Keynesianism into mainstream thinking. First, rigidity in price and wages and in investment would already be understood as potential sources of unemployment. Second, although Keynes claimed to be putting forward a general theory of unemployment, his was in fact a special case, one in which there is rigidity in money markets. Third, this does reasonably involve the replacement of Say's Law by Walras' Law – Keynes had highlighted that there could be a general glut of commodities if such excess supply was mirrored by an equal and opposite excess demand for money. And, last, the IS/LM framework allowed for a synthesis in the discussion of policy around which of fiscal or monetary policy is liable to be more effective. Essentially, is it better to move the IS or the LM curve to move the economy towards fuller employment? The answer depends upon what is thought to be the shape and position of the curves.

In passing, it should be observed that the association of the IS curve with fiscal policy (e.g. increase some component of effective demand through state expenditure) and the LM curve with monetary policy (e.g. expand the money supply) is fallacious. The one-to-one correspondence between the two curves and the two sorts of policies, respectively, is invalid as a simple consequence of the rejection of the classical dichotomy. As the IS curve represents the real economy in the short run, it must necessarily include real balances in the equations. But they are absent. In other words, real balances, and money, should be added to the IS curve. In their presence, the IS curve, and fiscal policy, are not independent of monetary policy. This is not to say that fiscal policy cannot be examined through the IS curve nor that it is necessarily ineffective (although see Chapter 8 on the policy ineffectiveness proposition), only that fiscal policy cannot be understood independently of monetary policy.

Putting this to one side, let us consider the liquidity trap in more detail. As observed, investments will be made, rather than money held in anticipation of a rise in the rate of interest, if the expected rate of return on the investment exceeds the current interest rate, if MEC ≥ r. Here the MEC is equivalent to the marginal product of capital in a production function, with profit maximisation leading to MEC = r, since all investments are made down the list of more profitable available projects.

But is this all that an investor would take into account? What if the necessary inputs were not available, or there was a potential strike on the part of the workforce? The MEC only materialises in practice as opposed to principle if the investment can be successfully completed, alongside production and, most important in this context, the output sold once it can be successfully produced. To capture this difference between what can be achieved in principle and what is liable to be achieved in practice, let the MEC in ideal circumstances be called the physical MEC, or PMEC, and the one contingent on realising sales etc. be the monetary MEC, or MMEC. Necessarily, PMEC ≥ MMEC, as the latter materialises as the former only if all constraints are overcome. But, for the purposes of making the investment, it is the MMEC that counts.

In particular, if there is deep pessimism over the level of demand in the economy then, whilst the PMEC may be greater than the rate of interest, the MMEC may be lower. So, even if the rate of interest is below the level required to generate full employment, if the MMEC is itself lower than this there will be insufficient investment to make for full employment.

Thus, for the neoclassical synthesis, because the distinction is not made between the PMEC and the MMEC:

$$r_{FE} < r = PPME = MMEC = MEC < r^*.$$

But, if that distinction is made, it is possible that:

$$MMEC = r < r_{FE} < PMEC.$$

In other words, the problem is not that the rate of interest is too high, since it could be below the full employment rate (think the minimal rates of interest in the global recession, see below); and the investment possibilities, at least in principle, are profitable since PMEC > r. But the investments are not made, and it is not because the cost of capital is too high. Rather, it is lack of confidence in the ability to sell the output. Moreover, it really does not matter what expectations are concerning the rate of interest, r^*. These could be higher or lower than r or r_{FE}. The reason for liquidity preference is not expectations about the rate of interest but expectations about future levels of effective demand.

This can all be looked at from a different point of view, from that of labour and consumption as opposed to investment and production. Suppose workers are unemployed. As a result, although willing to work even at lower wages, they are unable to buy consumption goods. As a result, firms are unable to sell those goods if they produced them. So they do not employ the workers who, as a consequence, do not have the wages to buy the consumption goods. The economy is caught in a vicious cycle of deficient demand. According to the IS/LM framework, this would lead to a fall in prices and wages, raise real balances and boost demand. But falling prices and wages might have the effect of both reducing effective demand and confidence, deepening rather than resolving the problem of unemployment.

These considerations raise serious doubts over whether the IS/LM approach, despite being the standard representation, fully captures the Keynesian approach to the economy other than in name. The neoclassical synthesis is primarily based upon the notion of what is termed Walrasian adjustment. Markets do not adjust properly because prices do not adjust or because supply and demand do not adjust to price adjustments. In other words, there is what is termed rigidities within markets or failure of Walrasian adjustment. By contrast, the Keynesian approach emphasises that prices as such are less important. They could all be at their equilibrium levels. But the market economy is dependent upon exchanges being made, with workers being able to get a job and spend on consumption goods, so that capitalists make a profit by employing workers and selling the output they produce. In this respect, Keynesian adjustment is one that considers quantities to change more speedily than prices. Changes in effective demand lead to loss of output more rapidly than reduction in prices, with knock-on effects for supply and demand.

This is taken up in Section 5.3. But it is also worth observing that the critique of the IS/LM framework offered here is more faithful to the Keynesian tradition in the way in which it treats expectations. For the neoclassical synthesis, it is a matter of what is the anticipated value of the future rate of interest, whereas the MMEC (and what Keynes himself understood as the MEC as a term he himself introduced) is more attuned to the state of confidence in the economy and whether there is or is not liable to be effective demand in the future. Indeed, Keynes' view of expectations was more focused on the presence or not of entre-preneurial 'animal spirits' and the potential impact of waves of optimism or pessimism.

Such considerations might be seen to be appropriate in the era of quantitative easing and minimal interest rates. It cannot be that the interest rate is too high to warrant investment because of the cost of capital. Rather, liquidity preference is so powerful because of severe pessimism over the prospects for making profitable investments in view of depressed demand with the recession, a situation which then appears to reproduce and justify itself.

In short, the appeal of the IS/LM lay not only in its formalisation of what is falsely taken to be Keynes' specific contribution but also in compromising with a Walrasian approach to the economy. In addition, the IS/LM framework allowed for each of these to be used as a way of posing fiscal and monetary policy, in which each could lever the economy through changes in government expenditure and the money supply, respectively. This inspired Coddington to dub the IS/LM framing of Keynesianism as 'hydraulic'.

5.3 Reappraising or Reducing Keynes?

In Section 5.2, we introduced the idea that the neoclassical synthesis may misrepresent Keynes by focusing on Walrasian price adjustment rather than quantity adjustment. This alternative view of Keynesianism was put forward in the 1960s as a critique of the IS/LM framework and enjoyed a brief period of prominence. Its focal point is that the market as a coordinating mechanism for supply and demand involves sequential, not necessarily simultaneous, exchanges, not least due to the need to meet budget constraints subject to how much credit might be made available, itself something that might be constrained. In order to buy, you have to have money, and to get that money, subject to what you might have kept under the mattress or elsewhere, you need to have sold something first. This is so whether prices are high or low, at their equilibrium levels or otherwise.

The starting point for taking account of market exchange as sequences has been what is known as Clower's dual decision hypothesis. Suppose there is a consumer who, for convenience, is assumed to live for just two periods, consuming in both but only working in the first from which savings must be carried over for consumption in the second. If the individual works for N hours at wage w, and faces prices p_1 and p_2 for consumption c_1 and c_2, respectively, with rate of interest r and initial assets A, then:

$$c_2 = (A + Nw - p_1c_1)(1 + r)/p_2$$

since, inside the first bracket is how much income is carried over to the next period, and this earns the rate of interest before being spent on consumption. The equation can be rewritten as:

$$p_1c_1 + p_2c_2/(1 + r) = A + Nw.$$

Let L be total hours available to the consumer and add Lw to both sides of the equation (for reasons to be revealed) and rearrange to yield:

$$p_1c_1 + p_2c_2/(1 + r) + (L - N)w = A + Lw.$$

This is the consumer's budget constraint, just like one for the standard optimising consumer after a little reinterpretation of the wrinkles. Because postponing consumption to the second period earns interest, the effective price of consumption then is $p_2/(1 + r)$ rather than p_2; and L − N is the leisure the consumer enjoys in the utility function, and it costs w for giving up the time that could be spent earning the wage; and, in this light, the consumer has total assets A + Lw available. Now, ideally, the consumer will maximise utility,

$u(c_1, c_2, L - N)$ subject to the budget constraint. Suppose we find the optimum as c_1^*, c_2^*, and $L - N^*$. This is where the consumer would like to go if they are able to make all sale and purchases at the given, fixed prices.

Now consider the representation of the consumer's position more generally by use of a two-dimensional representation through c_1 and N. Given that these are fixed, the value of c_2 will follow from the budget constraint. So, in Diagram 5.3, H represents where the consumer (or household) would like to be (with corresponding optimal value of c_2^*), but any other coordinates in the diagram will represent a less than optimal outcome. Just to be sure, for a higher value of c_1 and lower value of N than c_1^* and N^*, respectively, it might seem as if the household is better off with more consumption and less work, but this will be heavily at the expense of c_2, recalling that the optimum is at c_1^* and N^*, and so the consumer is worse off than at the optimum.

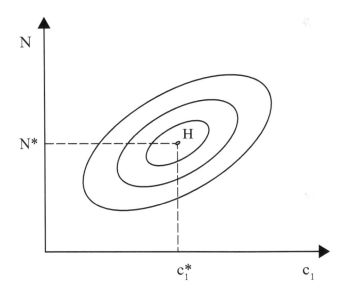

Diagram 5.3   Household pseudo-indifference curves

Indeed, the further away from c_1^* and N^*, the lower the utility of the household, as would be apparent if the utility function's indifference curves were represented in the three dimensions of c_1, c_2 and $L - N$. It is even possible to draw pseudo-indifference curves in Diagram 5.3, as illustrated by the concentric ovals around H. Each point on one of these is of equal utility for the household (taking account of implied c_2 through the budget constraint); and the utility is less the further away the pseudo-indifference curve from the single-point indifference curve represented by the optimum at H.

This apparatus has taken a little trouble to set up. But it will allow for the analysis to proceed relatively smoothly from this point. Suppose, for example, that all goods are freely available at the going prices and that the same applies to gaining access to work. Then the household will choose to go to H. On the other hand, suppose there is a constraint on the amount of goods available. For some reason, they are simply not available in the shops. This can be represented by a vertical line at the level of the constraint. Households will have to buy at or to the left of that line. If the line is to the right of H, it is no constraint at all as far as the household is concerned. But, if the line lies to the left of H, the household cannot get the consumption goods that it wants. As a result, how much work to provide needs to be reconsidered. After all, what's the point of working to earn income to buy consumption goods that are unavailable? So the household decides how much work to provide contingent on the availability of goods that can be purchased with the earned wage revenue. Accordingly, where goods are not available, the household will reduce the labour that it supplies in what is termed a dual decision. Ideally, or notionally, the household would prefer to go to H. Being unable to do so, it goes elsewhere.

But where exactly? Well, given the household is constrained by the availability of consumption goods as indicated by the vertical line, the best the household can achieve is where that line is tangential to the innermost pseudo-indifference curve. This is represented by B in Diagram 5.4. And, as the constraint moves to the left and right, B will trace out the line indicated, finishing at H above which the household, as observed, is no longer constrained.

A similar exercise can be conducted for when the household is unconstrained on availability of goods to purchase but is constrained by the availability of jobs. In this case, there is a horizontal line indicating the amount of work, N, available.

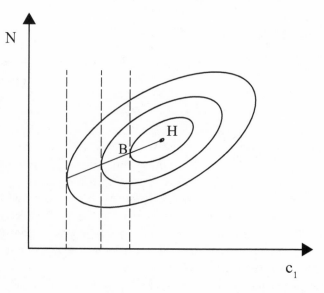

Diagram 5.4 Households constrained on goods

Again, if N is above N*, the constraint is not binding and the household can go to H. But if N is below N*, the constraint is binding, and the household has to reconsider how to divide available income between the two periods and come to a dual, instead of a notional, decision. In this case, as indicated in Diagram 5.5, the household will adjust to the closest pseudo-indifference curve to H and, as the constraint is tighter or looser, will trace out outcomes as also indicated in the diagram, with H as limiting point once more.

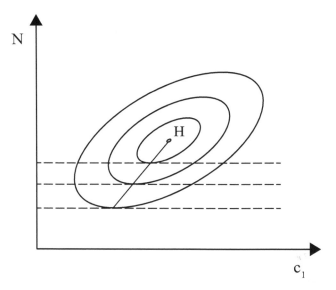

Diagram 5.5   Households constrained on labour

Putting these two sets of dual decision-making processes together gives rise to Diagram 5.6. It offers the 'wedge', DHS, with apex H which summarises all of the possible outcomes: for a demand-constrained household (for goods) along HD with a corresponding dual decision to reduce labour supply below the optimum at H; or a supply-constrained household (for labour) along HS with a corresponding dual decision to reduce consumer demand below the optimum at H.

This completes the analysis of the representative consumer/household. Now turn to consider firms. To conform with how consumers have been set up, these (or one firm as representative) will be able to produce in the first period only, employing labour but selling the output produced across both first and second periods. So the firm's decisions are how much labour, N, to employ and so output to produce, and how to divide it between sales in this period, c_1, and the next, c_2, given respective prices, p_1 and p_2, and rate of interest, r.

The effective price of output in the second period is $p_2/(1 + r)$, in present value terms, since if the sale were made in the first period the income could be saved and earn r. So, if $p_1 > p_2/(1 + r)$, then all output that is profitable to

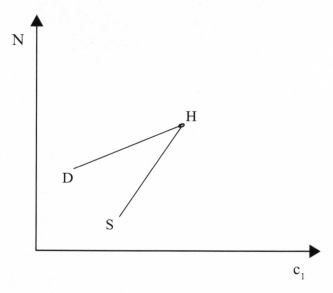

Diagram 5.6   The constrained household

produce will be sold in the first period, and vice versa, all output will be sold in the second period if $p_1 < p_2/(1 + r)$. If $p_1 = p_2/(1 + r)$, then it is indeterminate how much is sold in each period as prices are equivalent to one another.

This does not work for the model, so suppose that $p_1 < p_2/(1 + r)$ but that there are increasing unit costs from zero of passing over output from period 1 to period 2. Eventually, the marginal cost of storing the output will equal the price difference across the two periods, but output will be sold in both periods. With this device, and some underlying production function, f(N), there will be an optimum, profit-maximising outcome for the firm for choosing c_1^*, c_2^* and N^*. However, as with the household, once c_1 and N are specified, c_2 will follow as a result of what is left over from production, f(N), once c_1 and storage costs have been deducted. The optimum point for the firm can be represented in Diagram 5.7 by F, with c_2^* implicit, and the same applies for the whole of the diagram, with each point representing a set of values of c_1, N and, implicitly, c_2.

In this case, in parallel with the household, iso-profit lines can be traced as concentric ovals around F. And these can be used to work out what would happen should the firm not be free to attain its optimum point, F. In particular, suppose the firm is unable to sell the optimal output, in period 1, then this will be represented by a vertical line. It will be of no significance if it lies to the right of F, but, if to the left, there is no point employing the optimum amount of labour if the output produced cannot be sold as intended. As a result, a dual decision is taken on employment, traced out by FD', with typical point C, for which the firm's demand for labour is reassessed because the firm is demand-constrained

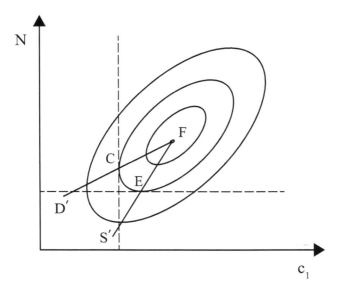

Diagram 5.7   The constrained firm

on its supply of goods. On the other hand, if there is shortage on labour supply, this is fine if the horizontal constraint lies above F. Otherwise, below F, being unable to produce all that it wants, the firm will adjust down from the optimal notional supply of c_1^*, tracing out FS' with typical point, E (see Diagram 5.7). As a result, there is a wedge for the firm, represented by D'FS'.

To find out what can happen within this model, it is simply a matter of putting household and firm behaviour together. There are four possible outcomes, with equilibrium being given by how the wedges are situated in relation to, and how they intersect with, one another (see Diagram 5.8). Each of these distinct outcomes is known as a regime. The first is the classic, unemployment regime. There is excess supply of labour and excess demand for goods. The reason is that the money wage is too high relative to prices. As firms want to go to F and workers want to go to H, firms are on the short side of both markets. They want to employ less labour and sell fewer goods than labour wishes to supply and purchase, respectively. The agent on the short side of the market prevails and so the economy will end up at F.

The second regime is known, possibly inappropriately, as an underconsumption regime (the idea of underconsumption is associated with a Marxist approach to 'monopoly capitalism' in which capitalists are unable to sell all that they can produce out of exploited workers). In this case, the money wage is much too low relative to prices. This is the reverse of the previous regime. Firms wish to sell much more than workers wish to buy, and to employ more labour

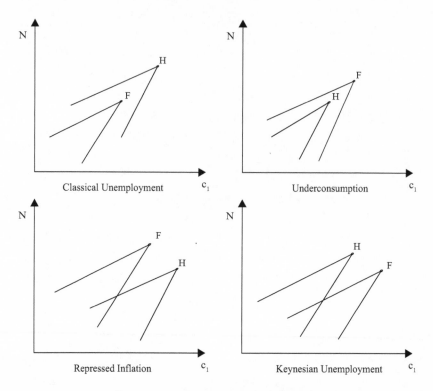

Diagram 5.8   Quantity-constrained regimes

than workers are prepared to supply. In this case, the household is on the short side of both markets, and the economy ends up at H.

The third regime is known as repressed inflation and is perceived as corresponding to the use of markets under Soviet central planning. In this case, the wedges intersect as indicated. For the household, there are insufficient consumer goods available to purchase. This leads to an undersupply of labour relative to the optimum (why work for consumer goods you cannot buy?). On the other hand, firms are constrained in the number of workers they can employ and so necessarily produce less than they would otherwise. Note that it is not necessarily the case that prices are at the wrong level in some sense (diverging, for example, from those that would prevail in a fully efficient, full employment equilibrium). Rather, at the prevailing prices, households would prefer to work and consume more, just as firms would prefer to employ and produce more. But their intentions are not coordinated properly through the market.

The fourth regime, at last, is the Keynesian. Households are constrained by being (partially) unemployed and so reduce demand for consumption goods. Firms are constrained in what they can sell and so employ less than they would otherwise like. Once again, the problem is not necessarily with prices. Rather, there is a lack of coordination through the market between what firms and households would prefer to do. Both would like to see more employment and output at the prevailing prices.

Finally, though, there is the potential for a fifth regime, or the one that is the other four combined. This is where F and H coincide with one another. It is the Walrasian, general equilibrium. Supposing the wedges are located randomly, then the chances of the Walrasian outcome are negligible (or measure zero, as mathematicians would have it).

Suppose, though, that the Keynesian, unemployment equilibrium, prevails. Would it persist? Given unemployment and potential excess supply of goods, it might be expected that wages and prices would fall as those on the long side of the market seek to meet their intentions. But falling wages hardly helps aggregate demand for goods even if they boost in principle the profitability to employers of taking on more labour (if what is produced can be sold).

In terms of modelling, to address such issues requires moving beyond the intraperiod analysis of the wedges to the following period for which it would be necessary to specify how the disequilibrium of the previous period affects the new round of prices for which a new set of wedges will be constructed. This is not undertaken here, but it is worth observing that prices and wages may be extremely sticky in view of the dual decisions of households and firms. The disequilibrium in whatever regime, apart from the Walrasian equilibrium, is one in which notional intentions of optimum outcomes are frustrated. There is no reason why these notional supplies and demands would be signalled through the market. Unemployed workers might go window shopping but they do not buy or order! So employers do not know whether, if they took on workers, they would create the demand that they themselves find deficient. This is just to reinforce the way in which the demand-deficient economy is being understood as a quantity, rather than as a price-adjusting system, and, as indicated earlier, a market economy that is sequenced in terms of buying and selling and not simultaneous interactions of supplies and demands.

It is certainly the case that, as demonstrated, this reduction of the role of prices, and the elevation of the role of quantities, has a peculiar effect. This is that, despite emphasis upon the role of the market as transmitting and coordinating, however well, supply and demand as a quantity-adjusting system, the role of money has become negligible. Indeed, as presented formally, the models above do not include money at all except implicitly in the fixed assets, A, that have no significance as such. Money may be the medium in undertaking exchanges but it seems to be a neutral veil in outcomes. The quantity-constrained market economy could also be based on barter!

This would appear to represent a departure both from Keynes and the neoclassical synthesis, given the importance that they both assign to money. Of course, the reappraisal can and did place considerable emphasis on money as a medium of exchange, not least because the speculative holding of money is liable to limit the volume of transactions undertaken in a Keynesian spirit. But, as presented above, the analysis does seem to have departed substantially from the emphasis placed upon two significant aspects of Keynesianism, both the role of expectations in underpinning economic activity and, in light of corresponding speculation over what is liable to happen to the rate of interest or animal spirits, the importance of the level of investment in generating demand. In short, in emphasising the role of the market in coordinating exchanges quantitatively, the reappraisal seems to have lost sight of the balance between the speculative use of money within the financial system as opposed to its use for expanding effective demand through real investment. As highlighted in Chapter 3, and in its own way by the neoclassical synthesis, the role of money both in facilitating transactions and in mobilising and allocating funds for investment are distinct (so much so that one tends to be treated as macro and the other as micro) but inextricably linked to one another. The reappraisal seems to have overlooked this altogether in perceiving the Keynesian economy as simply one of more or less efficiently coordinated and sequenced quantitative exchanges.

One reason for this oversight, although it can be corrected by incorporating quantity-constrained optimising for financial as well as real quantities, is possibly a consequence of a much more telling characteristic of the reappraisal – what has been known as its reductionism. As is only too apparent, its theory proceeds first and foremost from the optimising behaviour of individuals. In this respect, the approach represents at most a minor if significant departure from general equilibrium, one that does generalise it – a general, general equilibrium perhaps? Essentially, individual optimisation, and aggregation over individuals across markets for supply and demand, incorporates an extra constraint indicating previously required exchanges needing to be accomplished. If $E(p) = 0$ gives general equilibrium for a vector of excess demands, E, given a vector of prices, p, then the reappraisal is given by $E(p, X) = 0$ where X is a vector representing quantity constraints on individual transactions which must in turn add to outcomes from dual decisions in terms of supplies and demands as and when they are out of balance with their notional counterparts.

This is a somewhat abstract portrayal of the reappraisal, but it does suffice to indicate just how it is essentially a generalisation of general equilibrium and based upon the optimising behaviour of individuals. As a result, quite apart from how money and finance are treated, there is a total abandonment of systemic analysis, the macro being independent of the micro. Even the neoclassical synthesis does not go this far, as it seeks to postulate macroeconomic aggregates without necessarily grounding them in microeconomic foundations.

5.4 Further Thoughts and Readings

As mentioned, the reappraisal came to prominence in the mid-1960s as a reaction against the neoclassical synthesis that commanded a textbook monopoly in the interpretation of Keynes. However, within little more than a decade it had more or less lost influence, if not disappeared without trace. One reason for this was the emergence of stagflation that witnessed the monetarist counter-revolution against Keynesianism. The latter's emphasis on effective demand stalled on its apparent inability to explain how there could be a coincidence of both inflation (indicative of excess demand over and above full employment) and recession (indicative of excess supply). As if this were not enough to discredit Keynesianism in general, for the reappraisal in particular, models based on fixed prices must have seemed totally inappropriate in the face of rampant inflation, especially for a discipline increasingly geared towards econometric investigation. For a detailed account of the reappraisal, see Backhouse and Boianovsky (2013) and also Coddington (1983) (who coined the expressions hydraulic and reductionist for the IS/LM and reappraisal, respectively). The framework presented here first appeared in Muellbauer and Portes (1978), but see also Branson (1989).

Nonetheless, it would be mistaken to consider that the reappraisal's rapid rise and equally rapid demise have meant that it has not exercised any lasting influence, although this is something that can hardly be quantified. Whilst, not surprisingly, it can certainly be credited with incorporating the quantity-adjusting mechanism attached to the Keynesian paradigm, its departures from Keynesianism are equally striking, not least in its reliance upon methodological individualism – even to the extent of relying upon representative households. The role of money (to some degree paradoxically), let alone the financial system (as opposed to goods and labour markets), is minimal. Even the role of expectations in the narrowest sense is notable for its absence – quantity-constrained disequilibrium is self-sustaining whatever your expectations, given that you are in equilibrium.

What is remarkable, but not necessarily decisive or determining, is the way in which the future evolution of macroeconomics conformed with, or drew upon, these elementary aspects of the reappraisal. Indeed, it is important to note that these aspects were not always promoted by all of the reappraisal's proponents, not least as the reappraisal became captured by, and incorporated into, TA[2] and most obviously, as explained, as a generalisation of (demand-deficient) general equilibrium. Nonetheless, microfoundations and representative individuals, key aspects of the reappraisal's apparatus, became standard parts of the prospective NCE, the extreme form of monetarism and of the new (market imperfections) Keynesianism (see Chapters 7–10). The assumption of rigid or flexible prices became a critical point of debate between these two later schools. And wiping the slate clean around expectations and the role of money, let alone finance, allowed for macroeconomics to become even more pared down in its representation of Keynesianism, compared to the neoclassical synthesis that was the reappraisal's own critical point of departure.

This is to anticipate much that is still to come in this text and, as a result, what follows may warrant (re)visiting once the later material has been absorbed. The NCM that eventually came about is better seen as a synthesis of the NCE, with some other elements as opposed to a rejection of the latter. The relatively marginal adjustments to the NCE, in what has also become known as the new Keynesianism, completely tied Keynesian insights to microfounded market imperfections, fully based on TA^2, and also partially restoring the IS/LM approach (albeit with a modified LM curve to allow for rational expectations and corresponding foresight). Before discussing this in greater detail in Chapter 10, it is interesting at this stage to note two points regarding the real balance effect (RBE).

First, and as already mentioned, with Patinkin's incorporation of the RBE, fiscal (shifting the IS curve) and monetary (shifting the LM curve) policies are rendered interdependent. Nonetheless, the separation and implicitly assumed independence between monetary and fiscal policy continued, as can be prominently seen by the subcategorisation of macroeconomics between monetary economics on the one hand, and public finance on the other, with the other policy in each case considered exogenous, independent or simply passive as far as the other is concerned. Further, the NCM is directly derived from the monetary economics branch, whereby fiscal policy is exogenously taken to be passive (in light of Ricardian equivalence, see Box 5.1), and only monetary policy is seen as playing a role. The NCE's premise on fiscal policy ineffectiveness could have been influential, but, nonetheless, the separation of the study of the two policies preceded it.

Second, and as hinted at towards the end of Chapter 3, the role of the RBE in Patinkin's resolution of the classical dichotomy was different from the role posited earlier by Pigou – of price deflation increasing the RBE and demand, and ultimately leading to full employment. This explains why Keynes opposed Pigou's use of the RBE as a source of employment-creating demand, in principle viewing it to be of limited practical significance in conditions of very high unemployment (when confidence of the future is paramount). Nonetheless, by incorporating the RBE within the IS/LM framework, it can be seen to provide a stabilising role. As the monetarist Franco Modigliani demonstrated, the inclusion of the RBE in the real economy (wealth as an additional determinant of real consumption) renders the liquidity trap an ineffective explanation of involuntary unemployment. Thus, the Keynesian contention of an equilibrium below full employment becomes dependent solely on wage/price rigidities. The latter (particularly in the form of price rigidities) is the only characteristic that remains in the NCM. But, as already observed, this is to anticipate if only to signal now the extent to which the foundations of macroeconomics, and disputes over them, were being laid on the basis of the most arcane of issues.

Box 5.1
Ricardian equivalence theorem

For the purpose of the discussion of inside/outside money and net wealth effect, the Ricardian equivalence theorem postulates that even government bonds cannot be regarded as outside money. That is, government debt cannot be viewed as net wealth creation since there will be a corresponding tax liability down the line.

However, and as will become clearer in Chapters 8 and 10, the Ricardian equivalence theorem is essentially an elaboration of the neoclassical 'policy ineffectiveness' proposition: that fiscal policy (and monetary alike) cannot have real effects on economic activity. The essence is that bond and tax financing of government expenditure are equivalent and, within the argument of full crowding out, each is equally ineffective.

The argument relies heavily on intertemporal considerations of optimising individuals, and in a sense the pure distributional effect is now defined not across groups of agents as within a static framework (across those who hold the asset and those who wish to buy it), but across the same infinitely living agents (or, if you want to get fancy, overlapping generations of such agents).

An expansionary fiscal policy today, financed through government bonds, will entail an offsetting increase in future tax liabilities (to pay for the government's debts). Optimising rational individuals, realising they will have to pay more taxes in the future, respond to this by increasing savings today. Equally, if expansionary fiscal policy is tax financed, agents will spend less today to make provision for the higher current taxes. Thus, whichever way it is financed, the increase in government expenditure will be offset by an equal decrease of private consumption, leaving aggregate demand unchanged.

Besides lack of empirical confirmation (and basic common sense in suggesting government can never do anything much to the workings of the aggregate economy other than make it worse through microeconomic distortions), even on its own terms Ricardian equivalence relies on a set of very restrictive assumptions, not least perfect (capital) markets, no growth, particular types of intergenerational linkages and agents' hyper-rationality and extreme forward-lookingness. Along these lines, and despite its name, Ricardo was himself in doubt over whether agents would act in such a far-sighted manner, seeing through the 'intertemporal veil' (and rational expectations), as required by the theorem.

Nonetheless, the Ricardian equivalence theorem has been influential in both promoting the policy ineffectiveness thesis and in leading to the prominence of monetary policy, at the expense of fiscal policy, under the NCM (see Chapter 10). It serves in macroeconomics, in a sense, as the equivalent of general equilibrium for microeconomics – that is, the mythical standard against which to judge deviations from it by breach of the assumptions that are necessary for it. As it were, Ricardian equivalence does not hold because capital markets are imperfect or because individuals behave differently. This has the effect of consolidating rather than critically assessing mainstream methods.

6

Post-Keynesian Dilemmas

6.1 Overview

The post-Keynesian School of macroeconomics offers both a radical critique of mainstream Keynesianism and an alternative approach to the macroeconomy whilst retaining Keynesian features, not least emphasis on the determining role of aggregate effective demand. As is apparent from the simple Keynesian multiplier, the rate of saving is a key determinant of aggregate demand, as saving is presumed to take place at the expense of demand-boosting consumption. In Section 6.2, following an overview of the post-Keynesian approach, its treatment of savings in particular is presented. In this, the distribution of income between wages and profits has a profound effect on saving because of different saving rates out of different sources of incomes. This means that lowering wages and boosting profitability is perceived as potentially damaging to the economy since it reduces overall demand. Such an insight is reinforced on the supply side, as the increasing monopolisation of the economy is seen to increase prices and restrict output.

Not surprisingly, post-Keynesians see monopoly as damaging to the macroeconomy. But does this mean that it is distinctive from the mainstream? As shown in Section 6.3, even if from a different methodology and vision of the economy, the mainstream is able to model similar outcomes – hardly surprising given that mainstream microeconomics suggests that monopoly is price-increasing and output-decreasing. This suggests that some of the distinctive features of post-Keynesianism, especially its focus upon systemic factors, tend to be neutralised or excluded by being incorporated into the mainstream norm of mathematical modelling, not least since such modelling tends to be organised around equilibrium, and deviations from it. This begs the question of whether this is characteristic of the macroeconomy or, more exactly, how to conceive it – as something out of equilibrium as opposed to something that does not have an equilibrium as it is continually subject to dynamic change.

Interestingly, post-Keynesians tended to see the money supply as both endogenous and accommodating of the levels of effective demand generated by real factors (such as rates of saving and investment). Increasingly though, and unsurprisingly, post-Keynesianism has acknowledged the speculative role of money and how this can serve to dilute aggregate demand, quite apart from raising inequality. This is especially so where elements of uncertainty and/or Minksy's approach to finance are introduced. However, this has the effect of intensifying the tensions between formal modelling and incorporating factors that involve systemic change.

6.2 Post-Keynesianisms?

The post-Keynesian approach to macroeconomics certainly takes Keynesianism as its starting point, not least in its emphasis upon aggregate effective demand as a key determining variable. Indeed, a major part of post-Keynesianism is to construct such a theory of effective demand and leave the economy to get on with the business of supplying it, more or less unexamined. What distinguishes post-Keynesianism is how it constructs its theory of demand. In this respect it is distinctive, and diverges both from other Keynesianisms as well as from Keynes himself. In other words, in this respect the 'post-' is not so much after- and pro- as anti- (and to some degree ante-) Keynesianism as far as other interpretations are concerned.

This can be brought out by five fundamental features of post-Keynesianism. First, it understands the economy in terms of systemic structures (and so, by immediate implication, is antagonistic towards reductionism to methodological individualism). The most obvious structure on which post-Keynesian relies is that between capital and labour, as classes. And this is important for distributional relations, not least the structure of revenues between wages and profits. How these are distributed and spent is an important element in forming aggregate demand, although wages are also an important element in costs and, to that extent, in the level of profitability (see Section 6.3).

Another important structural element in post-Keynesianism is the relative weight of monopoly in the economy (see the counterpart *Microeconomics* volume, chapter 4). For this, the greater the degree of monopoly, the more output tends to be restricted, for the price level to be higher and for the level of aggregate demand to be lower (see Section 6.3). Although not covered here, post-Keynesianism can also understand the global economy in structural terms, roughly divided between developed and developing countries with different characteristics, not least in what they produce, and what they import and export, with the developed countries tending to be advantaged by these structures albeit at the expense of the developing and overall levels of global demand – although, in a developing country context, post-Keynesianism, symbolically, tends to go by the name of structuralist macroeconomics.

This is in part a consequence of a second feature of post-Keynesianism: its incorporation of systemic processes. In this case, for example, much emphasis can be placed on the declining terms of trade faced by developing countries and their increasing dependence upon developed countries for imports for processing and consumption, quite apart from the high rates of interest to be paid upon loans to fund them. In this respect, post-Keynesianism has resonances with what is known as dependency theory, in which developing countries suffer a process of surplus transfer to developed countries which undermines their potential for development and reproduces the global structure of developed and developing within which they reside. To some degree, a similar process is involved in the domestic (closed) economy in which wages are held down by monopolies, both favouring profits but also reducing growth through deficient demand. Equally, then, post-Keynesianism can appeal to a range of processes such as monopolisation but also globalisation and, drawing upon Schumpeter and evolutionary economics more generally, the idea of creative destruction in which the issue of technical change and its impact on macroeconomic performance can be incorporated.

Third, post-Keynesianism is theoretically distinctive. In part, as indicated, this derives not so much from its emphasis upon effective demand as such but on how this is constructed out of distributional and monopolised structures and processes. As a result, the school does tend to sustain a dichotomy between the real and the money economies, but in a way that totally departs from the mainstream. This is because the money supply tends to be seen as endogenous, not exogenous – responding to facilitate supply in meeting whatever degree of effective demand is generated. Famously, Kaldor gave the example of an Irish banking crisis over Christmas severely affecting the availability of liquidity, but with shopkeepers more than ready to offer credit in the interim even though the supposedly fixed money supply was confined to the banks' vaults.

More recently, though, especially in the wake of the global crisis, post-Keynesians have been in the forefront, alongside Marxist political economy and much social science – but not mainstream economics – of embracing and advancing the understanding of financialisation. In this respect, there is reinforcement of the idea of an endogenous money supply (as speculative finance and financial markets have mushroomed), but this is no longer seen as exclusively serving the transmission from effective demand to supply (and output and employment). It can also lead to differential rewards for those working or owning assets in the financial sector with corresponding implications for the (lower) level of effective demand from redistribution towards those with lower propensities to consume. And it can result in the allocation of such finance away from serving real to speculative investment, again at the expense of effective demand.

This dovetails with the post-Keynesian attraction to the economics of Minsky (and his financial instability hypothesis), in which the viability of firms' finances comes under scrutiny in an account of speculative bubbles (and bursts) over the business cycle. Whilst the economy is booming, borrowing to invest is exuberant and, as long as the boom continues, there is the possibility of returns from those investments more than meeting the interest payments on them: so-called hedging finance. But, as the boom slows, for whatever reason, some firms are only able to cover the interest and not the capital on their borrowings: so-called speculative finance. For some firms, this may tip into Ponzi financing, where the borrowing is increased to cover the repayment of interest, increasing firm indebtedness without the ability to repay. But now any default has knock-on effects to those who own the firm's liabilities. This can lead to a collapse of the value of financial assets, the so-called Minsky moment, and a financial crisis. For Minsky, and increasingly post-Keynesians, the modern financial system is systemically subject to a cycle of bubbles and bursts in light of the uncertainties underpinning the returns to real investments and whether these can and do meet the expectations of returns to corresponding financial assets that are placed upon them.

Fourth, post-Keynesianism is heavily inductive in its methodology, drawing upon institutional analysis and empirical regularities rather than exclusive reliance upon a deductive methodology, in constructing its theory. Thus, as mentioned, declining terms of trade for developing countries may be deployed as well as, for example, mark-up pricing on costs as a reflection of monopoly structure. The reliance on induction at the expense of deduction (what is optimal pricing on the basis of costs and other factors) is in part pragmatic, but it also reflects a departure from the mainstream that is reproduced in other respects as well. For example, post-Keynesian is strongly associated with the idea of the economy being subject to radical uncertainty as opposed to rational or other forms of expectations formation (and, in this respect, exhibiting an affinity with Keynes as opposed to Keynesianism and strengthening the appeal of Minsky, especially in the wake of the global crisis).

Last, and by no means least, post-Keynesians are generally strongly wedded to an anti-capitalist position, ranging from proposing major reform, especially to neoliberalism (across structures, processes and distribution), to seeking some form of socialism (with the first as the means of achieving the second). Of particular importance is raising the real and social wage (to expand employment and living standards through higher aggregate demand) and, increasingly and unsurprisingly, to regulate the financial system to underpin the expansion of aggregate demand.

As should be apparent, the post-Keynesian approach draws upon a mix of methodologies, conceptualisations, theories and traditions. For this reason, it is tolerant, eclectic and so remarkably free of internal dissent, even though some post-Keynesians will be fiercely critical of Marxist political economy whilst others positively draw upon it. But an identifiable and major divide within post-Keynesianism (although specific individuals can contribute to both sides of the divide) is whether it draws upon formal mathematical modelling or not. If it does, there is clearly some affinity with the mainstream, and this is more than a formality since, with mathematical models, the systemic and uncertain processes that are part and parcel of post-Keynesian tend to be reduced to a deterministic content. Indeed, the result tends to be one in which the post-Keynesian analysis offers a distortion from the equilibrium or even the dynamics of the mainstream itself. As it were, the model of monopoly pricing, or of distributional outcomes, or of financial speculation means that the economy functions badly but by reference to an equilibrium that would prevail if prices were reduced, wages increased or speculation curbed.

This is not to say that the formal modelling of post-Keynesianism leads to the same sort of economics as the mainstream. It not only models differently to some degree (leading to deviation from some ideal) but it also understands or interprets economic processes differently (as distributional, the power of monopolies, etc.). Nonetheless, as shown in Sections 6.3 and 6.4, there are striking potential affinities between the results of post-Keynesian modelling and those of market imperfection macroeconomics. This is in sharp contrast to those strands of post-Keynesian that are not open to modelling as such, especially those dealing with the processes of monopolisation, creative destruction, financialisation, etc., for which there can be neither a corresponding mainstream model nor equilibrium as points of analytical departure. Thus, this divide within post-Keynesianism – between formal modelling and more qualitative approaches – is indicative of the more general tension between what models can and cannot do. At most, as argued by Keynes himself, they can clarify reasoning to which might be added both their capacity to explore implications of (axiomatic) assumptions and capture particular aspects of how an economy can be conceived, if only at the expense of doing so in a deterministic (if potentially probabilistic) way and at the expense of what is excluded.

6.3 Kaldor–Pasinetti Savings

There are, however, two standard elements in the post-Keynesian modelling toolkit. One is the impact of monopoly on output and pricing. This will be addressed later, but its formal substance is covered in the counterpart *Microeconomics* volume. The other is the saving function. For this, in the post-Keynesian tradition derived from Kalecki, national income is disaggregated by its distribution into profits and wages, prior to its disaggregation into savings and consumption (or the more traditional Keynesian starting point as $S = sY$ and $C = (1 - s)Y$). Thus:

$$Y = W + P$$

where Y is income, W is wages and P is profits.

It is also presumed, in the first instance, that all wages go to workers and all profits go to capitalists. Further, each class has a different propensity to save, s_p for capitalists and s_w for workers, with the further presumption that richer capitalists have a higher propensity to save than poorer workers, $s_p \geq s_w$. Accordingly, total saving for the economy, S, is given by:

$$S = s_p P + s_w W.$$

This means that the level of saving will depend upon the (functional) distribution of income between capital and labour. If α is the share of profits in income, Y, and so $(1 - \alpha)$ the share of wages, then the average saving rate, s, depends on α as follows:

$$s = S/Y = s_p P/Y + s_w W/Y = \alpha s_p + (1 - \alpha)s_w.$$

So s is a weighted average of the higher s_p and the lower s_w, and therefore lies somewhere between them.

Suppose, in simple multiplier Keynesian fashion, that the level of investment is externally given by I. Then:

$$Y = I/s \text{ and } s = I/Y = \alpha s_p + (1 - \alpha)s_w.$$

Solving this for α yields:

$$\alpha = (I/Y - s_w)/(s_p - s_w).$$

As long as $s_p \geq I/Y \geq s_w$, this can be sensibly solved. But if $I/Y > s_p$, then even if all income goes to profits the saving rate will not be big enough to provide for the required level of investment. And, if $s_w > I/Y$, even if all income goes to workers, savings will be too high and will lead to an excess when compared to investment.

Subject to these conditions, an equilibrium between savings and investment can be found through varying the distribution of income. There might even be an adjustment mechanism to bring this about. Suppose savings were too high (low), then there would be too much savings and capital with a corresponding relative shortage of labour (too little savings with relative shortage of capital). This would put pressure on the rate of profit to fall (to rise), shifting distribution in favour of labour (capital), until savings and investment were themselves equalised.

Kaldor offered a special case for this model of saving, the so-called classical savings function (supposedly corresponding to classical political economy) in which stylised capitalists save everything and consume nothing, $s_p = 1$, and workers do the opposite, with $s_w = 0$. For the latter alone:

$$S = s_p P = I \text{ and } P = I/s_p.$$

The last equation led Kaldor to view the model in parallel with the widow's cruse (a magic goblet, not an ocean holiday for bereaved wives, or cruise). The cruse refills itself the more that is consumed from it. With $P = I/s_p$, the same is true of capitalists! The more they invest, the more profits they get; and the more they consume, that is the lower is s_p, the same applies. This is because of the Keynesian nature of the generation of profits. The expenditure of capitalists creates markets for other capitalists and boosts their profits. As Kaldor puts it, capitalists (as a class) earn what they spend, whilst workers are deemed to spend what they earn in passive response to whatever employment and wages come their way. And there is a paradox here in that if profitability is increased by whatever means, such as increased productivity or reduced wages, then this will lead to the generation of sufficient saving for investment at a lower level of output and lead to a decline in national income. This indicates, as it were, that the model is purely determined on the side of effective demand, with improved conditions for profitability even harming the economy. Indeed, if wages were increased, this would boost the economy too (although all of this is contingent on there being excess capacity).

There is, however, even on its own terms, another striking paradox or anomaly in Kaldor's account outside of the classical saving function for which $s_w = 0$. This was pointed out by Pasinetti. It is that for $s_w > 0$, although workers save they do not appear to receive any profits, since the saving rate out of all profits is s_p with none at s_w even though workers are presumably receiving some profits in return for their savings, and, as part of income alongside wages, it would be expected that these would be saved out of (workers') profits at the rate s_w and not s_p. For Pasinetti, why would workers put wages as part of their income in one pocket and save at rate s_w but put profits in another pocket and save at rate s_p (although there are reasonable behavioural and cultural theories suggesting use of money income differs according to its source and may also reflect intrahousehold or other forms of access to, and control of, money)?

Taking account of Pasinetti's insight makes the model much more complicated. First, it is necessary to divide profits according to whether they go to workers or capitalists. Assume that K_p and K_w represent the total capital of capitalists and workers, respectively. Assume also that each gets the same return on their capital so that, for profits P_p and P_w:

$$P_p = rK_p \text{ and } P_w = rK_w \text{ so that } P_p/P_w = K_p/K_w,$$

i.e. workers and capitalists each receive profits at the same rate and in proportion to their ownership of the capital stock – equal shares, as it were.

In addition, recall that $Y = W + P$, so that $Y = W + P_p + P_w$. Now consider a steady-state balanced growth path – one in which all ratios remain the same over time. This is necessary to get any results since, presuming that capitalists began with all the capital, workers would always be playing catch-up in terms of steady-state ratios (although they would eventually get there in the 'long run'). This means that in the steady-state the ratio of capital stocks will be the same as the ratio of savings or:

$$P_p/P_w = K_p/K_w = S_p/S_w.$$

But $S_p = s_p P_p$ and $S_w = s_w(W + P_w)$. From the previous equation, this implies:

$$P_p/P_w = s_p P_p/s_w(W + P_w).$$

P_p cancels from both sides, and the equation simplifies to:

$$s_p P_w = s_w(W + P_w).$$

Although it is apparently innocuous, this simple equation is of dramatic significance. It finds, even if it is a bit of a mouthful, that workers' savings (the right-hand side) are identical to the extra that capitalists would save if they were in receipt of workers' profits. This is possible because workers save at lower rate, s_w, out of their profits but add to their savings from their wages as well. But these two effects always combine to make workers' savings equal the higher level of saving that would have been made by capitalists if they had been in receipt of the workers' profits (if not their wages).

This has a remarkable effect on overall saving since:

$$S = S_p + S_w = s_p P_p + s_w(W + P_w) = s_p P_p + s_p P_w = s_p P.$$

In other words, as implied in the earlier discussion, the level of saving is totally independent of the workers' saving rate, s_w, and only depends on the capitalists' saving rate, s_p. So, if workers wanted to change the long-run saving rate of the economy, either up or down, they would be frustrated from doing so. For, if they increase their saving rate, this would lead to a compensating redistribution of profits to them and combine with their reduced saving rate relative to capitalists to leave the overall saving rate unchanged.

Now suppose that the investment level, I, is exogenously given. Then, since $S = I = s_p P$:

$$P = I/s_p$$

and, as this too is independent of s_w, workers are unable to affect the absolute amount of profits in the economy. And, finally, consider the rate of profit, r, for the economy, P/K. This equals I/Ks_p. But I/K is the rate of growth of the economy, externally given, say, by rate of growth of labour force and given technology, and equal to g. This means that $r = g/s_p$, once again independent of s_w.

How are these results to be interpreted? Basically, capitalists rule OK. The functional distribution of income between profits and wages, the amount of profits overall and the rate of profit cannot be affected by the workers' saving rate. In other words, whilst workers can get a bigger share of profits by saving more, they cannot save their way to socialism and eliminate the influence of capitalists by a gradual erosion of their share in the capital stock. This is a negative result as far as a commitment to a universal shareholder capitalism is concerned if this means more than sharing in profits by saving to include in addition some exertion of influence over the underlying properties of the economy.

Of interest, though, is Kaldor's response to Pasinetti's suggestion that he made a mistake in overlooking the fact that workers make savings but do not appear to receive corresponding profits in return for those savings. Possibly as an ex post justification, Kaldor argued that the use of saving for investment is primarily controlled by the corporate sector, even if it is nominally owned by some, or all, workers in the form of shares or, possibly more important, pension funds. In practice, the saving rate out of workers profits is that of, and determined by, the capitalists who manage and control workers' savings on their (and in part, their own) behalf. Paradoxically, Kaldor's emphasis on the power of corporate capital over workers' savings means that the Pasinetti result, with those savings having no influence on much of the economy other than distributional outcomes, no longer holds.

So much for the demand side of the economy within the post-Keynesian tradition, although (especially in the wake of the current crisis) it is open to much refinement in terms of the way in which financialisation swings the distribution of income against labour (and against effective demand) and against investment in favour of speculation (ditto). As suggested above, the rise of financialisation has led to tensions, or at least refinements, in post-Keynesian analyses, by incorporating a much more significant role for money in distributional outcomes (towards finance within profits) and in raising the potential weight of speculative as against real investment, with both of these at the expense of effective demand and working class incomes. In addition, post-Keynesianism has been drawn towards a stronger attachment to Minsky-type analysis, but with attention broadened from the viability of industrial finance to incorporate other Minsky moments across other forms of financing, such as housing markets, private finance in general and state finance in particular.

This would all reflect a finer disaggregation for the economy in order to get at the level of effective demand in a financialised world. Now, though, consider the supply-side of the economy. In the Kaleckian theory of the degree of monopoly, covered in some detail in the counterpart *Microeconomics* volume, the modern capitalist economy is seen in terms of being highly monopolised. This leads to higher prices and lesser output at firm, sector and economy-wide levels, with a corresponding reduction in the real wage as money wages are deflated by higher, monopolised prices. This means that the post-Keynesian economy tends to be depressed below full employment on both the macroeconomic demand side (because wages are too low to generate sufficient demand) and on the supply side, as monopolies raise prices, restrict output and reinforce the lack of demand through reduced real wages.

6.4 Post-Keynesianism as Mainstream?

This overall thrust of post-Keynesian modelling across its demand and supply sides taken together (with ineffective demand underpinned by increasingly unfavourable distributional and monopoly relations, potentially reinforced by financialisation) allows for further analysis of the distinctiveness of the tradition from the mainstream. Consider, then, a mainstream model of the economy in which there is one sector (adding more sectors does not make a lot of difference) with n firms. Each firm only uses labour as an input, and charges price, p, for output. Households supply labour and derive utility from goods, X, and from holding money assets, M'/p, with Cobb–Douglas utility function $U = X^c(M'/p)^{1-c}$, leaving aside disutility of labour for the moment (see below). Let nominal income be $Y = pX$ and the exogenously supplied money endowment be M. Assuming all households are the same (one can be taken as representative of them all). The household maximises:

$$U = X^c(M'/p)^{1-c}$$

subject to assets $Y + M$ being available to spend on X and to hold money.

With such a Cobb–Douglas utility function for which expenditure shares are constant and equal to exponents, the amount spent on X will be $c(Y + M)$, and $(1 - c)(Y + M)$ will be held as money balances, M'. So, for macroeconomic equilibrium in which these desired money balances, M' equal available money, M:

$$M' = (1 - c)(Y + M) = M.$$

This simplifies to $Y = cM/(1 - c)$ as the determination of nominal income. Note that, as there is no investment in this model, the same result can be obtained by realising that consumption, $C = c(Y + M)$. As this is the level of effective demand in the economy, it generates nominal income, Y, so that $Y = c(Y + M)$, giving $Y = cM/(1 - c)$ once more. This is also equivalent to $X = c/(1 - c)(M/p)$ (since $Y = pX$).

Suppose labour is supplied in what is effectively an independent optimising process to utility maximising (this requires utility of leisure simply algebraically added to U, what is called additive separability), with labour supply equal to $N_s(w/p)$ and with $N_s'(w/p) > 0$. Each profit-maximising firm has a labour demand $N_d(w/p)$ with $N_d'(w/p) < 0$. Adding up over n firms, this will have a solution N^* and w^*/p^* (as indicated in Diagram 6.1), with * to indicate equilibrium values. With n firms, $Y = npX$, where X is what is produced by each identical firm from whatever labour N is chosen. This means, for equilibrium that:

$$Y^* = np^*X^* = cM/(1 - c), \text{ so } p^* = cM/(1 - c)nX^*.$$

This has been a bit of a rush through the model and algebra so it is worth a review. There are n firms, each with a supply function and labour demand given price p and wages w. From this, aggregating over the firms, there are economy-wide functions for supply of goods and demand for labour in terms of w/p. These work out the long-run real economy, for real output nX^*. For the households, aggregate effective demand is derived from the overall income available from nominal income, Y, and money balances, M, with expenditure from these assets divided between consumption and holding of money balances (leading to a total value for aggregate demand of $cM/(1 - c)$). This is spent on the output produced (for consumption), leading to the determination of the equilibrium price, p^* through the last equation. Not surprisingly, p^* is bigger, the bigger are M (more money available to hold) and c (more effective consumption demand with multiplier effects) but the smaller are n and X^* (the less output on which

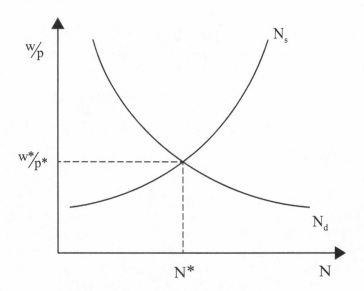

Diagram 6.1 Labour supply and demand

to make expenditure). These will give the long-run, competitive equilibrium for output and employment (nN^* and nX^*) and relative prices w^*/p^*.

Essentially, this is one of the simplest possible models of competitive general equilibrium in which account is taken of money demand by households (but not by firms – so despite real balances on the household side, its absence on the firm side will mean lack of consistency with Walras' Law, see Chapter 3). But what happens in case there is monopoly on the supply side? As can be seen from any microeconomics text across a wide range of models, individual firms, sectors and hence the economy as a whole are liable to reduce output and employment and increase prices relative to the competitive situation. Accordingly, the industry supply for labour curve in case of monopoly elements will lie below that for perfect competition (as illustrated in Diagram 6.2). This will lead to lower output, N_M^* and X_M^* employment (with subscript M to denote monopoly) and a lower real wage. This will also carry through to a higher price level.

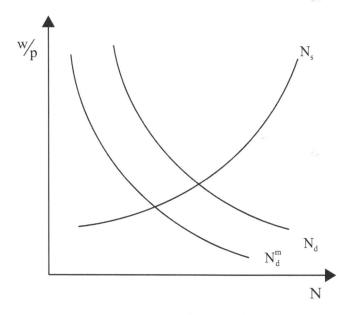

Diagram 6.2   Monopoly supply of goods

The model can also be used to suggest what happens in case of monopoly, or monopsony, on the part of labour. This is supposed to correspond to the presence of trade unions. This raises the issue of how to model the impact of trade unions. Not surprisingly, it is common to treat them as if they had a utility function (to fit with the microeconomic technical apparatus) in which there is some sort of trade-off, for example, between the levels of employment and wages achieved. In other words, the more the wage is held above the competitive

outcome, the less the level of employment. As a result, the labour supply curve
will always lie above that for perfect labour market competition (as in Diagram
6.3). In this case, in equilibrium, there will be lower output and employment but
higher real wages than in the perfectly competitive equilibrium.

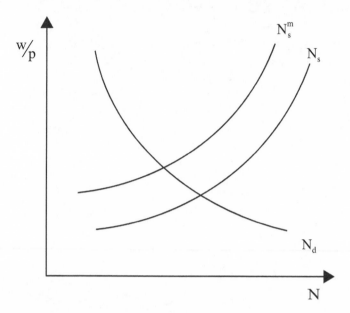

Diagram 6.3   Monopoly supply of labour

Finally, suppose that there is both monopoly on the supply side of goods and
monopsony on supply side of labour. The supply and demand curves are both
shifted as previously, leading to the equilibrium as illustrated in Diagram 6.4.
The real wage relative to perfect competition is indeterminate (being subject
to both upward and downward shifts), but the downward shifts in employment
from the individual divergences from perfect competition reinforce one another.

Significantly, with a bit of monopsony on the labour side thrown in as a bonus,
these results strengthen those previously derived from the post-Keynesian
modelling. This reinforces the point already made that, once modelled in such
ways, post-Keynesianism tends to conceive the macroeconomy as a deviation
from some sort of more ideal equilibrium (that might be achieved through
fairer distribution, less monopoly and, more recently, curbing speculative
financialisation). There also tends to be a separation between, or independence
of, short-run dynamics and long-run equilibrium. As a consequence, this
suggests that post-Keynesian modelling is less a departure from the mainstream
in its substantive results (as the latter can allow for less than ideal short-run
outcomes by appeal to market imperfections, including monopoly). Rather,
post-Keynesian modelling is primarily distinctive in interpreting less than

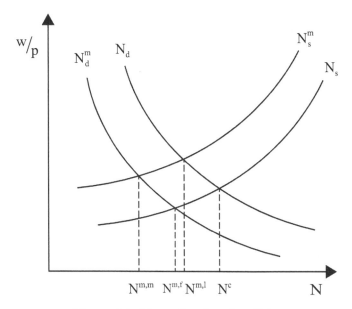

Diagram 6.4 Monopolies of goods and labour

N^c shows equilibrium employment level under perfect competition; $N^{m,m}$ under monopoly in both goods and labour markets; $N^{m,f}$ under monopoly in the goods market and $N^{m,l}$ under monopoly in the labour market.

ideal outcomes in terms of systemic factors such as the underlying influence of distribution and monopolisation, rather than as the consequence of individual optimisation in the context of imperfect markets.

6.5 Further Thoughts and Readings

The last point can be made in another way. As will be seen in Chapter 12, a system of equations for short-run macroeconomics will yield long-run solutions in which outcomes depend upon the more or less complicated multipliers that derive from the short-run equations and the parameters within the equations. Without going into formal details, much the same will be true of post-Keynesian models. The parameters in the long-run solutions will be different and differently motivated, but otherwise there is much that the two sorts of modelling will share in common.

Does this mean that informal post-Keynesian analysis is better than the formal in some sense? It does have greater capacity to deal with systemic and other factors, such as the path of technical change, the role of power, conflict and institutions, and the uncertainties attached to these – together with the acknowledgement that the long run is not an equilibrium around which short-run movements can be otherwise independently understood. But, at one level, the question is not sensible. As emphasised, economic theory should be assessed on how it interprets the capitalist economy, what it includes as well as what it leaves out, and how and why. This is so even where the conclusion might be drawn that the economy simply cannot work in that way. So post-Keynesian models might tell us how distribution between wages and profits affect outcomes through aggregate demand in an economy conceived as tagged to a long-run equilibrium. But it does not tell us more than that.

For the treatment of post-Keynesianism here at greater length, see Fine and Murfin (1984a, 1984b). For post-Keynesian modelling with financialisation, see Stockhammer (2004) as an early illustration which has gathered pace in the wake of the Great Financial Crisis. See also Stockhammer (2012). The mainstream of monopoly/monopsony and macroeconomics is taken from Dixon and Rankin (1994).

7

Keynesian Revolution: What Keynes, What Revolution?

7.1 Overview

Over the previous chapters, a number of different interpretations of Keynesian economics has been presented – IS/LM, the reappraisal and post-Keynesian versions in particular. Not surprisingly, they not only compete with one another as different ways of understanding the macroeconomy, but also in offering themselves as the legitimate inheritors of the Keynesian tradition and even of Keynes himself. It might reasonably be thought that claiming the mantle of Keynes is something of an indirect and unnecessary route to laying out an approach to macroeconomic theory. Why not just present the latter and judge it on its own merits? One reason for claiming to be Keynesian is to be able to benefit from the legitimacy and prestige that it carries. It is worth recalling the popular academic slogan that arose during the post-war boom, until and even beyond the stagflation of the 1970s, that 'we are all Keynesians now', a phrase paradoxically deployed by Milton Friedman in 1965. Inevitably though, the strength underpinning this motive has declined in the wake of the monetarist counter-revolution, inspired by Milton Friedman himself. Are we all monetarists now (see Section 7.3)?

Another motive for adopting the Keynesian label derives from the distinction between the economics of Keynes (the individual) and Keynesian economics (the evolving schools of thought which carry his name). Serious scholarship on Keynes' own economics reveals that Keynesian economics, especially initially in the form of the IS/LM approach, rapidly and considerably diverged from its original inspiration (see Section 7.2 for some elements of this). In other words, Keynesian economics has taken on a life of its own, allowing for it to be developed in various different and competing versions. These can be assessed on their relative merits, but is there a core that they have in common even if they reflect their differences as well (in macroeconomic theory and, possibly, interpretation of Keynes himself)?

This question, and others related to it, are addressed in Section 7.2, by examining the sense in which there was a Keynesian revolution in economic thought. Did economics become different and, if so, in what way and with what lasting effects? This will be traced in terms of scholarship, how macroeconomics became conceived within its home discipline of economics, but account will also be taken of the broader ideological and political role of Keynesianism and its influence on policy in practice.

7.2 The Revolution Portrayed or Betrayed?

Was there a Keynesian revolution, and if so what form did it take and what were its consequences and effects (bearing in mind the old joke about Chou En Lai's comment on the impact of the French Revolution that it was too early to tell)? The case in favour of there having been a revolution is strong for the following eight reasons.

First and foremost, Keynesianism came to the fore in the context of consolidating, even cementing, the division of the discipline of economics, primarily into a dualism between microeconomics and macroeconomics (although a third category could be added of a ragbag of everything else). Whatever the content of macroeconomics and the influence of versions of Keynesianism upon it, macroeconomics and microeconomics became the two core elements in teaching and research. Even those who might deny or regret the influence of Keynesianism upon the discipline can hardly fail to recognise this influence and outcome. Further, at least during its heyday, (Keynesian) macroeconomics enjoyed at least equal prestige as microeconomics (although microeconomics has gained the upper hand in the wake of the monetarist counter-revolution, see Chapter 8).

Second, within macroeconomics the Keynesian revolution brought the aggregate level of effective demand to the fore as a determinant of employment and output. This is most apparent in the simple Keynesian multiplier but applies equally to monetarist views of the role of effective demand in determining nominal income (although this derives from an initial stimulus from the money supply as opposed to real expenditure, such as investment, however this might be determined if not taken as exogenous).

Third, with aggregate effective demand to the fore, macroeconomics became, and remains, preoccupied with its constituent components. In macroeconomic theory, and in building macroeconomic models, attention has been focused on the aggregate consumption function, the aggregate investment function, the aggregate demand for money, and so on.

Fourth, especially but not exclusively in light of the so-called liquidity trap, the supply of and demand for money has occupied an important place in macroeconomics. Money has been seen as exerting an important influence, directly and indirectly, on the rate of interest, the level of effective demand and the absolute price level (as well as the exchange rate, if flexible, in international macroeconomics).

Fifth, by the same token, with some exceptions such as for the money wage relative to the price level (to help deal with aggregate supply of, and demand for, labour) or the extreme real business cycles theory (see Chapter 9), the role of relative prices (the subject matter of microeconomics) has become secondary if not absent in macroeconomics. Whether the economy is working efficiently in some sense or not (by reference to Pareto efficient general equilibrium) comes a distant second behind consideration of the level of economic activity at which it is working.

Sixth, this is also associated with a preoccupation with the short run as opposed to the long run, with the latter taken too much for granted (like short-term efficiency). Indeed, macroeconomics has primarily been focused around analysis of short-run deviations around a given equilibrium or long-term trend.

Seventh, expectations have come to occupy an increasingly significant role in macroeconomics. This is apparent in the liquidity trap of the IS/LM approach (where the interest rate needs to go down but is expected to go up) and, subsequently, adaptive expectations have given way to rational expectations (see Chapter 8).

Eighth, policy considerations have been consolidated around the effectiveness (or not) of, particularly specified, monetary and fiscal policies. The former is primarily identified as changes in the supply of money (or the interest rate), and the latter with government expenditure changes. Policy conclusions may vary considerably, but preoccupation with (the impact of) demand management policies is present even if only, in the extreme, to reject their possible efficacy (see Chapter 8 on the NCE).

Each of these aspects of modern macroeconomics is so familiar that they can all be taken for granted. But this is precisely indicative of the presence of a Keynesian revolution, since they are a product of the incorporation of Keynes' influence upon the evolution of the discipline. This remains the case even though some of these aspects have been subject to erosion, not least in the extreme position of the NCE that there is no macroeconomics distinct from microeconomics and that macroeconomics essentially just becomes general equilibrium with money and expectations added (see Chapter 8).

With these common elements across Keynesian macroeconomics, what light do they shed on the various different versions of Keynesianism and their relationship to Keynes' own economics? Interpreting the latter is not straightforward, since Keynes offered complex and evolving (and not always consistent) views. In addition, especially in his magnum opus, *The General Theory of Employment, Interest and Money*, Keynes was mindful of persuading fellow economists of key points on their own terms rather than his own. But Keynes' terms are sufficiently clear in some respects, such that it is possible to conclude that each of the versions of Keynesian economics departs considerably from Keynes' own.

This has already been seen for the IS/LM approach, not least through the critique launched by the reappraisal (for which Keynes is appropriately seen as proposing capitalism as a quantity-adjusting as opposed to price-adjusting macroeconomy). In addition, it is worth adding how expectations have taken a far from subtle shift in meaning between Keynes and IS/LM (and, much more so, subsequent mainstream macroeconomics). Keynes' view of expectations, having himself written *A Treatise on Probability*, was based on the idea of uncertainty as opposed to risk (see Section 6.5 in the counterpart *Microeconomics* volume). For the IS/LM approach, expectations are about what values will be taken by future variables, such as the rate of interest (and many other variables such as inflation and output in subsequent macroeconomic models). This is what is understood as risk. It is distinct from uncertainty, which is what Keynes had in mind, as he focused on much more general and subjective notions of the future state of the world – crudely, should I be optimistic or pessimistic?

Moreover, for Keynes such uncertainty was attached to waves of pessimism and optimism associated with the animal spirits of the capitalist class in general, and of those working in finance in particular. In this sense, expectations are not simply individual but systemic, subject to collective movement, herd behaviour and herds of intelligent sheep, but sheep nonetheless, as opposed to independently minded cats. The financial system was perceived by Keynes to be analogous to a beautiful baby contest in which the idea is not to judge the best baby (or investment) but to guess who others will judge to be the best baby. Accordingly, opinion will tend to swing in one or another direction. The result is that the financial system will be subject to waves of speculative movements and, if pessimistic, will lead to deficient levels of investment and aggregate demand. For Keynes, as a liberal, this implied that the state needed to intervene to guarantee adequate levels of aggregate demand since there was no doubt that the financial system would fail in this regard from time to time.

In short, in its treatment of money (as an aspect of the financial system) and expectations, Keynesianism does seem to have departed from Keynes (although post-Keynesians have a much more fluid understanding of money than one that sees demand being brought into equality with a fixed supply). But this runs much deeper than simply giving rise to ineffective demand that is reproduced through the quantity-constrained optimisation of individual agents, such as representative households and firms. Keynes was also antagonistic to the idea that macroeconomics could be satisfactorily reduced to the optimising behaviour of individuals. This is apparent from his deeper philosophical stances, but is revealed explicitly in his previously discussed attitude to the financial *system* and how it is subject to waves of pessimism and optimism. Such a social organisation of financing investment, where the costs and benefits involved take second place relative to speculative assessment of share prices, say, needs to be supplemented by overall social coordination of the level of aggregate demand rather than relying upon better informed or behaved individuals. It is also worth mentioning that Keynes was antagonistic towards mathematical models within economics (other than as a device for clarifying explanation) and particularly towards estimating models and using them for policy purposes. The reason is simply that he saw the performance of the macroeconomy in terms of uncertainties that would not be amenable to capture by fixed models or parameters.

In many of these respects in which the Keynesianism of the IS/LM and the reappraisal approaches deviate from Keynes, post-Keynesianism by contrast seems to fare better, not least since its foundations are derived from those who worked closely with Keynes. However, whatever the merits of doing so, the post-Keynesian emphasis on structural factors, such as distribution and monopoly, have no place in the macroeconomics of Keynes himself.

This is important, for it points to the role of the Keynesian revolution not only in bringing in some common aspects to macroeconomics and of leaving out some elements of Keynes' own economics, but also that Keynes himself took a selective view of what comprises the macroeconomy. For him, it was short-run deviations around an otherwise given long-term trend (although he had, generally wrong, views about what shape this might take as economies grew richer, not least massive reductions in working times and falling profitability). There is, however, much more to the functioning of the macroeconomy than aggregate demand, as observed by post-Keynesian structuralism, in addition to monopoly and distribution, sources of productivity increase, the health and education of the workforce, and the role of the state in providing and coordinating these, not least through industrial, welfare and other policies. In this respect, the Keynesian revolution, and Keynes himself, can be seen to have been both limited and responsible for drawing attention away from the major determinants of macroeconomic performance.

One way of seeing this is through asking the question of whether Keynesianism caused the post-war boom. Prior to the stagflation of the 1970s, the conventional wisdom was definitely that it did so, with Keynesian macroeconomic management having been held responsible for sustaining full employment and correspondingly higher growth rates than previously. One way in which that conclusion was disputed was to disaggregate the sources of aggregate demand during the post-war boom. This tends to find that growing levels of international trade and private investment were the major stimuli to demand as opposed to government expenditure (although this did grow as well with welfare states, etc.). But this cannot disprove the virtues of Keynesianism policymaking, since this is supposed to provide a short-term stimulus that is self-sustaining even after it is withdrawn. Charting the ex post composition of demand cannot prove or disprove whether Keynesianism did or did not improve the performance of the economy (and, perversely, most models today might suggest that Keynesianism simply had no effect at the macro-level given how state intervention is neutralised by compensating reactions by representative agents, see Chapter 8).

However, disaggregating effective demand into its constituent components does begin to point to alternative explanations for the post-war boom going beyond the role of short-term macroeconomic policy, particularly when this is placed in historical context relative to the interwar period. For the latter, the world was divided into more or less formal segments, with trade and investment heavily oriented between advanced countries and their colonies or spheres of influence, and considerable protection impeding free flows of trade and investment. Under US hegemony in the post-war period, the situation changed dramatically, with investment and trade flows becoming primarily focused within the advanced countries, most notably with the rise of multi-plant, multinational corporations. In addition, state intervention through provision of health, education and welfare, together with extensive industrial policy (including many publicly owned industries) promoted high levels of investment, productivity and real wages as well as effective demand.

This all leads to three important conclusions. First, the erstwhile notion, itself heavily undermined by 30 years of neoliberal ideology, that the post-war boom was primarily the consequence of a Keynesian revolution in thought applied to policy in practice is incorrect. Short-term macroeconomic manipulation of aggregate demand may have had some effect, although deciphering what this is depends upon full and complex models of the economy, but other factors both need to be taken into account and can be seen as having been far more important. These include the extensive reorganisation of the international economic order and the depth and breadth of state economic intervention. Each of these is simply overlooked, or heavily reduced, if viewed through the prism of Keynesian effective demand.

Second, at most the case can be made that Keynesianism did support an ideology and politics of interventionism that went beyond its own preoccupation with short-run macroeconomic policy. This can be seen as coupling Keynesianism with welfarism and modernisation, for example. But it should immediately be added that to whatever extent this is a valid interpretation of the broader impact of Keynesianism, it does not follow from its analytical thrust as macroeconomic theory. For this, interventionism is focused on, if not confined to, short-run management primarily through fiscal and monetary policy broadly interpreted.

Third, this does itself reflect the consolidation of the distinction between macroeconomics and microeconomics within the discipline of economics, as well as the separation between the short and long runs, something that derives from Keynes as well as characterising his successors. In short, whatever the extent to which Keynes has been misinterpreted by Keynesianism, and to the extent that there was a Keynesian revolution, it was a shift in economics that discarded many positive features of interwar economics, not least the wish to relate growth to cycles and to take account of major changes in the capitalist economy such as sources of productivity, the role of institutions such as trade unions and corporate monopolies, and the distribution of income. Even Keynes' major contribution in this respect – emphasis upon the speculative unreliability of the financial system in generating adequate levels of investment and aggregate demand – became anaesthetised in Keynesian macroeconomics by being couched in terms of the supply of, and demand for, money and interest (and, later, exchange) rate determination. The theoretical chickens of such a treatment of finance came home to roost with a vengeance in the wake of the crisis at the end of the 2000s, as the supposedly microeconomic impact of bank failures could hardly be neglected as constituting a macroeconomic phenomenon. Yet, this is merely the tip of the analytical iceberg as far as the way in which Keynesianism, to some extent complicit with Keynes whatever other deviations there might have been, has been responsible for precluding major elements in defining and understanding what macroeconomics is.

7.3 Further Thoughts and Readings

One striking and persisting aspect of the literature on Keynes, Keynesianism and the Keynesian revolution is that it remains highly contested. It is interesting to dwell upon why this should be so (alongside other great contributors to the history of economic thought) as opposed to the far less controversial interpretations of monetarism in general and Milton Friedman in particular (although the nature of neoliberalism and its relationship to monetarism are both heavily debated). Why are there so few articles on 'What Did Milton Really Mean?'. Even to ask the question is more or less sufficient to provide its own answer, and it has two aspects. On the one hand, whilst themselves subject to dispute from Keynesian perspectives and otherwise, the propositions of monetarism are relatively simple and primarily not open to disagreement in terms of interpreting their core content. On the other hand, unlike the enigmatic economics of Keynes, monetarism has the effect of closing down rather than opening up inquiry in terms of a broader set of issues and how these are broached. This is especially so regarding the nature of the financial system and the nature and role of expectations, with scope for other considerations too in the post-Keynesian tradition.

It is also important to observe that the rise of Keynesianism, the forms that it has taken and their influence in scholarship, ideology and policy in practice, are not simply a matter of academic debate. They have all been heavily influenced by external and political influences. And much the same is true of the monetarist counter-revolution.

On Keynesianism, see Fine and Milonakis (2009) and Milonakis and Fine (2009), and for neoliberalism, see Fine (2012).

8

From Monetarist Counter-Revolution to Fundamentalism

8.1 Overview

Towards the end of the 1960s, macroeconomics seemed to be set for good, like the capitalist economy following two decades of unprecedented levels of growth, albeit unevenly distributed. Although the Cold War and strife in the developing world still loomed large, if ever there was an end of history then this was it for macroeconomic theory and its application to the worlds of policy and complacent ideology. The situation, within economics at least, exhibits remarkable parallels with the self-satisfaction that equally marked the NCM, which reached its peak of influence just before the great crisis broke at the end of the first decade of the new millennium (see Chapter 10).

Of course, even whilst Keynesianism was at its height, it was subject to differing interpretations as well as challenges from monetarism (and from radical critiques of capitalism and the limitations of what Keynesianism could achieve on a lasting basis). Within a decade, the stagflation of the 1970s had not only discredited Keynesian conventional wisdoms (which would never be the same again, let alone be restored) and shifted the balance of the discipline towards its monetarist alter ego. In addition, traditional Keynesian methods in approaching the macroeconomy were turned upside down through a process we will chart in this chapter.

It all began as the post-war boom was running out of steam, with Friedman's theory of the vertical Phillips curve (Section 8.2). This had the effect of introducing more or less self-fulfilling expectations of inflation into macro-economics, thereby undermining the notion that there existed a simple trade-off between unemployment and inflation that could be exploited by policy. That unemployment could be affected at all by policy then became targeted by Friedman's descendants in the form of the NCE (Section 8.3). This not only substituted rational for adaptive expectations but drew upon the assumption of perfectly working markets. As revealed in Section 8.4, this had the effect of reducing macroeconomics to general equilibrium theory with all the extremes in methods, conceptualisations and assumptions that this entails. And, in particular, the headline policy implication of the NCE, that state policy is ineffective, became the very simple consequence of relying upon unquestioned microeconomic fundamentals (in extreme form) and a collapsed understanding of the nature of the state itself (what it is, what it can do, etc.). With an emasculated state in the context of perfectly rational individuals and perfectly working markets, is it surprising that the state becomes ineffective?

8.2 From Vertical Phillips Curve ...

Following the Keynesian revolution and its orthodox representation through the IS/LM framework, all became Keynesians – not least through modelling with macroeconomic aggregates and a policy synthesis in which either IS or LM curves could be shifted as fiscal and monetary policy, respectively. The differences between Keynesians and monetarists were more a matter of degree. The macroeconomy was perceived by both to be determined by aggregate effective demand which itself determined nominal income, pQ say, with p as the price level and Q as real output. Macroeconomics revolved around the transmission mechanisms, or multipliers, by which one market impacted upon others, and so on to other markets, eventually coming back to the original source of the stimulus and ready to go again (presumably at a reduced level or otherwise leading to instability).

As a result, the differences between monetarism and Keynesianism revolved around the size and nature of these multipliers. In general, then, increases in effective demand go into either prices, p, or into quantities, Q, with monetarists tending to favour one and Keynesians the other, respectively. In contrast to Keynesians seeing a need to provide a stimulus to sustain effective demand, monetarists believed that markets work well if left alone and oiled with sufficient but not too much money. Thus, for example, Friedman's permanent income hypothesis suggests that a temporary decrease in income will have limited impact upon current consumption and effective demand, since the reduced income will lead to consumption expenditure being optimally spread over the remaining lifetime of those unlucky enough to have suffered decreased income. With say an average of 30 years left to live, this would reduce, at a stroke, the marginal propensity to consume, and hence the simple Keynesian multiplier, by a thirtieth.

This common frame of analysis between Keynesianism and monetarism broke down with the emergence of the stagflation of the 1970s. How could there be increasing unemployment and accelerating inflation, as this would indicate both deficient and excess demand at the same time? Friedman gave an answer in terms of the vertical Phillips curve. Previously, the Phillips curve had been based upon the idea that there was a potential policy trade-off between higher unemployment and lower inflation. Increasing aggregate demand (above the so-called natural or equilibrium rate of employment) would lead to excess demand for labour and goods and hence inflation. This is indicated in Diagram 8.1. It seems as if unemployment can be held artificially low (less than its natural rate) if at the expense of inflation.

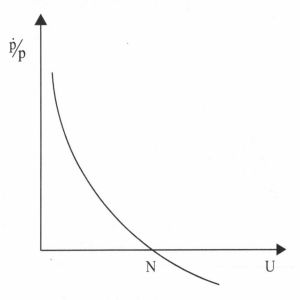

Diagram 8.1   Phillips curve

N is the so-called natural rate of unemployment.

Friedman argued that this argument is fundamentally flawed. If inflation is running at 3 per cent as a result of such policies, then everyone would get used to such an inflation rate and would factor it into their labour market demands or goods pricing in anticipation of the inflation that has become normal. The result is to shift the Phillip Curve up by that 3 per cent so that in subsequent periods, if the same lower rate of unemployment is to be sustained, then inflation will turn out to be 6 per cent. This shifts the short-run Phillips curve up once more by an ever-increasing rate of inflation if persisting with the lower rate of unemployment.

It follows that lowering unemployment to some degree permanently below the natural rate leads to ever-accelerating, not constant, inflation. Thus, the so-called long-run Phillips curve is vertical, with inflation (deflation) of prices infinitely high (low) if unemployment is held below (above) the natural rate of unemployment. At most, employment can be held at the natural rate at whatever is the current rate of inflation. With (expected) inflation at 3 per cent at the natural rate of unemployment, this is the rate at which the money supply will need to be increased to allow for unemployment to remain at this level, with the inflation rate remaining constant. At most, there will be some temporary scope to lower (raise) unemployment but at the expense of inflation (deflation) that needs to accelerate. Hence the moniker vertical Phillips curve, at least for the long run, whilst the short-run Phillips curve intersects the natural rate of unemployment at the current rate of inflation (see Diagram 8.2).

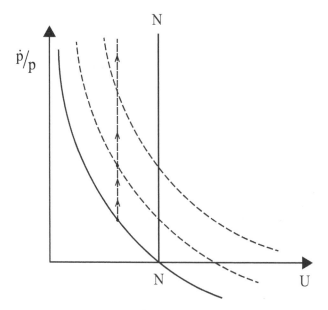

Diagram 8.2   Friedman's vertical Phillips curve

N becomes the NAIRU, the non-accelerating-inflation rate of unemployment. For sustaining U below N, increasing money supply at an accelerating rate is necessary with accelerating inflation.

The vertical Phillips curve, first put forward in 1968, had a huge impact upon macroeconomic theory for four reasons. First, it was credited with having predicted the stagflation of the 1970s. Second, it introduced expectations at the heart of macroeconomic thinking, but in a way that essentially eliminated any understanding of expectations that involved any element of uncertainty as opposed to risk. In a nutshell, expectations were simply about what you thought the price level (or other variables) might be (estimated to be) as opposed to more amorphous notions of confidence, or not, in the future of the economy. Third, as such expectations can only be formed by individuals (as opposed to being the systemic consequences of how the financial system operates, for example), emphasis within macroeconomics was given a push towards greater reliance upon microeconomic foundations (and the optimising behaviour of individuals in light of expectations around future economic variables). Fourth, despite all of this there did remain residual Keynesian elements within the monetarist counter-revolution. After all, government could affect the level of unemployment, lowering it below its natural rate, if only at the expense of accelerating inflation (although possibly equally important is the conclusion that the only way to reduce even constant inflationary expectations along the vertical Phillips curve at the natural rate is to have a period of unemployment higher than the natural rate).

8.3 ... To New Classical Economics

It was, however, the goal of the so-called NCE to eliminate all such Keynesian influence from macroeconomics, and it did so over the course of the 1970s. The prime target was the notion that the state could lower the rate of unemployment through reflationary policies, even if at the expense of accelerating inflation. This would be to accept that markets do not work perfectly in the absence of state intervention (not least as the rationale for disliking inflation seemed to have no basis within macroeconomics other than possible increased volatilities around relative prices, thereby affecting microeconomic decision making). So, from a perfect market point of view, how was it that unemployment could be affected according to the vertical Phillips curve?

The answer requires a close examination of the process. There is a current rate of inflation, say, which will be factored into the price-setting of economic agents (money wage demands and pricing of goods). To sustain unemployment below the natural rate, the state will have to raise the money supply by this amount, and by some more as well according to the short-run, expectations-augmented Phillips curve à la Friedman. As a result, there will be excess demand and inflation will turn out to be higher than anticipated. Agents will have underestimated the inflation rate and are liable to increase their expectations of inflation but, at least in the meantime, unemployment will have been lower than the natural rate. In effect, because the price level has been underestimated, agents believe they will have more real balances, M/p, than they actually will (having underestimated the price level), and this is what creates the excess demand.

There are two closely related critiques of this account from the perspective of the NCE. The first concerns expectations. For the long-run vertical Phillips curve, agents have what are termed adaptive expectations. We got inflation wrong so we will adjust our expectations to close the difference between what we expected and the actual outcome. This is what is known as adaptive expectations. Whatever we anticipated before, we adjust to correct any discrepancy in our expectations by moving them in the direction of our most recent experience of the variable concerned. The problem is that – especially in the context of the vertical Phillips curve and unemployment being below the natural rate – inflation (fuelled by increasing the money supply to allow for it) is persistently and indefinitely underestimated by agents. The expectations never catch up with the outcome (which is why real balances are persistently thought to be higher than they will actually be). This would appear to be unreasonable – a bit like the clown kicking the ball ahead in trying to pick it up and never learning not to do so. Surely agents would realise that they keep on getting inflation wrong – too low – and would revise the way in which they form expectations? For this reason, the NCE replaced what are termed adaptive expectations (just described), in which expectations are simply moved in a direction to close error, with rational expectations (see below).

The second related or, more exactly, deeper critique of the vertical Phillips curve by the NCE is to insist that economic agents need to work with a theory or model of the economy in order to form expectations. This is not provided by adaptive expectations, as these simply rely upon a behavioural rule which has nothing to do with economic theory (see Box 8.1). It is precisely because agents with adaptive expectations do not work with a model of the economy that they are able to persist in underestimating inflation despite the evidence of what they are estimating to the contrary. For this reason, the NCE draws upon rational in place of adaptive expectations, with agents modelling the economy in doing so. In this respect, there is a huge difference between the way in which the model forms expectations about how the economy will evolve and how agents do the same. In particular, the model with adaptive expectations takes account of state policy in increasing the money supply in deciding what future prices will be, but the model does not allow agents to do so. They have to wait until that increase in the money supply works its way through the economy to change prices before these can be allowed to modify their (adaptive) expectations.

But exactly how are rational expectations to be formed? For adaptive expectations, it is relatively easy to modify previous expectations in light of new evidence. The same is not true of rational expectations, since new evidence is not simply used to modify existing expectations but needs to be run through a model, or models, to determine which is best. Possibly with new evidence, it is not only the estimates that need to be changed (what do we think the price level will be on the basis of our model?) but also the choice of model itself as one might become better performing compared to another as new evidence (i.e. data) becomes available. This means that the agents' (potential) models become part of the model itself. As it were, the model uses expectations of prices to work out agents' behaviour, and the agents use their own model of the economy to work out their expectations. So our model of the economy depends upon the agents' models, and the agents' models must be as good as our own or they could do better by adopting our model (if it were known to them). In a sense, the agents' models of the economy are a variable of our own model, and neither model can do better than the other in modelling, since a worse performing model would then be abandoned for the better performing model by agents within the model itself, and economists modelling the economy and the agents (and their expectations).

Box 8.1
Adaptive expectations are behavioural and non-theoretical:
The Koyck transformation

Suppose the price level (or some other variable), p, is known for all earlier periods, and that an agent wants to form expectations, p_t^* about the present unknown value, p_t. Adaptive expectations are defined by the agent choosing to take a weighted average of the last observed value, p_{t-1}, and the previous expectation of it, p_{t-1}^*, so that, for some $0 \leq \alpha \leq 1$:

$$p_t^* = \alpha p_{t-1} + (1 - \alpha)p_{t-1}^*.$$

Essentially, the agent is correcting the past mistake by moving the expectation towards the actual value. Note that, if $\alpha = 1$, the agent sticks with p_{t-1}, but if $\alpha = 0$ the agent sticks with the old expectations despite having been wrong and as if p_{t-1} had not occurred. With expectations formed in this way, the equation holds for all t, so that:

$$p_t^* = \alpha p_{t-1} + (1 - \alpha)p_{t-1}^*$$
$$p_{t-1}^* = \alpha p_{t-2} + (1 - \alpha)p_{t-2}^*$$
$$\vdots$$
$$p_{t-s}^* = \alpha p_{t-s-1} + (1 - \alpha)p_{t-s-1}^*$$
$$\vdots$$

Leave the first of these equations alone, multiply the second by $(1 - \alpha)$ and the sth by $(1 - \alpha)^{s-1}$ and the sequence of equations becomes:

$$p_t^* = \alpha p_{t-1} + (1 - \alpha)p_{t-1}^*$$
$$(1 - \alpha)p_{t-1}^* = \alpha(1 - \alpha)p_{t-2} + (1 - \alpha)^2 p_{t-2}^*$$
$$\vdots$$
$$(1 - \alpha)^{s-1}p_{t-s}^* = \alpha(1 - \alpha)^{s-1}p_{t-s-1} + (1 - \alpha)^s p_{t-s-1}^*$$
$$\vdots$$

Now add up these equations. The first term on the left-hand side (after the first equation) will cancel the second term of the equation below on the right-hand side. The overall result will be:

$$p_t^* = \alpha\{p_{t-1} + (1 - \alpha)p_{t-2} + (1 - \alpha)^2 p_{t-3} + ... + (1 - \alpha)^s p_{t-s-1} + ...\}.$$

This means that expectations are formed purely out of a numerical sum of past, observed values. The sum of the weights on past values is 1 (because $1 + (1 - \alpha) + (1 - \alpha)^2 + ...$ sums to $1/\alpha$). So it is called a distributed lag of past values (since it is a weighted average). And because each weight declines in the same proportion, $(1 - \alpha)$, it is called a geometrically distributed lag. The shift from the adaptive

▶

expectations to this lagged expression is called the Koyck transformation. It is useful in empirical work because there may be no observations of expectations. By assuming adaptive expectations, and subject to the parameter α, the expectations can be replaced by the distributed lag of past values that can be observed (noting that the coefficient on the lagged variables becomes small after a few time periods as $α^{t-s}$ declines with s).

But what of the theoretical significance of adaptive expectations? The Koyck transformation shows very clearly, whether such expectations are sensible or not, that they are not the result of any theory. They are simply the more or less arbitrary weighted average of past values of the variable for which the expectations are being calculated. Put another way, they are the result of a behavioural rule on how to make use of available data. Significantly, the same rule could be used for any such data series, reinforcing the point that adaptive expectations are theoryless (equally applicable to the temperature as to economic series).

Note also that we have laid out the Koyck transformation (which can go in the opposite direction too, from a geometrically distributed lag to adaptive expectations that are exactly equivalent to one another) without putting in any random disturbances in the equations, such as:

$$p_t^* = αp_{t-1} + (1 - α)p_{t-1}^* + u_t.$$

In this case, with the Koyck transformation, the random disturbances after the transformation become complicated: $u_t + (1 - α)u_{t-1} + (1 - α)^2u_{t-2} + (1 - α)^3u_{t-3} + ...$ This will make estimation complicated.

This does not get us much further in forming rational expectations other than in realising that with rational expectations models become recursive – dependent upon themselves – as the model is a part of the model. It is possible to take this forward somewhat easily by making the assumption that everyone has the same, single model – both us as economists and agents as modellers. The consequences of doing so can be demonstrated with the following simple model.

Suppose the economy is only subject to uncertainty about the supply of money, M, and let all variables be in logs. The money is made up of a known, systematic part M' plus an unknown, unsystematic, 'surprise' or random component, u. This has mean zero (otherwise we would revise our estimate of the systematic component, M', by the non-zero mean u). Let Q be short-run output, Q_N the equilibrium level of output, and P and P* be prices and expected prices, respectively. If the price level facing a particular individual is higher than expected, presume they have no idea whether this is because of a general increase in prices or is only specific to their sector (agents are said temporarily to be isolated in non-communicating islands until the general rate of inflation is known in the next period). As a result, with P > P* (P < P*) supply will be increased (decreased) to the extent that relative prices are presumed to have become (un)favourable. Across all agents, it follows that there is a short-run supply curve:

$Q = Q_N + a(P - P^*)$ for some parameter, a.

Clearly, $Q = Q_N$ if $P = P^*$. Now suppose the aggregate demand curve is given by:

$Q = b + c(M - P^*)$ for parameters b and c.

Recalling that variables are in logarithmic values, this means that demand is dependent on expected real balances, M/P^*, given $\ln(M/P^*) = \ln M - \ln P^*$. This means, for the short run, that there are *two* equations for *three* unknowns – prices, P, quantity, Q, and expected prices, P^*. To complete the model for the short run, it is also necessary to specify the process of expectations formation (see below).

But for long-run equilibrium $P = P^*$, since, if otherwise, expectations of prices would be permanently incorrect and they would need to be changed (unless, unrealistically, allowing unchanged expectations when they remain wrong). It follows that $Q = Q_N$, and long-run price, $P_{lr} = M' + (b - Q_N)/c$. The long-run equilibrium output, unsurprisingly, is Q_N, and the long-run equilibrium price level depends directly upon the money supply.

Now return to the short run. From the two equations for supply and demand:

$Q_N + a(P - P^*) = b + c(M - P^*)$.

For rational expectations, P^* must be consistent with the workings of the model, i.e. whatever the model expects P to be, so should the agents' expectations of P. So, taking expectations, E[...] say, of both sides:

$E[Q_N + a(P - P^*)] = E[b + c(M - P^*)]$.

With $E[P] = E[P^*] = P^*$ (these three terms are, respectively, all equal to one another but conceptually different, being what the model expects prices to be, what the model expects expected prices to be and what agents expect prices to be, respectively), it follows that:

$Q_N = b + c(M' - P^*)$.

Hence $P^* = M' + (b - Q_N)/c$. Note, this is non-stochastic (i.e. independent of u) and equals the long-run equilibrium price. In other words, agents should always expect the price to be at its equilibrium level.

Substituting for P^* in the short-run demand equation gives:

$$Q = b + c(M - M' - (b - Q_N)/c) = Q_N + cu.$$

From this, substituting into the supply curve, it follows that $P - P^* = cu/a$. This simple outcome captures the essence of the Lucas 'misperception' model. In the absence of unanticipated changes in the money supply ($u = 0$), the economy will always be at its long-run equilibrium, given by $Q = Q_N$ and $P = P^* = M' + (b - Q_N)/c$. In turn, Q_N is determined by the supply side of the economy, based on production technologies, endowments and workers' preferences that will essentially determine the supply of goods and labour (a retrieval of the classical dichotomy and in contrast to IS/LM). The deviation of expectations of the short-run price level from its actual level only depends upon the unsystematic component of the money supply. This means that both short-run output and short-run prices only depend upon unanticipated changes in the money supply.

This seems to be a remarkable result. By increasing the money supply, government would merely do no more than create a new equilibrium price level increased in proportion to the increase in the money supply. There is no boost to the short-run level of output, since future (equilibrium) price increases are fully and immediately anticipated by agents as soon as the money supply is increased (and there is no illusion of increase in real balances). In other words, money and monetary policy are neutral in the long run, as well as in the short run, so long as changes in money supply are anticipated. The only way in which government can increase output in the short run is to increase the money supply without agents knowing about it, as an element of the random shock, u. Such a surprise increase in the money supply might itself become self-defeating as agents begin to anticipate that this is what government is doing. Interestingly, this opens up the possibility that agents must not only have expectations about prices (and other variables) but equally about what government will do. This has implications for the so-called reputation of government, as agents' expectations will be formed on the basis of past experience. It leads to the argument, first, that using shock reflationary policy can only work temporarily in the short run, after which it will damage reputation and make control of inflation even harder. And, second, as this is purely a technical matter of inflation control, it should be taken out of the hands of government that might be tempted to abuse its position for short-term gain (temporary boost to the economy) at the expense of longer term reputational losses. This leads to the argument for an independent central bank to control the money supply (see also Chapter 9).

The difference between rational and adaptive expectations can now be highlighted. For adaptive expectations, the equilibrium of the model (the long run) is exactly the same, with $Q = Q_N$ and $= M' + (b - Q_N)/c$ and $P^* = P_{1'}$ but in the short run expectations are formed differently, with P not adjusting in the first instance as an immediate jump to the new equilibrium level in response to the increased money supply, since its effects have yet to be felt on past price levels out of which adaptive expectations are formed. With the illusion of extra real balances, the price level will increase as a result of the expected demand (as predicted by the model but not by agents) which means that the expectations will be wrong and take time to catch up with the new equilibrium level of prices (and the correct rational expectations) (see Diagram 8.3).

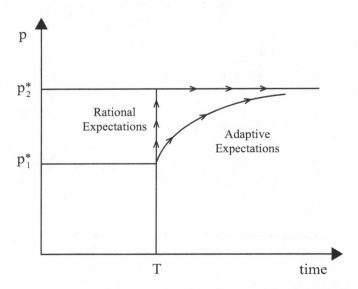

Diagram 8.3   Adjustment to money supply increase for adaptive and
rational expectations

These results of the NCE are devastating for Keynesianism. On the one hand government intervention, in this case through discretionary increases in the money supply, is seen to be totally ineffective. It is simply neutralised by the countervailing reactions of agents who fully anticipate what will happen to the price level and do amend their actions accordingly. On the other hand, the NCE also argued that all previous models of the economy deployed for policymaking had been fundamentally flawed for not taking account of such countervailing action by economic agents. Consider, for example, the Phillips curve itself. It may well be that random shocks lead to an inverse relationship between employment and inflation, since some accidental and unanticipated increase in money supply is liable to lead to increases in both output and inflation. But this does not mean that (known) policy can exploit this supposed relationship, since agents can and will take such deliberate policy into account so that the relationship will no longer hold as it does if random.

A neat illustration of this is to consider the safeguarding of a bank. It may well be that, for whatever reason, there are temporary shortages of security staff. But we may not observe an increase in the number of bank robberies at these times. Empirically, this would seem to suggest that there is no relationship between the presence of guards and the number of bank robberies. So we save money on wages by announcing a policy that there will no longer be any bank guards, fully expecting there to be no impact on the number of bank robberies. Of course, rational bank robbers know otherwise! The problem arises because we have estimated the relationship between bank robberies and security staff without taking into account the fundamental and underlying rationale for bank robberies (potential gain against potential cost and optimising behaviour of the robbers). Instead, improperly specified relationships have been estimated empirically that are correct only for responses to random variation that cannot be used as the basis for policy and systematic variation.

But the economy is not a bank and agents are not robbers. Consider, then, a more general formulation of the NCE. Let $M(x_t, x_t^*)$ be a model of excess demands in the economy, where x_t are the values of a vector of economic variables at time, t, chosen by agents, subject to random shocks, u_t, with mean zero. At this time, presume there has been no government intervention and that we know all previous values of x at earlier times. This is the basis on which expectations (x_t^*) are formed. Now make the crucial assumption that all markets work perfectly, especially in the sense that prices adjust immediately so that supplies and demands are always equal. It follows that short-run equilibrium is given by $M(x_t, x_t^*) + u_t = 0$ where u is the vector of random shocks with $Eu = 0$. Let long-run equilibrium be given by $M(x, x) = 0$ with expectations of x, necessarily at the same value as equilibrium values, x.

Now suppose that government intervenes by shifting values in each market by the vector of values g, with y_t^* the expected value of overall economic variable outcomes. In the short run:

$$M(x_t + g, y_t^*) + u_t = 0.$$

For adaptive expectations, y_t^* will be exactly the same as if g had not occurred, simply because no change has yet appeared to agents in the past variables on which the adaptive expectations are formed. We will need to solve the above equations and, in doing so, the new values of x_t will depend upon g (and the past values of x out of which $y_t^* = x_t^*$ has been calculated). Government, i.e. g, clearly has an impact in the short run, although the long-run equilibrium will still be given by $y = x$, the previous equilibrium since $M(x - g + g, x) = 0$ (with private, expected activity, $x - g$, ultimately neutralising government intervention, g).

For rational expectations, the situation is entirely different: y_t^* changes immediately with g rather than waiting for the impact of g to work through, although agents still work with the same data as those using adaptive expectations, i.e. the previous values of x_t. As already indicated, this means the model M, in determining x_t^*, is part of the model. So now, with g taken into account, expectations will also take the g variables into account straight away and not through their subsequent effects. And y_t^* will also be estimated through a model, not mechanically through working arithmetically on past values. How can this model be found, given that it depends upon itself? Well, take expectations. If the model is linear, then the expectations operator can go inside the M brackets. Because, as observed earlier, the expectations of the model, of the agents, and the expected outcomes themselves should all be the same, it follows that:

$$M(x_t^* + g, y_t^*) = 0.$$

This has a solution, $x_t^* + g = x = y_t^*$, since $M(y, y) = 0$. So, with $x_t^* = y - g$, rational expectations are expected to neutralise government intervention, g. In other words, private agents shift their actions in equal and opposite amounts to government, and short-run expectations are immediately and instantaneously in long-run equilibrium. Note that this holds true for whatever the government intervention is, not just for an increase in the money supply. This gives rise, for example, to the Ricardian equivalence theorem: that government expenditure boosting effective demand will be neutralised by private agents' equal and opposite anticipation of later taxation and/or inflation (see Box 5.1).

This is possibly unnecessary, although simple, mathematics to suggest that, with rational expectations as defined, agents always expect the economy to be in equilibrium other than as a result of short-run random shocks, u. Shocks are the only reason why the economy is not always in equilibrium, with two factors involved. The first, and most obvious, is that expectations in the short run cannot be exactly correct because of the random shocks. Second, and as a result of these, the model's and agents' estimation of the economy will not be perfect but subject to the random evidence generated. So, even if $u_t = 0$, the expectations are liable to be incorrect insofar as there is randomised error in estimating the economy. Such estimation should improve the longer the period over which expectations are formed.

But what of the assumed linearity of the model? Is this necessary for the results? Essentially, the answer is no, and we only need the assumption in order that the argument can proceed on the basis of what are termed point estimates, that is, estimates of the value of the particular variables, P, or the parameters involved such as a, b and c. More generally, rational expectations should involve estimating the probability distribution of the model's values and not just their means, for example. This makes estimation much more complicated, but it would be a bizarre result for something as important as whether the state is ineffective or not to depend upon whether the world is linear or not.

8.4 From the Not So Sublime to the Even More Ridiculous

There are, however, much more important assumptions made by the NCE which do need to be highlighted. Some are so standard that they are taken for granted without comment, let alone critical reflection. There must be some sort of efficient, unique general equilibrium underpinning the long-run solution to the economy, as represented in the highly aggregated form of a single sector. There is the separation between the long run and the short run, with no scope for dynamic or other change. In addition, there are a set of other assumptions all of which would otherwise upset the outcome. These include the need for each agent to have the same model of the economy (although different models might work as well as one another) and for individuals to form models in undertaking their decision making (this can be justified on the grounds that they can use the models made by others).

Whether as a cause or consequence of the model's needs, the NCE seemed to adopt (and encourage subsequent adoption even by its critics) the view that such sinful necessity was a virtue, by consolidating the assumption of representative individuals, one household and one firm for the economy as a whole. This wipes out at a stroke differentiation within the economy whether it be by distribution, knowledge, modelling or whatever. Equally, whether driven to the extreme of representative individuals or not, the NCE insists that macro models should be based on what are termed fundamentals, by which is meant the exogenously given determinants of general equilibrium based on fixed preferences, endowments and technologies. A very peculiar logic is involved. On the one hand, the so-called Lucas critique argues that government policy cannot take empirical relations (such as the Phillips curve) as the basis for policy, since agents will respond differently to known policy than to random shocks. This is why it is necessary to go back to fundamentals and examine why individuals make the choices that they do, and why they would be different if responding to known policies. Using a model to do so is, after all, merely being consistent in optimising the use of information as well as in optimising supply and demand.

On the other hand, despite this appeal to 'fundamentals' as the underlying determinants of outcomes, not a single moment or effort is shed in asking what determines these fundamentals – why should it be optimising individuals and, even so, why would preferences be the way they are and might not they change (similarly with technologies and endowments)? Just by asking such questions, it becomes immediately obvious that by appeal to fundamentals the NCE is simply privileging their preferred approach to economics and not rooting out fundamentals at all, unless these are dogmatically taken as given as they most unrealistically specify them.

Such a privileging of this preferred approach is also apparent in the assumption of perfectly working and clearing markets. This is reflected in setting the excess demand functions, $M(x_t, x_t^*)$, equal to zero. If this assumption is not made then, whenever there is government intervention, $M(x_t + g, x_t^*) \neq 0$ also. And so, setting expected values equal to their equilibrium values is no longer a short-run solution. In addition, it is necessary to question how government intervention, g, might affect the inequality or imperfections in the workings of the market. If the right-hand side of the equation is not zero, it might be affected by g as well as the left-hand side. As will be seen, this opens the way to allow for Keynesian approaches even in the presence of rational expectations, highlighting the extent to which rational as opposed to adaptive expectations are not the key to the NCE so much as the assumption of perfectly working markets. After all, with such an assumption (on top of the existence of a stable, unique Pareto efficient equilibrium), it is hardly surprising that the only thing that can go wrong is the (irrational, adaptive expectations) behaviour of individuals.

However, a much more serious and readily overlooked aspect of the NCE is its reduced understanding of the state/government. Again, within macroeconomic theory this has become so commonplace as to be uncritically accepted. The point is that the nature and role of the state has been extraordinarily reduced – to such an extreme that it is hardly surprising that it should have become ineffective, especially if intervening in the context of the other assumptions made and approaches taken. This is not the place to offer an account of the role of the state and how it might affect macroeconomic functioning. But in the NCE, and more generally, it is essentially confined to the status of some sort of special individual, with powers and motives of its own that are confined to shifting supply and demand as indicated by the variable, g. As a result, the state has no powers to affect a given long-run equilibrium. And, with agents able to anticipate and neutralise its every action in the context of perfectly working markets, that long-run outcome is immediately brought forward to the short run.

8.5 Further Thoughts and Readings

Where does this leave the NCE? First is to reiterate that it drove to extraordinary extremes of extremes how the macroeconomy is understood in terms of a unique long-run, stable and efficient equilibrium, independent of the short run, entirely dependent upon representative optimising agents, perfectly coordinated by the market and capable of totally frustrating the minimal interventions that the state is empowered to make. Second, but for random shocks, this economy would be in the same equilibrium forever. Third, this is indicative of the almost empty theoretical content to the NCE. Markets work perfectly, leave them alone. Fourth, this would appear to spell out the euthanasia for the economist

– why would they be necessary? Fifth, the answer is that, whilst we might believe the economy works perfectly, we do not know what its fundamentals are (themselves ideologically and arbitrarily reduced to individual preferences, etc.), and we need to estimate these in light of the data that the economy itself provides in response to the random shocks that it suffers. This allows rational expectations to be formed in the wake of economic outcomes. However, beyond linear models this becomes extremely complicated because of the dependence of a model upon itself, so that rational expectation models can only be properly estimated with fancy econometrics and numerical methods (see Chapter 9).

Box 8.2
From adaptive through rational expectations to econometrics

Suppose we toss a coin that is equally liable to be heads or tails but we are not sure and need to estimate the probability as p and $(1 - p)$, respectively, giving a score of 1 if heads comes up and 0 if tails does. Obviously, the expected value of the score is one-half. If we take a sequence of throws with scores, x_i, adaptive expectations will predict p as $\alpha\{x_{t-1} + (1 - \alpha)x_{t-2} + (1 - \alpha)^2 p_{t-3} \ldots + (1 - \alpha)^s x_{t-s-1} \ldots\}$ for some α. This is a theoryless estimator of the value of p. Note that on average it will be correct, since each x has an equal chance to be heads or tails. But it will be skewed towards the most recent values as these count more. As a result, the estimator is not biased but it is not least variance.

By contrast, rational expectations depend upon theory. In this case, we know we are throwing a coin that may or may not be biased. So any one throw is as good as any other irrespective of the order in which it was thrown. Using this knowledge, the best estimator is just to take the simple average of x. This will have correct mean *and* least variance.

Essentially, this is how the New Classical Economics views the economy, or a model of it. The model will generate, subject to shocks or probabilities around the variables and relationships, a set of probabilistic outcomes. The model should be used to predict both what happens and what we expect to happen, and the two should be consistent with one another.

Most teaching of econometrics starts off with the Gauss–Markov theorem, and the conditions and tests for BLUE (Best Linear Unbiased Estimator). When statistical tests show that the conditions for BLUE do not hold, this is interpreted as a problem that has to be solved. So, we have to deal with heteroscedasticity or serial correlation, and find ways of doing so.

This is not the most appropriate way of looking at econometrics. It is best seen as putting forward theoretical hypotheses, derived from economic theory, together with statistical hypotheses concerning the randomness around the data or the specified relationships. Then, you test the hypotheses as a package. If your hypotheses fail, this is not a problem to be addressed as such. Rather, it means you need to look for new hypotheses, either theoretical or statistical. If you are confident in your theory, you are liable to put forward alternative statistical hypotheses, but that is what you are doing, not otherwise dealing with a problem.

In short, the NCE ultimately came to rest upon advances in econometrics in the absence of advances, or regression to coin a phrase, in macroeconomic theory (see Box 8.2 for some discussion). In case of its theory of real business cycles (as covered in Chapter 9), it did seek to recognise that the economy grows whilst accompanied by cyclical movements in employment. It explained this in terms of choice for leisure over labour when technical progress is randomly slower (faster) and potential wage levels and employment less (more) attractive. However, despite its flimsy foundations and substance, the NCE both served as the major mainstream response to the collapse of the post-war boom and, as will be seen in Chapter 10, heavily influenced the form taken against the extreme, putatively critical postures that it promoted both in terms of their substance and scope. In other words, NCE set the standard despite being so extreme, thereby considerably limiting the substance and scope of critical reactions against it.

On the NCE, see relevant chapters in Snowdon and Vane (2005) and also in de Vroey (2016). For spirited defences of NCE which do more to expose their deficiencies on careful reading, see Chari et al. (2009) (a critique of NCM, see Chapter 10, for not relying on the fundamentals of individual optimisation which it itself dogmatically privileges) and Ball (2009) (for defence of the efficient market hypothesis, see Box 1.1, which allows financial markets to work as efficiently as possible given deficient information).

9
Forging the Consensus: Monetary Policy and Real Business Cycle Theory

9.1 Overview

NCE set a new ethos for the study of macroeconomics, in terms of how short-run fluctuations were to be understood and studied. One aspect of the new ethos was to base macroeconomics on microeconomic principles. Another was to appeal to 'rigour', meaning the analysis should depend exclusively on deductively derived propositions (from microeconomics) as opposed to the inductive (empirically based assumptions, such as the Phillips curve, and the systemic irrespective of microfoundations). Taking the so-called fundamentals of NCE (representative individuals, rational expectations, given preferences, endowments, technologies) as more or less given, this gave rise to two parallel lines of research that would eventually become consolidated into what came to be known as the NCM (see Chapter 10). One of these lines of analysis, which remained true in its own way to the principle and practice of the NCE, is RBC theory (see Section 9.3). It extends the short run to the long run whilst retaining the extreme posture of reducing the macroeconomic to the microeconomic, necessarily leading to the exclusion of money and monetary policy altogether, presuming that markets work perfectly, and deeming any sort of policy intervention as unnecessary. At the same time, and as a partial response to the extremes of the NCE and the RBC positions, mild renewals of 'new' Keynesianism were developed in numerous contributions, scattering their attention across different dimensions of macroeconomic phenomena by reference to, and by incorporating, market imperfections. Some of these insights, judiciously selected alongside the RBC toolkit, would then be combined to allow for the NCM, neatly constituting a macroeconomics based on (rational expectations) microeconomic foundations but apparently restoring a limited Keynesianism (with some, but equally confined, role to be played by the state).

At the same time, the NCE prompted another line of investigation, focusing on the role and conduct of monetary policy, and this will be taken up in Section 9.2. The NCE managed to square a circle or two in its approach to monetary policy. Whilst it seems to be irrelevant given perfectly working markets and state ineffectiveness, room is found for it to play a role in light of the ability of the monetary authority to stimulate or deflate the economy through 'surprise' changes in the money supply. If, however, the monetary authority does this in pursuit of aims that defy Pareto efficient equilibrium, as it can due to the time inconsistency nature of policymaking (effectively not keeping to policy promises after agents' actions based upon them have already been made), it loses credibility with agents as a policymaker. As a result, it becomes costly to squeeze inflation out of the system, as lack of trust has to be squeezed out as well. The conclusion drawn is that politics are distortionary and so should, in effect, be removed from policymaking, with monetary policy ideally devolved to a supposedly independent authority or central bank (in the sense, essentially, that the latter can be better trusted to know and represent the nation's economic interests than government).

Section 9.4 highlights how the legion deficiencies of the RBC have been veiled by prodigious reliance upon empirical investigation in place of substantive theoretical analysis. Such extremes to which macroeconomics had been driven in methods, assumptions and conclusions provided ample potential for future developments as more or less critical points of departure as will be seen in subsequent chapters.

9.2 Monetary Policy Under the NCE

The NCE, through its monetarist origins, provided an alternative explanation for the stagflation of the 1970s, as well as a way of explaining business cycle fluctuations. Indeed, the essence of the Lucas misperception model (Chapter 8) is exactly to achieve that. Price expectations may deviate from long-run values if, due to incomplete information, agents cannot distinguish between specific and general price disturbances, brought about by unanticipated or erratic money supply changes. Short-run deviations of prices and output/unemployment from their long-run equilibrium values are canonically attributed solely to unan-ticipated changes in the money supply, although other shocks could shift the economy in principle (and do for the supply side with RBC). The long-run equilibrium output, Q_N, and corresponding natural rate of unemployment, derived from the supply side of the economy, will prevail in both the short run and the long run, as long as price expectations are set correctly, or as long as there are no monetary 'surprises'. Essentially, the economy is only out of long-run equilibrium because of shocks.

The policy ineffectiveness proposition of the NCE is a remarkable implication of the framing of the macroeconomy, and devastating for any sort of Keynesian policy intervention. It suggests that systematic (i.e. no shocks or surprises) monetary policy is neutral, leaving real variables unaffected in the short as well as the long run. A systematic (what came to be called 'announced') increase in money supply would only increase prices (and inflation), with no boost to output or employment, not even temporarily. This was in line, albeit more extreme, with the monetarist explanation for stagflation whereby continuous increases in inflation are not accompanied by reductions in unemployment in the long run. However, this policy implication also has a perverse effect that could not (and did not) stand well within NCE. For, the policy ineffectiveness proposition also implies that a successful disinflation can be attained easily and quickly and at no real cost. All a government has to do, if deciding to reduce inflation, is to 'announce' it. Within a rational expectations environment, a systematic reduction in money supply would lead to a clean reduction in inflation, leaving output and unemployment at their 'natural' levels.

To some degree, this bizarre result (inflation is not a policy problem) is a consequence of the more general failure of macroeconomics in general, and of monetarism in particular, to specify why inflation matters at all. As long as relative prices are correct and markets are working perfectly, who cares what the absolute price level is or how it is changing? In a sense, extreme monetarism in the form of the NCE had rendered its own proponents redundant – who needs economists if markets and individuals are all perfect? At most all that is needed is to take monetary policy out of the hands of those who might manipulate it for their own purposes, especially surprise increases in the money supply for electoral advantage by fooling voters into thinking they had been made better off than they actually were.

This argument – that macroeconomic policy in general, and monetary policy in particular, might be exploited by politicians for electoral purposes – predates the rise of monetarism. After all, the Phillips curve had seemed to offer a trade-off between employment and inflation, and why not go for employment (and higher government expenditure) prior to an election and deal with the resulting inflation after being elected. With the rise of the NCE, the scope for such electoral cycles was perceived to be considerably limited, precisely because agents with rational expectations would preclude manipulation of demand through increasing the money supply, and hence demand until inflation is fully anticipated. But, for the NCE, the inflation is always immediately anticipated. Consequently, only unanticipated inflation can deliver short-run deviation of output from long-run equilibrium levels, and this requires surprise monetary policy.

Remarkably, by this device the NCE was able to turn 'the inflation is not a policy problem' outcome on its head with attention to what became known as the time inconsistency and credibility problems, covered below. For a simple exposition, all that is needed is the Lucas aggregate supply curve, as before:

$$Q = Q_N + a(P - P^*)$$

and an additional function, f, that describes the government's (or monetary authority's) objectives, which are presumed to underpin their policy decisions. These are assumed to reflect society's preferences towards output (or unemployment) and inflation as a whole, and became conventionally referred to as the 'social welfare function', S, although open to capture by particular interests in the absence of central bank independence. So:

$$S = f(Q - Q^T, P - P^T)$$

where Q is a 'good' thing in the utility function, f, P is 'bad', and Q^T and P^T correspond to society's target levels of the variables Q and P, with $f_1 > 0$ and $f_2 < 0$. For example, typically, f might be taken to be quadratic and be equal to $a(Q - Q^T)^2 + b(P - P^T)^2$ for parameters a and b.

It is also assumed that the monetary authority controls inflation directly through monetary policy or, in other words, $dM = dP$ and, in what follows, P and P^* will stand for inflation and inflation expectations, respectively, Q for output and Q_N for the natural level of output. So, other things being equal, government would wish for Q and P to be as close as possible to their targets Q^T and P^T, although there may be, as will be seen, some potential to tradeoff one against the other despite rational expectations.

This raises two questions. The first is, why should government wish to depart from the equilibrium values of Q and P and, in particular, to choose target output above its equilibrium level, $Q^T > Q_N$? On the one hand, it might be motivated by pursuit of electoral advantage as previously discussed. On the other hand, and whilst NCE is distancing itself from the past theory of electoral cycles based on the Phillips curve, its own version of deviation of Q^T from Q_N might be justified by reference to the wish to correct some externally imposed Pareto inefficiency that renders Q_N 'too low'. Thus, for example, in the presence of a scheme for unemployment insurance (dulling the incentive for workers to take employment), the government can efficiently reduce insurance payments and increase employment. Similarly, if trade unions exercise power over labour markets, unduly raising money wages, it might make sense both to increase employment even if at the cost of inflation (thereby reducing the real wage despite the monopsony power of labour). These explanations can be combined, as indeed they were within rational expectations electoral models, to complete the central bank independence argument (see end of section).

The second issue concerns not just the rationale for non-equilibrium targeting, but where the capacity to achieve it comes from. Recall that, whilst anticipated monetary policy has no real effect, unanticipated monetary policy does have a short-run effect, whereby a surprise increase in money supply (or inducing inflation directly as assumed here) could lead to a temporary boost in real activity, as a result of errors in expectations due to agents' (or the representative agent's) misperceptions of the money supply. As a result, government can only 'distort' the economy away from its equilibrium by deploying surprise monetary policy. One way of allowing for this is to sequence decision making in the following way – with the representative agent forming expectations, after which government chooses the money supply.

This, though, has two further implications. One, as is readily apparent, is that the agents will learn what the government has done after the event and be mindful when forming expectations next time around. This will create what is termed a 'credibility' problem for the government. The more it increases inflation unexpectedly to boost employment, the more it will be expected to do so. How credible will its future announcements of monetary policy (or inflation targets) be?

Any announcement – for example, to reduce inflation by a systematic reduction in M (e.g. whilst intending to leave output at some level lower than Q^T, at Q_N) – will not be credible, as the government's incentive to boost the economy unexpectedly is inherent in its objectives. Or, in other words, agents start to form expectations or gain knowledge of government's excessive ambitions (within its objective function) and would, ultimately, be able to neutralise these too. But, as will be seen below, the effects are not entirely neutral in light of credibility problems when the goal is to reduce inflation.

This reflects the other implication: that the government is subject to what is known as the problem of time inconsistency. This is because the 'best' policy for the government to announce before the agents form expectations is different from the best policy that will be adopted after the agents have adopted those expectations. This is easily shown from the aggregate supply curve. As soon as P^* is set to a fixed value, if M is set so that $P > P^*$, then actual output Q will be greater than Q_N and closer to the social optimum, Q^T. The consequence, though, will be higher inflation at a later period.

It follows that those setting discretionary monetary policy always have an incentive to adopt surprise inflation (via a surprise increase in M) given they can do so after the agents' expectations are set. In short, under rational expectations, agents are aware of the policy goals that determine the behaviour of the government (that is, the model that describes both the economy's structure and the government's social welfare function with leaning towards setting Q^T above Q_N). Consequently, they are aware of the government's time-inconsistent problem and take it into account whilst forming their expectations. This gives rise to so-called inflationary bias. If output is to be sustained at the level Q_N, M will have to be increased to a higher level than would otherwise be necessary because this is what agents will be expecting.

In this light, consider what happens if government decides to undergo a dis-inflationary strategy. Agents suspect that any such announcement to reduce excessive inflation is not credible. As it were, it is just a con to get agents to reduce their expectations, after which the announced goal will be abandoned. This is a bit like the famous Charlie Brown cartoon in which, whenever Lucy places the ball for him to kick, she always whips it away as soon as he begins to do so – however much she promises to do otherwise. For how long would he remain the sucker? Similarly, as soon as agents adjust their expectations downwards, a surprise monetary policy will kick in.

That is, unless government can genuinely convince agents that there will be no future surprises. It is presumed that it can only persuade agents of its true intentions through convincing actions rather than unconvincing words. Government has to adopt disinflationary policy for as long as it takes for agents to believe this represents a change in policy (or objective function), thereby allowing them to lower their expectations without suspecting that a surprise increase in the money supply will result (and if government does this as soon as expectations come down, it will once again lose agents' confidence). Costly dis-inflations in the UK and US during the early 1980s were thought to be explained on the basis of government credibility. Inflation had been so bad in the seventies that no one believed government was committed to reducing it.

Such conundrums gave rise to the further conclusion that inflation control is better taken out of the hands of government because it is liable to be unduly subject to political considerations and short-sightedness. It will be tempted to increase M unexpectedly for short-run gains to the detriment of longer-term losses in both excessive inflation and reputation. Accordingly, a central bank, independent from political pressures, should be responsible for monetary policy. The independent central bank should enjoy a relatively long term in office and adopt a higher degree of inflation aversion than government, thereby ensuring an appropriate weight on the long-term benefits of the primacy of price stability.

Such an analysis of the role and conduct of monetary policy provides yet another clear illustration of the reduced modelling and understanding of the state, as well as the beginnings of the macroeconomic consensus that ultimately settled as the NCM (see Chapter 10). Similar results are obtained by substituting the supposedly more Keynesian assumption of fixed (or sticky) nominal wages. In effect, an identical aggregate supply curve can be generated not from misper-ceptions, but from multi-period fixed nominal wage contracts of otherwise optimising agents with rational expectations. In this way, monetary policy is endowed with a secure stabilisation role in the presence of exogenous shocks, whilst also being enabled in its capacity to boost the economy beyond its natural position even if at the expense of stimulating inflationary momentum by doing so.

This also sets the basis for the modern version of the rules versus discretion debate, in which the balance tips towards following a well-established policy rule, rather than discretionary optimising in every period. This policy rec-ommendation is similar to Friedman's proposition, in the context of the expectations-augmented Phillips curve, whereby to avoid inflationary episodes the government should be better off following a stable rule for the growth in the money supply. In its modern version, as shown in Chapter 10, it takes the form of a feedback rule for the interest rate, known as the Taylor rule.

Even on its own terms, the model and its motivation are highly artificial, more driven by forced rationalising of the assumptions that are necessary for the desired results than any inner coherence. The presence of a fixed social welfare function is presumed even though government has objectives that are divorced from both agents and a putative independent central bank. This is both to allow for conflicts of interest and to leave them, and conflicts over them, unanalysed. With representative agents, it is not clear how these can be separate from government itself, let alone those who run the independent central bank (with motives that seem to differ from those of government but represent those of agents). Remarkably, then, despite the absence of any account of the political process and distributional or other issues, it is the exogenously, unexamined political process that is deemed to blame for excessive inflation and the cost in terms of deflation in bringing down inflationary expectations and inflation itself. Unsurprisingly, market forces of any sort are entirely blameless.

As revealed in its pure form above, at the core of the argument is the implicit presumption that the democratic process has too short a time horizon and it is better for it to be displaced by the longer-term horizons adopted by a putatively independent, benign central bank. Elections take place too often to allow for politicians to develop and sustain a long-term commitment to the primacy of price stability. On its own, however, such an argument (and theoretical premise) could not support the advocated superiority of central bank independence. In a peculiar combination, then, of dubious empirical evidence and an appeal to the old political business cycles (albeit with rational expectations) the government is rendered not only short-sighted but also subject to undesirable leaning towards satisfying electoral goals. This completes the rationale in favour of an independent central bank being responsible for monetary policy, following a simple and transparent rule, enjoying a long term in office and a high degree of autonomy from political influences. In light of recent events, not least the global financial crisis, it scarcely seems credible, to coin a phrase, that bankers should be entrusted to serve long-term, social interests!

But there is more. The corresponding presumption – that there could be a pure depoliticisation of monetary policy – was coupled with legitimising the use of unemployment as the necessary cost of building government reputation, or credibility, in the fight against inflation. Monetary policy is merely a technical instrument in the control of inflation with no distributive and social implications, and better left in the hands of autonomous technocrats. In effect, politics is the means by which the state can be made effective, if distortion-ary, and so the conclusion is drawn that the state should be neutralised by transferring its means of being able to intervene to what is presumed to be an apolitical regulator.

9.3 Real Business Cycle Theory

RBC theory is not so much an extreme version of the already extreme NCE as the latter's exposure beyond the short to the long run. It emerged at the beginning of the 1980s, incorporating the basic theoretical presuppositions of NCE and, on its own terms, sees itself as rigorously formalising the new research methodology for the study of all aspects of macroeconomics – at least in principle. In practice the extremes of the methodology and methods, such as reliance upon representative individuals, tend to place issues such as distribution beyond its scope. The result has been the construction of more or less artificial models from what are perceived to be solid microeconomic fundamentals and principles that are then deployed to fit the 'stylised facts' quantitatively. The latter refers to statistical properties and co-movements of aggregate macroeconomic variables in the short and long runs.

A great variety of RBC models has emerged, but each shares the common ground of viewing the economy as a moving Walrasian equilibrium that is buffeted by real supply shocks (although more recent models in the RBC vein do allow for imperfectly working markets as well, see DSGE discussion below and in Chapter 10). A crucial distinction is made between impulse and propagation mechanisms. The first refers to the shock hitting the otherwise stable economy, whilst the second refers to the mechanisms by which this initial impulse transmits into aggregate variables and produces fluctuations. The aim is to explain theoretically how these induced fluctuations in aggregate variables in response to random shocks can be made to match empirically observed movements of economic variables.

With this research programme and aim, the novelty of RBC theory rests on the presumed resolution of two of the previously discussed tensions, those between micro and macro and the short- and long-run nexus. With the economy constructed as a micro-based general equilibrium, continuous market clearing (that is, perfectly flexible prices and perfectly clearing markets) prevails, whilst money simply disappears from the picture altogether. This partially justifies the word 'real' as a label, but also indicates a departure from the use of monetary disturbances as the driver of fluctuations as identified by the Lucas NCE misperceptions model. This departure from monetary considerations was driven by the reasonable dissatisfaction, as far as it goes, with the misperceptions explanation and its implied confusion about the nature of nominal monetary shocks, with all variation in the economy swinging on temporary failure to distinguish individual from general price movements. This lever does not fit well with the notion that underlying microeconomic 'fundamentals' are not only subject to shocks themselves but that these shocks are the sources of induced fluctuations (including those of prices themselves) as agents respond to the shocks as best they can, given informational imperfections. But also, and equally important, not least in extending the scope of analysis and justifying its extreme forms, is that RBC theory overcame the shortcomings of the NCE in its inability to address well-established stylised facts (particularly the moderate pro-cyclical movement of real wages).

In addition, although RBC theory is fundamentally framed by, and derived from the NCE, it also exhibits some significant departures from it. Most obvious is the exclusion of money from the analysis altogether, possibly motivated by its short- and long-run neutrality in the NCE policy ineffectiveness analysis. Whether or not it is deliberately motivated by this, the absenting of money sidelines debate about its role across Keynesians, more traditional Friedmanite monetarists and New Classicals. Consequently, with no role for money, let alone monetary policy, only relative prices and real variables are relevant, themselves derived from optimising representative individuals. Given this and representative agents forming expectations rationally, the presumption becomes that agents are continuously optimising, and nothing prevents the Walrasian general equilibrium from being obtained at all times across all markets.

What might move the economy to generate fluctuations? This is answered through a particular way of resolving the relationship between the short and long runs. The 'unification' of the two arguments entails two aspects. First, it is shown that short-run business cycle fluctuations can be studied within what is known as a stochastic growth model. This brings a particular type of dynamic element to the study of business cycles, and a break from earlier representations in which dynamics were previously derived purely from being out of, and the time to get to, equilibrium (steady-state balanced growth). It also brings technological progress to the fore in a stochastic, if minimal, way. The second part of the 'unification', as mentioned, seeks to incorporate some degree of empirical consistency between short- and long-run regularities in the movement of aggregate data.

Traditional exogenous growth models (see Chapter 4) identify technological progress as the fundamental source of long-run per capita growth, whilst previous macroeconomic theories focused on the determinants of aggregate variables in the short run without considering long-run growth. In contrast to neoclassical growth models, in which a deterministic smooth process of technological advance is assumed and a steady-state balanced growth path results, RBC theory continues to assume the rate of change of technology to be exogenous but also stochastic. When randomness in the rate of technological change is incorporated into the growth model, the growth rate of output will be also moving in a random manner, and the economy will display fluctuations that resemble business cycle phenomena. Elementary though it may be, such technological shocks are taken by RBC theory to be the main impulse mechanism in explaining growth and cycles (which are now one and the same), warranting the use of the term 'real' as a qualifier in its name, signifying that only real supply shocks are responsible for the observed fluctuations.

In addition, the stochastic growth paradigm is deemed to derive from sound microeconomic principles, with rational agents optimising not only intra-temporally at one moment in time, but also intertemporally (over time), not least taking into account whenever possible the random supply shocks. The cyclical fluctuations do not then become (as previously explained) deviations from potential (full employment) output, reflecting some form of disequilib-ria. Rather, they are simply variations in the outcomes attached to continuous full employment output. More specifically, agents are presumed to respond optimally to random technological shocks, and any observed variation in output is an optimal and full employment response to the evolving technical conditions. In short, the fundamental propagation mechanism, through which cyclical fluctuations are produced, is the intertemporal substitution (in the supply) of labour. The representative household is responding to changes in real wages brought about by random changes in TFP by optimally substituting between labour and leisure over time. In a nutshell, when productivity increase is growing faster than usual, real wages are rising, and everyone wants to work more, with the opposite when technical change is randomly increasing slower than normal. With perfectly working markets there is no involuntary unemployment, since all observed fluctuations in employment over the business cycles are voluntarily chosen by representative households in light of the fluctuations in real wages induced by the supply shock.

In this way, RBC theory prompted a new, more general research programme, and a modelling method going under the name of DSGE models. These entail, first, a 'dynamic' element in the sense that the passage of the economy over time is emphasised (although this is, to a large degree, a formality with intra-temporal and intertemporal optimisation based on the same principles with, in effect, different goods at the same time treated in the same way as the same good at different times). The path taken by the economy is analysed through the prism of dynamic (intertemporal) optimisation in which rational expectations far into the future (indeed, the whole life span of the economy, i.e. until infinity) are a crucial determinant. Second, business cycles are explained solely in terms of exogenous stochastic shocks to the system that result in fluctuations in output and other macroeconomic variables through a number of propagation mechanisms. These may include investment lags, inventory building and consumption smoothing, but, most prominently, intertemporal substitution of labour (and consumption). And third, the models are built on the microeco-nomic principles of continuous optimising and general equilibrium. Although nowadays DSGE models are coterminous with the NCM (see Chapter 10), they originated from RBC theory, and this merely reflects the terms around which the consensus of the NCM was built, not least with DSGE modelling as the common analytical toolkit for the study of business cycles, albeit with market imperfections embedded.

Of equal importance, the RBC paradigm prompted an influential shift on the empirical front in macroeconomics. It involved getting real in a rather different sense, not just theoretically as opposed to monetary, but also empirically by reference to data. The goal became one of constructing a model, or computable DSGE model for the economy, and judging it by its predictive power in numerically fitting statistical properties of observed aggregate time series. The means to achieve this became known as the calibration technique, bringing the DSGE model to the heart of macroeconomic empirical analysis, whilst breaking away from classical econometrics methods.

In brief, the calibration exercise entails first solving the model numerically and then generating simulated fluctuations by feeding a series of synthetic real shocks into it. The induced fluctuations in macroeconomic aggregates and their statistical properties are then to be compared with observed data. The aim of the calibration method is to quantify a theoretical model in order to be able to assess its fitness with observed stylised facts of interest, and to answer concrete quantitative questions. The procedure of quantifying the model is the essential aspect of calibration. For more details, see Appendix A.

To meet the empirical goal, the calibration method requires a set of conditions. First, and building on the NCE tradition, the theoretical models must be built from microeconomic fundamentals and optimising rational agents, and thereby be rendered immune to the Lucas critique. In other words, the models have to be 'structural' with parameters and propagation mechanisms that are invariant to systematic policy changes. Structural is a term used here to denote that the parameters of the model are derived (and hence can be identified) from fundamentals of optimising individuals whereby expectational effects from changing economic conditions are accounted for (as opposed to ad hoc behavioural equations). It has nothing to do with the conceptualisation of the structure of the economy, as it is about individuals, not structures.

Second, the numerical values attached to the structural parameters should not be chosen arbitrarily, but from existing microeconometric empirical studies (pitched at the individual or household level) and/or from long-run historical averages. This way, the parameterised theoretical model would be consistent with micro data (and long-run observations) and 'unified' with reality. For example, the coefficient that describes the share of labour in a (Cobb–Douglas) production function is given the value of the historical average of national income paid to labour (commonly set around 0.7), or the relative weights attached to consumption and leisure in the representative agent's utility function are parameterised using estimated values from empirical studies that explore individual allocations of time to market and non-market (leisure) activities. Along the same lines, the coefficients that underpin the form of random shocks hitting the model economy should also be parameterised, using information from well-established previous studies (e.g. estimates from Solow residuals for technology shocks).

Third, particular statistical techniques were needed that would systematically and convincingly refine the derivation of stylised facts and render them consistent with the theoretical model. This refers to unravelling the dynamics of time series aggregate data – for example, how to disentangle and isolate the trend from cyclical and seasonal components of time series (e.g. GDP or investment), as well as examining co-movements among variables (e.g. how income and consumption relate to one another over time, and how to distinguish between lead and lag correlations). Not surprisingly, especially with the availability of large data sets and cheap and enhanced computing power, a rich literature evolved around improved empirical techniques for the study of data properties, alongside development of algorithms and computing techniques for the solution and simulation of theoretical models.

In some respects RBC theory was a product of its time, drawing upon the NCE, growth theory (even if prior to NGT) and developments in econometrics, albeit with idiosyncrasies of its own (not least the absence of monetary factors altogether, although this was itself a product to some degree of postures of policy ineffectiveness and short- and long-run neutralities of money). Not surprisingly, though, RBC attracted a degree of criticism for the extremes of assumptions adopted. However, the majority of such criticism is more indicative of the consensus that was being created around the more general DSGE models that merely built the possibility of market imperfections and nominal rigidities within the framing provided by RBC theory (after all, a market imperfection can be rendered as more or less equivalent to an imperfectly known shock).

In short, an account of many of the criticisms of RBC can best be seen as steps and refinements in a transition to DSGE models in the NCM framing. In response to the latest financial crisis a new wave of criticisms emerged, producing a new round of refinements to the NCM-DSGE models, as discussed in Chapter 10. First, for example, RBC theories were criticised for their sole reliance on real supply shocks, particularly technology shocks, as the source of impulse mechanisms. Beyond well-known problems with the measurement of TFP and the restrictive assumptions required for its derivation (see chapter 5 in the counterpart *Microeconomics* volume), relying upon technological change to explain business cycle fluctuations is difficult, especially when they are large, as in a major recession. A natural step was to introduce other shocks, whether on the supply side (oil prices and wars) or as real demand shocks (unanticipated government expenditure), as well as nominal ones.

Second, there has been dissatisfaction with the calibration method, and, in particular, with how consistently the values for the structural parameters had been chosen. As mentioned, the parameters of the theoretical model were assigned numerical values from existing micro studies and/or long-run averages for the country under study and, although some of the selected values became well accepted, others have been more controversial or even deemed inconsistent. Inconsistency is a problem either where there are diverging microestimates for a parameter (and hence which value to choose) or where no estimates exist (and hence on what criteria is a value assigned). In operationalising DSGE models there is considerable ambiguity in choosing the different parameters that make up the model, and this is of pivotal importance given the quantitative goals.

The calibration debate has evolved around one parameter in particular, reflecting deeper objections (see below) and setting the pace for future internal developments. This is the parameter for the intertemporal elasticity of substitution in the labour supply (to what extent do households optimally prefer to supply present as opposed to future labour?). Microeconometric evidence suggests that the elasticity of labour supply is quantitatively small. However, in its simple form the RBC model fails to match the observed sizes in the movements in employment over a business cycle with those that would be implied by the estimated elasticity value. In other words, for the model to account for the stylised facts on employment variability, a large value (contrary to microeconometric evidence) needs to be assigned to the labour supply elasticity coefficient. Apart from suggesting measurement errors in the employment data, this weakness of the RBC prediction has been attributed to the modelling of the labour market, whereby employment volatility is derived solely from changes in hours worked by employed individuals (whilst, in reality, the largest part of variation in labour supply stems from movements in and out of employment – or the presence in reality if not in the models of involuntary unemployment). Attempts to incorporate voluntary unemployment in extensions of the RBC model have not managed to resolve the 'puzzle', or they have generated mismatches with other stylised facts (e.g. in the correlation between hours worked and wages), whilst at the same time imposing even stricter assumptions (notably, that workers can fully insure against the probability of becoming unemployed, so that their income is the same irrespective of their employment state). Alternatively, account of other types of shocks (e.g. government expenditure disturbances) have been used to reduce the intolerable burden that is placed on the role of intertemporal substitution of labour in explaining fluctuations in levels of employment.

Dissatisfaction with the above led to a move away from calibration and towards estimation of DSGE models (or a combination of the two), so that instead of using estimates from other studies, a set of the 'structural' parameters could be jointly estimated from the same model that serves as the basis for the theoretical and empirical investigations. This gave a tremendous impetus to econometrics techniques (such as GMM, VAR and variants, and Bayesian estimation) in their own right – since the theoretical models are of general equilibrium, and hence all variables are endogenously related to one another – and its stochastic basis also implies that that the shocks hitting the economy should be specified and both identified and matched with the data in light of the theoretical model. However, even with estimation of DSGE models that became prevalent with the rise of the NCM, tensions across the theoretical and empirical work remained. On the one hand, in principle more and more refinements are open to being incorporated into a DSGE model (provided that they can be micro-founded) and potentially provide a better empirical match and resolve 'puzzles'. On the other hand, being the sole source of variation in the theoretical model, more and more shocks need to be added to account for empirical variability. Given its rigid methodology, there then seems to be a trade-off between theoretical complexity (i.e. more variables and more transmission mechanisms) and more impulse mechanisms or shocks. And if enough shocks are incorporated then an estimated DSGE model may guarantee a good empirical fit, leaving open the question of what the systematic component of the model is able to explain.

But the third, and most commonplace, objection to RBC theory is its neglect of any sort of failure in the market price mechanism in explaining frustrated exchanges, and involuntary unemployment in particular. This is, after all, the extreme to which RBC theory had gone in explaining cyclical fluctuations as the consequence of continuous, optimal Pareto efficiency through time – as opposed to its denial as part of the rationale for a macroeconomics distinct from micro-economics. Particularly galling in this respect, for anyone with the slightest of Keynesian sympathies, is the reliance upon representative agents' optimality in withdrawing hours worked (or getting out of the labour force) when real wages decrease as a consequence of a negative transitory productivity shock, in anticipation of higher wages in the future when the shocks are anticipated to be more beneficial, and conversely for particularly positive shocks. This is a criticism that draws upon but goes beyond the parameterisation debate on the size of the relevant (intertemporal) elasticity of labour supply that is required to explain excessive movements over time in what is presumed to be full employment, in the presumed absence of involuntary unemployment. In other words, labour supply decisions reflect demand-side constraints in the short run, rather than optimal supply-side equilibria.

The last objection also relates to the extreme postulate of RBC theory relative to the policy ineffectiveness proposition of NCE. With business cycle phenomena viewed as optimal responses to exogenous shocks, stabilisation policy is not only ineffective but also irrelevant. However, if business cycles, and recessions in particular, are to be viewed as consequences of market failures (and hence as deviations from potential levels) then some role for policy can be reinstated.

9.4 Further Thoughts and Readings

To reiterate, RBC theory takes NCE's methodological approach a few steps further and in a different direction, first by adopting an extreme resolution to the micro/macro and short-run/long-run tensions and, second, by dropping monetary factors altogether. The aggregate economy is conceptualised as a dynamic microeconomic general equilibrium system that is subject to exogenous random technological shocks. Short- and long-run analyses are integrated by essentially assuming that equilibria from short to long runs, and all points in-between, are always continuously and smoothly attainable; the short and long runs coincide apart from interference from random shocks. This is not surprising given that all variables are allowed to adjust instantaneously, all markets are complete and continuously clearing, and expectations are formed rationally. By completing the total subordination of macro to micro, RBC theory renders money irrelevant (as it becomes super-neutral across all time and space) and inevitably provides for a purely supply-side explanation of cyclical fluctuations with household preferences exogenously given in all respects (although also allowed to be subject to random changes). Importantly, however, business cycle phenomena are no longer viewed as deviations from potential long-run output; rather, the observed fluctuations are all equilibrium positions and Pareto efficient. Recessions and economic booms alike are ideal responses of the economy (representative agents) to exogenous changes in the real economic environment. The only blot on the economic landscape is the stochastic uncertainty that the economy (i.e. agents) face in distinguishing the underlying parameters of the economy. This is unavoidable, just as we cannot tell if a toss of a coin is going to come up heads or tails even if our life, or employment, depends upon it. The idea that policy intervention might make things better is an illusion. Essentially it is at best only ineffective, and otherwise simply undesirable, unnecessary and potentially distortionary.

Paradoxically, by reducing the scope of macroeconomic theory, not least to microeconomic principles of the narrowest content, the so-called fundamentals, RBC also sought to extend its scope of explanation to the workings of the economy as a whole over an indefinite time period. The tensions involved in such reductionism were essentially resolved, or glossed over, by close, detailed and increasingly refined attention towards empirical validation of co-movements of aggregates, rather than the causal factors and social costs of busts and recessions.

Consequently, the RBC's research methodology has three important implications. First, qualitative aspects of economic analysis were subordinated to narrow quantitative modelling. Second, econometric analysis shot to prominence, occupying the vacuum vacated by theory. Third, models function primarily as tracking devices, neither true nor false other than being 'rigorously' grounded in micro-foundations, and are not to be judged on the basis of realism of assumptions (although these are given the name 'fundamentals'). Their sole purpose, and hence basis for assessment, is their ability to fit the 'stylised facts' as far as possible. One model is preferred if it fits the chosen evidence better and, in case of a tie between competing models, then refinement of existing stylised facts or inclusion of new ones offers a way forward.

Such ways of proceeding lie at the extremes of methodology in terms of negotiating the nature of theory, and its relationship to realism and evidence. Leaving this aside, it is important to observe a certain circularity or *cordon sanitaire* around the approach, reflecting a weak negotiation of the far from neutral relationship across theory, statistical technique and data. The HP (Hodrick–Prescott) filter – a statistical technique for detrending a series – offers a simple illustration. Its construction is based on the RBC theoretical presumption that deviations from potential output are short-lived and quickly corrected. In other words, a protracted recession, like the one observed in many countries during the latest financial crisis, will be theoretically self-fulfilling in its interpretation of the deepest of recessions as a decline in potential output, rather than a deviation from it, and consequently in viewing the economy as being close to its potential throughout the cycle. This will be confirmed by HP detrended data.

The appeal of RBC theory rests on overlooking its negligible content in economic theory for which it has substituted potentially evolving and contested empirical investigation. The circularity across theory and empirics can also go the other way. The internal propagation mechanisms (predominantly inter-temporal substitution), in conjunction with rational expectations and perfect markets, have proven to be weak in mimicking an important aspect in the dynamics of macroeconomic aggregates. In particular, empirical evidence shows that macroeconomic aggregates move slowly during the business cycle – in other words, economies take time to recover from recessions. On the basis of its microeconomic principles and its weak internal mechanisms, the RBC theory needs to appeal to exogenous factors to replicate this stylised fact. It needs to assume implausibly large and persistent types of exogenous shocks to explain what would otherwise be considerable inertia and persistence in macro-economic variables. Simply put, a negative technology shock is assumed to have a long-lasting impact and that is why output (and other aggregates) only recover slowly, albeit endogenously, within the system. In the name of meeting its goal (i.e. the stylised facts), whilst being committed to its sacrosanct principles (inter-temporal optimisation, rational expectations, etc.), the RBC theory appeals to and superimposes external sources of persistence.

The responses that followed the surge of NCE and its extreme counterpart, RBC theory, paved the way (together with a corresponding revision of monetary analysis and policy) for an apparently more rounded approach, the NCM, as covered in Chapter 10. The developments leading up to this consensus can in part be better understood through reference to the influence of the NCE/RBC duo. Just as there is a neat dualism between the NCE and RBC theory in handling the short and long runs on the basis of extreme assumptions and model framing in the monetarist tradition, so there is a corresponding dualism across the initial 'new' Keynesian responses that took the NCE as its corresponding critical point of departure and the subsequent responses to RBC theory that were consolidated into the NCM. It is a moot point, however, whether the NCM accepted the NCE/RBC partnership more than it departed from it, and whether it addressed the empirical conundrums and theoretical and methodological extremes that the latter had created.

See relevant chapters in Snowdon and Vane (1997) for the initial support for, and responses to, RBC theory. See Buiter (2006) and Pesaran and Smith (2011) for critiques of the DSGE approach both theoretically and empirically, covering both the original RBC models and the NCM versions (including market imperfections and money). For an insistence on explaining the recent financial crisis from an RBC perspective, see McGrattan and Prescott (2014). For an illuminating discussion on calibration in relation to the estimation of DSGE models, see chapter 11 in DeJong and Dave (2007). On monetary policy within the NCE and central bank independence, see critiques by Bibow (2013) and Forder (1998, 2004).

Appendix A: Solution and Calibration of a DSGE Model

Without going into too much detail, a calibration exercise entails the following steps. The first three involve setting up and solving the model and are common to any further analysis, be it to calibrate or estimate the model to fit stylised facts or answer quantitative questions.

First, a fully articulated microfounded model is created, framing who the agents are and what the markets are. Second, the optimisation problems for the representative agents (households and firms) are derived. These are solved to yield the optimal time paths for the choice variables (e.g. consumption, employment and new capital stock) and can be expressed as time-invariant decision rules contingent on the state of the economy (given by state variables, i.e. those, and the results of those, previously chosen, and shocks) – in other words, given this is how things are, this is what you do into the foreseeable future given how things turn out as you go along.

However, the first-order conditions of the optimisation problems (together with constraint equations) constitute a system of non-linear stochastic difference equations with rational expectations embedded in them, and in practice cannot be solved mathematically. Thus, the third step engages with mathematical methods to render the system into a form that can be solved by known mathematical methods. An approximation is necessary before the equilibrium decision rules can be computed. The 'local' approximation method converts the original nonlinear system into a system of linear stochastic difference equations via an approximation of each of the equations in the neighbourhood of a reference (the local) point. Thus, the approximation process involves two elements, first choosing the point around which to approximate the system, and second the approximation method itself.

There are many approximation techniques. However, the most usual is a Taylor series expansion. This is a mathematical representation of a function as the (infinite) sum of its derivatives at a given point, first formulated by James Gregory, not Brook Taylor as the name suggests. It should not be confused with the Taylor rule for monetary policy (different Taylors for different suits!). A linear approximation makes use only of the first term in the Taylor expansion. The typical reference point used for the approximation is the steady-state of the model with no shocks to technology. That is, it is that point where the economy would be if there were no shocks (or if shocks had taken place a long time ago, and the economy has since converged on its steady-state). The reference point could also incorporate a deterministic trend (so that the economy would be moving on a balanced path, rather than being at a fixed point).

Fourth, the parameters of the model are assigned numerical values so that the model can be solved numerically. Given that the model is derived from micro-economic principles, the postulated parameter values need to be consistent with microeconometric studies and long-run averages. Some common parameters that can be found in the optimisation problems of the representative agents are: shares of labour and capital in production, the depreciation rate of capital, the subjective discount factor of households, the leisure/labour weights in the utility function and the intertemporal elasticity of substitution of labour/consumption.

Some standard assigned values might be set as follows. Long-run averages from historical US data show, for example, that the shares of labour and capital in production are about 0.7 and 0.3, respectively, while US microeconometric studies show that, on average, households allocate about two-thirds of their time to non-market activities and one-third to labour. The representative household's discount factor is, at the equilibrium, related to the long-run steady-state real interest rate. Again, historical data show that an interest rate of 4 per cent per year would imply a discount factor of 0.9615. At the same time, the distribution of shocks needs to be specified and parameterised as well. For example, as usually assumed, the technology shock, call it z_t, follows an autoregressive structure, say $z_t = \rho z_{t-1} + \varepsilon_t$, and hence numerical values should be selected for the coefficient that determines the degree of persistence of the shock (ρ) and its variance (σ_ε^2). These values can be obtained from estimates on the Solow residual for total factor productivity (see the counterpart *Microeconomics* volume).

Fifth, the model is solved numerically and the optimal decision rules are obtained. In passing, note that the solution of the linearised approximate system is complicated by the presence of rational expectations, and many mathematical algorithms, and standardised software packages together with computer power, have been developed for obtaining the rational expectations equilibrium (as opposed to having adaptive expectations that are formed solely on the basis of past values, see Box 8.1).

In the sixth step, the model is simulated. Randomly generated values for the shocks are fed into the system which generates a simulated time series for the variables under scrutiny. A corresponding set of statistics, predominantly variances, autocorrelations and cross-correlations, are computed from the artificial variables. The same moments are calculated from actual data. The final step is to compare the moments of the variables generated by the model with the ones computed from actual data, to check how well the theoretical model's predictions match the actual fluctuations of a (developed) economy, and then also use the model to answer quantitative questions.

In a sense, calibration of the model can be viewed as an informal and somewhat arbitrary matching exercise, whereby an ex ante selected set of statistics are matched exactly with the data (that is, the parameters take values from previous studies), and then a different set of model-computed statistics (variances, etc.) are matched with empirical data. The new estimation techniques of DSGE models take this informal matching technique as the point of departure, and proceed in statistically formalising the ways by which the parameters are jointly estimated and the model's fit is assessed.

10
From New Classical Fundamentalism to New Nonsensus Macroeconomics

10.1 Overview

One of the consequences of the NCE was to bring the control of inflation and monetary policy to the fore, at the expense of boosting employment through fiscal policy, albeit in the heavily circumscribed ideological context of policy ineffectiveness. RBC theory completed the argument by rendering monetary policy irrelevant. The relationship between this extreme posture in macroeconomic scholarship and the implementation of policy in practice is another story, not one to be covered in this volume. Certainly, though, the NCE reinforced what can be taken to be the thrust of what we now term neoliberalism across scholarship, policy and practice, and ideology.

In addition, policymakers do require a little more room for manoeuvre, and support from scholarship, than to be informed of their ineffectiveness as the best for which they can aim. As a result, the NCE gave way to a broad 'new' Keynesian approach – a new and milder form of Keynesianism, and itself a peculiar amalgam of much that had gone before if heavily under the influence of the NCE as the mildest critical point of departure. Along similar lines, the extremes to which RBC theory had taken macroeconomics led to reactions from selective elements of the new Keynesian pallet, albeit in a dynamic and stochastic general equilibrium framework. Eventually, and with the traces of RBC theory remaining visible, it all settled around the NCM (see Box 10.1, summarising all these different strands). This is outlined in Section 10.2, together with the substantive content of the NCM, as underlined by the simplest form of the three fundamental equations derived from its basic DSGE basis. Section 10.3, on the other hand, discovers that the NCM found itself in a state of total disarray in the wake of the global crisis despite, or even because of, its complacency immediately before or even as it was emerging. Whilst able to pinpoint some of its own deficiencies in light of unavoidable aspects of the economic realities revealed by the crisis – not least that money does not cover finance, and finance is not micro – these cannot be readily remedied since their

Box 10.1
Models typology: how many new Keynesians are there?

In contemporary macroeconomics, as with the discipline more generally, given the systematic disregard for the history of economic thought, there prevails a habit of casual attachments of what are inappropriate monikers to new developments, an early and leading example being the New Classical Economics (NCE, which has as much affinity to classical political economy as general equilibrium has to Marxism). Subsequently, the use of different terms interchangeably and indistinctly has, in many instances, created confusion and ambiguity. Here is a somewhat simplified typology of the different terms and how they are used here, although, more broadly, there remains a disciplinary lack of discipline as far as collective consistency is concerned.

The *new Keynesian* 'approach' is a broad approach to macroeconomic theorising, distinguished by its (non-Keynesian) reliance upon microfoundations, drawing upon all sorts of market imperfections and real/nominal rigidities. It developed in response to NCE and its reliance upon perfect markets, particularly incorporating rather than rejecting rational expectations. It encompasses many different theoretical models (e.g. efficiency-wage theories and credit rationing, with a predilection for drawing upon imperfect information). It started off as static and not necessarily within a general equilibrium framework. The inspiration for, and main preoccupation of, the new Keynesian approach has been to show that market non-clearing (and involuntary unemployment) can still emerge in the presence of rational expectations.

Dynamic stochastic general equilibrium (DSGE) is a generic modelling device with three major elements: general equilibrium, stochastic shocks and dynamic microfounded optimisation. When employed by *Real Business Cycle* (RBC) theory (RBC DSGE), the microprinciples and technical apparatus assume perfect markets, continuous market clearing and only relative prices (i.e. no money). The short run becomes synonymous with the long run and business cycles are viewed as sequences of optimal equilibrium points over time – individuals and markets adjust perfectly in response to external shocks with, for example, workers becoming voluntarily unemployed when productivity is temporarily growing more slowly. When used by new Keynesianism (new Keynesian DSGE) the modelling device is the same, but the microeconomic principles allow for market imperfections of a particular kind (e.g. monopolistic competition) and nominal rigidities (price and/or wage stickiness). The *new Keynesian DSGE* modelling came as a response to RBC, with the main aim being to reintroduce monetary policy (of a particular, peculiar and narrow scope). Money is 'endogenised', but only in a token fashion, and there is little if any preoccupation with involuntary unemployment. From this perspective, business cycle fluctuations are no longer optimal (due to price stickiness), and monetary policy is used to stabilise the economy around the RBC equilibrium (contingent upon monopolistic competition). There are numerous new Keynesian DSGE models introducing, for example, more rigidities, or capital/investment and fiscal policy, and now, more than before, a financial sector to allow for bubbles and the like.

▶

New Consensus Macroeconomics (NCM) is the term used to summarise the three main reduced-form equations of a (basic) new Keynesian DSGE model. That is, a new IS (Euler equation, first-order condition, of intertemporal utility maximisation), a new Phillips curve (first-order condition of profit maximisation by monopolistic intermediate firms) and a Taylor rule (for monetary policy). Adding more 'bells and whistles' to the microfoundations of the DSGE model would change the three main equations, but the gist would remain the same.

Last, but by no means least, is the notion of *computable general equilibrium* (CGE), a term we have not used in this text although it is commonplace and refers to the use of general equilibrium models for quantitative analysis, by employing economic data to estimate policy (and other) changes. A special case of CGE is the quantitative (calibrated or estimated) DSGE models, discussed in Chapter 9.

absence is the consequence of the deeply rooted and long-evolved nature of contemporary macroeconomics. From a position of 'if it works, don't fix it', the NCM found itself in a position of 'it don't work, and we don't know how to fix it'. For this reason, as reflected in this chapter's title, we refer to it somewhat clumsily as 'nonesensus' as opposed to 'consensus'!

10.2 Consensus is Borne ...

Not surprisingly, the extremes to which the NCEs drove macroeconomics provoked a 'Keynesian' reaction. The form that this took was heavily influenced both by developments going on more generally within economics at the time and by the extent to which this involved considerable concessions. Thus, for example, the displacement of adaptive by rational expectations by the NCE, which had signalled the death of the vertical Phillips curve as the basis even for minimal discretionary policy, remained in place in what was to become the new Keynesianism. After all, rational expectations had first been proposed in the early 1960s by John Muth, long before they were adopted by the NCE. They represented an attempt to forge consistency over how expectations are formed (optimal use of information) and how they are used in supplying and demanding goods (optimal pursuit of self-interest). To the extent that macroeconomics becomes based on microeconomics, and microeconomics becomes based on optimising individuals, it becomes essential to adopt rational expectations.

In short, whilst important for absolutely undermining the idea of the policy effectiveness of the state (to undermine even the vertical Phillips curve with its accelerating inflation as the cost of having an effect), the assumption of rational expectations did not originate with the NCE. Instead, it represented a move towards further underpinning macroeconomics with microeconomic foundations, and doing so consistently with individual optimisation. In this light, far more significant for a Keynesian point of departure from the

NCE, and RBC alike, has been the assumption of perfectly working markets. And, here, a number of different influences runs together to provide for a Keynesian alternative.

The first, and most important, was the emergence of asymmetric information, market imperfection microeconomics (see the counterpart *Microeconomics* volume, chapter 1). Originally inspired by Akerlof's market for 'lemons', this provided a rationale for why markets might not clear, or prices adjust downwards, even in the presence of excess supply and freedom for them to do so. Employers, for example, prefer to keep wages higher than they need to in order to attract a more productive and compliant workforce, given they do not have the information to distinguish the productivity of one worker as opposed to another. In other words, labour markets can be sticky and not adjust to clear excess supply even though there are no institutional impediments to adjustment. In the same vein, the movements in the interest rate may fail to bring equilibrium, and agents may be credit rationed when lenders have limited information on the type of borrowers or their ex post behaviour. More generally, despite perfectly working markets, they may not clear in the presence of asymmetric information. Besides asymmetric information, an alternative type of imperfection popularised by new Keynesians was monopolistic power in goods (or labour markets) and price (or wage) stickiness.

Second, note that such an emphasis on market imperfections, potentially if not necessarily endogenously generated rather than exogenously given, places information – more or less as statistical knowledge – at the centre of micro-economic, and hence macroeconomic, functioning. This consolidates the role of expectations as crucial (as opposed to systemic functioning or variables such as class, power and conflict). As a result, the new Keynesian is fully capable of embracing the concept that most symbolised the NCE: rational expectations. Even in the absence of perfectly clearing markets, rational expectations make sense since this will mean that economic agents will be consistently rational in their use of resources and available information to reflect the pursuit of their own self-interest. With the restoration of market imperfections, rational as opposed to adaptive expectations are of lesser significance and the dispute between Keynesianism and monetarism can be resumed, only with self-fulfilling inflationary expectations to some degree accompanying the trade-off between output and prices in case of a boost to aggregate effective demand. Whatever disputes may have existed in the past between monetarism and Keynesianism, they could now be rerun with expectations-augmented, self-fulfilling inflation as an added bonus and token deference to economic realities – after all, it should be remembered that very high rates of inflation began to be seen both as the norm and problematic after the experience of the 1970s.

Third, as should be apparent from the previous points, the new Keynesianism incorporates as much if not more from the NCE as it rejects, not least its potential reliance upon representative individuals as the extreme form taken by micro-economic foundations. By the same token, and in the light of the emergence of RBC theory, the macroeconomy is conceived in terms of short-run deviations around a trend or long-term equilibrium, with these deviations determined by a mix of random shocks *and* market imperfections or rigidities.

Fourth, with such limited points of departure from the NCE, the new Keynesianism does allow for the state to be effective. But, once again reflecting how much of the NCE has been incorporated rather than rejected, the extent to which the state can alter outcomes is extremely circumscribed together with, or as a result of, the narrow conceptualisation of the state itself.

The different strands and dimensions of new Keynesianism ultimately settled on what came to be called the NCM. This entailed an eclectic selection of new Keynesian sources of imperfections and rigidities, albeit succumbing to the general equilibrium and stochastic paradigm of the RBC theory, and fully embracing the DSGE analytical framework for the study of business cycles. The NCM was seen by many, up to and even beyond the financial crisis at the end of the 2000s, to have resolved both how to understand the macroeconomy and to formulate (monetary) policy. Within the closed economy, it became fundamentally based on the three main (reduced form) equations of the new Keynesian DSGE model (see Appendix B for more details). Let y represent (log) income, i and r, the nominal and real interest rate, respectively, and Π the inflation rate. Let E be used to express expectations, and * for long-run, 'natural' equilibrium values, with t as a subscript for time. The deviations between short-run and long-run values are defined in terms of speed of adjustment of prices. In the long run, prices are fully flexible, able to move fully to clear markets; in the short run, some prices are sticky, hence it is quantities that move to clear the markets. The long-run equilibrium values, then, are determined by the supply side, consistent with the natural rate hypothesis and RBC theory. However, given sticky prices, the short-run equilibrium may be demand-determined. This difference also characterises the distinct short- and long-run responses of the economy in the presence of exogenous shocks.

The new Keynesian DSGE model also assumes monopolistic competition in the goods market, but this plays no essential role other than to provide justification for the key assumption of nominal price rigidities. It does, however, imply that, in contrast to RBC models, equilibrium values are potentially Pareto inefficient (both in the short and the long runs).

The first equation is given, with $a_1 > 0$, $a_2 > 0$ and $a_3 < 0$, by:

$$(y - y^*)_t = a_1(y - y^*)_{t-1} + a_2 E(y - y^*)_{t+1} + a_3(i_t - r_t^* - E\Pi_{t+1}).$$

This is like the old IS curve, as actual demand and output are below long-run equilibrium if the expected real interest rate is above its equilibrium, natural level (r_t^*), as this tends to depress demand. But demand is also expected to be higher if it has been higher in the past and if it is expected to be higher in the future. The lagged term, itself a later addition to the canonical NCM model, assumes that the output gap is persistent in that, if $(y - y^*)_{t-1} > 0$, this will mean more expenditure in time t as a result of higher income (optimally spread over a lifetime). Nonetheless, the principle that steams out of rational expectations and intertemporal optimisation is that the current output gap is primarily determined by the (representative) agent's expectations about future economic conditions. This is so both for the case of expected future economic activity, and output, and expected future real interest rates.

The second equation is given by:

$$\Pi_t = b_1\Pi_{t-1} + b_2 E\Pi_{t+1} + b_3(y - y^*)_t.$$

This parallels the Phillips curve, with $b_i > 0$ and $b_1 + b_2 = 1$. The anticipated inflation rate will be higher, the higher it has been in the past and the higher it is anticipated to be (as a weighted sum), since past inflation will have an inertia of its own and the future inflation will be factored into decision making. In addition, excess demand will fuel inflation.

The third equation, unlike the LM curve, arises out of the independent role played by the central bank in setting its policy instrument: the nominal rate of interest. Money supply is supposedly endogenised, but a closer look at the underlying DSGE model and its presuppositions reveals a trivial, residual role for the money supply, and not much scope for money per se (see Appendix B).

Thus, for $c_i > 0$:

$$i_t = r_t^* + E\Pi_{t+1} + c_1(\Pi_t - \Pi^T) + c_2(y - y^*)_t$$

where Π^T is the bank's targeted rate of inflation and y^* potential (natural) output. This is known as the Taylor rule for setting the rate of interest (and implicitly, or as a consequence, the money supply to accommodate it), with the central bank raising the interest rate to deflate the economy to the extent that the inflation rate and the level of demand exceed target or equilibrium, respectively. The Taylor rule essentially reflects the way monetary policy is assumed to react (optimally) to changing economic developments (i.e. exogenous shocks) with the aim of stabilising the economy around its long-run values.

Note, first, that the long-run equilibrium for this economy is given with $\Pi - \Pi^T = 0$, i.e. when the rate of inflation hits its target level, which is fully expected, together with $y = y^*$, and $i = r^* + \Pi^T$.

Second, why is the economy not at full employment all the time, given there are rational expectations? It is important to note, firstly, that there exist two distinct and independent sources of distortion in the NCM model. One is monopolistic competition in the goods market that, as already mentioned, makes the long-run equilibrium level of output, y˙, Pareto suboptimal. And as a well-learned lesson from the NCE central bank independence paradigm (see Chapter 9), monetary policy, following its rule, should not and does not attempt to do anything about this (full employment cannot be achieved without leading to self-defeating time inconsistency and credibility problems). The second distortion, sticky prices, does not allow for both attaining the constrained natural level of output, y˙ (in the short run), and for an efficient response to an exogenous disturbance.

Third, it is because of rigid prices that a role for monetary policy emerges. The block of three equations describes the scope and mechanism of monetary policy in stabilising the economy in the presence of exogenous shocks. Suppose a shock hits the economy such that actual inflation and output deviate positively from their target and equilibrium levels, respectively. The Taylor rule mechanically prescribes that the central bank should react by increasing the nominal interest rate. Due to sticky prices, this nominal increase will translate into a rise in the real expected rate of interest, and (through the IS curve) this will depress consumption (and investment) and signal a commitment to control the inflation rate as well, thereby reducing inflation both through reducing excess demand and by reducing inflationary expectations (via the Phillips-like curve). Both output and inflation move downwards towards their targeted levels. The situation is similar in the case of an opposite shock, where both inflation and output deviate negatively from their targeted levels. The central bank lowers its nominal interest instrument, leading to a lower real interest rate, an increase in consumption and demand, as well as an increase in inflation.

As is apparent, the NCM has an RBC supply-side equilibrium as its basis and as its target (minus the implications of monopolistic competition that monetary policy does not attend to). Deviations from it are the outcome of exogenous shocks, rather than endogenous systemic forces within the system or even due to systematic lack of effective demand. And the stabilisation mechanism provides for an evident exposition of much of the RBC (and NCE) that has been accepted, rather than rejected, certainly relative to the old neoclassical synthesis. To put it another way, imperfections and rigidities are appended to an otherwise purely Walrasian RBC frame, and monetary policy is given the role of bringing the economy in line with it. All of this might look like it reflects 'Keynesian' features, not least when the response to a positive shock is to reduce the interest rate and reflate the economy. But on the occasion of a negative productivity shock, for example, that affects both the short-run and the long-run (natural) positions of the economy, inflation and output deviate positively from their target inflation and (suppressed) natural level, respectively. The corresponding increase in the central bank's interest rate brings them towards being in line. In other words, and in light of a negative technological shock, monetary policy assists output to contract further than it would otherwise, and down to the reduced y_t^* (see Appendix B for more details). The NCM is, almost by chance, 'Keynesian' only half of the time, when adjusting the economy upwards to long-run equilibrium, but reinforcing adjustment when in a downward direction to squeeze out inflationary expectations.

As a mild departure from its origins, nominal shocks that are absent in RBC theory are now in the NCM, and are seen as being able to cause business cycle fluctuations, necessarily without affecting the natural level of output. In as much as the response to such shocks may seem more 'Keynesian', preoccupation with monetary disturbances generates a further conundrum. This is because systematic policy (via the Taylor rule) has a stabilising role whilst, at the same time, unanticipated shifts in the central bank's interest rate (an error term in the Taylor rule) are unambiguously destabilising. Beyond the problem of interpreting what is or is not a monetary shock, it is a moot point whether monetary policy, the imprint of the NCM, is to be praised for its ability to cause fluctuations rather than to tame them.

Fourth, as is apparent, all the (scope for) adjustment in this model comes from the monetary side of things. This leaves it open to two criticisms, quite apart from all of those associated with the framing around the extremes of representative individuals or the ways by which stabilisation is achieved, etc. On the one hand, there is simply no account taken of fiscal policy, and it is a well-observed property of the NCM that it relies exclusively upon monetary policy to trade-off inflation against output.

On the other hand, leaving this and other simplifications and assumptions aside, the model takes the simplest possible view of the monetary, i.e. financial, system. It is merely a source of demand through the leverage of the interest rate, and thereby takes no account of potential malfunctioning of the financial system should there be any sort of failure, not least a crisis of confidence both in provoking downturns and undermining remedies to them (lowering the interest rate). Indeed, only after the global crisis of the 2000s was well underway was it realised that the financial system might malfunction in this way, despite no signalling of this in either inflation or the output gap. In other words, and as a justification for the suppression of a (meaningful) financial market in the canonical model, there stood the belief that should something bad be building up in the financial sector (however much understood), it would reveal itself in the two terms to which systematic monetary policy is responding: inflation and the output gap. If the price system (in whichever market, however narrowly perceived) is allowed (or helped) to adjust flexibly, then the price mechanism will ensure convergence to the long-run equilibrium, because the unconstrained price mechanism would reflect the 'fundamentals'.

Despite quantitative easing, in which interest rates were lowered to minimal rates and money made readily available, recession persisted as banks were not prepared to lend in case they were not repaid. Indeed, the liquidity trap seems to have reasserted itself with a vengeance (if not as understood by the neoclassical synthesis in which interest rates are too high, and are expected to rise but need to fall as opposed to the apparent lack of confidence underpinning lack of economic activity irrespective of high or low interest rates). The NCM was shown to be toothless policy-wise since, with interest rates at rock bottom, there was nowhere else for it to go.

10.3 ... and Shattered?

As can be seen, the NCM made the previous macroeconomic consensus, or IS/LM neoclassical synthesis, seem like child's play compared with its own achievement in compromise. It embodied not only ingredients from the erstwhile synthesis itself, but also the careful assembling of elements from the NCE (microfoundations and rational expectations), from market imperfection economics (markets do not work perfectly), and interactions between monetary authorities and economic agents (reflecting how much market imperfections could be manipulated given how much they had been manipulated previously). There was also the added advantage of the neatness of the three (reduced-form) equation system describing the main mechanisms of adjustments to shocks, that could always be made more complicated.

Not surprisingly, these developments inspired a wealth of criticism from more radical Keynesians, as well as some self-criticism from those who had been complacent over the theoretical and policy achievements of the NCM. But the NCM is extremely close-knit and self-contained, with relatively little potential for piecemeal reform. Consider allowing for some impact from fiscal policy. It has been proposed that this could be done by adding a fiscal stimulus, a_0, term in the first equation, the pseudo-IS curve. This then becomes:

$$(y - y^*)_t = a_0 + a_1(y - y^*)_{t-1} + a_2 E(y - y^*)_{t-1} + a_3(i_t - r_t^* - E\Pi_{t+1}).$$

The idea is that such a stimulus from government, as opposed to reducing the interest rate, could increase output and reduce inflationary pressures in this way, rather than simply relying upon squeezing out demand.

In principle, this would appear to be sensible, especially where reducing the interest rate is not having any effect. But within the model as such it is ill-conceived. This can be seen by taking the revised equation set and finding equilibrium. It would require that a_0 be equal to zero, as this is the value of every other term! Of course, this does not mean that fiscal stimulus is impossible, only that it is ruled out by the model itself. It would appear as if the Ricardian equivalence theorem must hold and there will be a countervailing and neutralising response by rational, optimising agents to any attempted fiscal stimulus. In a sense, the NCM is being consistent by discounting fiscal policy, and attempts to reintroduce it within the NCM framework are liable to be undermined by the unyielding influence of an externally given long-run equilibrium determined by 'fundamentals'.

At a deeper level, this applies equally to all other factors that determine long-run growth, and hence the potential for short-run variation and the capacity of the state to affect both. This is highlighted once again by what have been acknowledged to be the deficiencies of the model without fully taking account of the corresponding limitations exposed by their implications. Consider the case of the money/finance dualism. As observed, the treatment of money as such fails to allow for bankruptcy (the so-called transversality condition in which firms or individual agents in general have to satisfy some degree of intertemporal solvency rather than borrowing indefinitely to cover any debts if it is optimal to do so), with systemic knock-on effects through the financial system. But this ought to be seen not simply as an occasional event for individual agents that may or may not occur, and as such is an oversight for not being allowed within the model. Rather, its potential presence challenges the dichotomy between money and finance and how the latter bridges, or undermines, the dualisms on which both the NCE and the NCM, and less extreme variants, rely – that is, between the short and long runs and the microeconomic and the macroeconomic, not least as finance is imperative in determining levels of investment and their efficacy, bridging the divides across these dualisms.

In short, whilst the much lauded consensus of the NCM has been discredited even to its own practitioners by the global crisis, with any number of omissions being able to be highlighted as marking its limitations (bankruptcy, fiscal policy, and so on), these are neither accidental nor readily remedied. They are the consequence of a long history of evolution of macroeconomic theory that has seen the macro displaced by micro, the short run rendered independent of the long run, and the long run organised around general equilibrium. Whilst it is possible to point to any number of absences from the NCM that follow from this, putting them back in a meaningful way even on a piecemeal basis is challenging if not impossible given how deeply entrenched is their exclusion. This is obvious once issues are raised around the role of the state in the economy, of corporate power, technological change and distribution, let alone the financialisation that brought the NCM to its knees. When change is impossible, old habits die hard. As a result, macroeconomics is more or less characterised today by the idea: 'The NCM is dead; long live the NCM'!

10.4 Further Thoughts and Readings

As macroeconomic theory stands today, it can be understood as allowing for a wide range of choice across the contents of a large toolkit. First, and easily overlooked for being taken for granted within a set of models, is how a model is disaggregated into sectors (or what is often thought of as its structure). The simplest models have very few sectors, possibly for goods and money alone, for example (to which might be added a market for government credibility). The more complex can be highly disaggregated with many different sectors, possibly across the real and the financial sectors. More disaggregated models might be thought to be more realistic in some sense, but also tend to be intractable both technically and empirically. It is worth bearing in mind that the more sectors a model has the more likely it is to exhibit instabilities of one sort or another. Significantly, the practice of macroeconomic modelling has swung between the simplicity (and presumed insight) of highly aggregate models (such as IS/LM, NCE and NCM) and the more demanding construction and putting together of the various components of aggregate supply and demand within these more aggregated framings. Should models focus on the woods or the trees, or neither if, to pursue the metaphor, the object of study is more akin to a more fluid and stormy ocean?

Second is whether, and which, markets clear or not within the structure of supply and demand. Clearly the NCE stands at one extreme, whereas Keynesians allow for some failure for markets to clear. For the latter, it is a matter of which markets fail to clear and how they interact with, have knock-on effects for, or have multipliers to other markets whether these themselves clear or not. The simplest example is the simple multiplier. More generally, once the model is written down then solved in terms of its parameters, the multipliers will be represented by the coefficients in the solutions between one variable and another. $Y = I/s$ is just one elementary example, as the multiplier is confined to the relationship between income and investment, via consumption. But if this is mediated by other intervening markets, such as those for money, imports and exports, and so on, then the multipliers will be that much more complicated. For the simple multiplier, an investment creates demand and income which is spent and creates more of the same at the rate $(1 - s)$, then $(1 - s)^2$, and so on. If this increases the demand for money at some rate, then this might equally raise the rate of interest to some degree, dampening the amount of investment and the multiplier effect with more complex multiplier effects (equally with change in the trade balance, possible devaluation, and so on).

In this way, it is possible to see that the macroeconomy is perceived to be a set of interlinked markets in which multipliers summarise the effects of mutual interaction. Formally, in linear terms, $Ax = b$ for some vector of endogenous variables x, parameters of adjustment within markets given by the matrix A, and exogenous parameters b. It is also possible to throw in time subscripts and expectations. But the equilibrium solution to the model at the end of the day is $x = A^{-1}b$ (we find equilibrium by wiping out time subscripts so that lag structure has no effect on the solution), with the inverse of the matrix A giving us our multipliers just as $S = I = sY$ gives us $Y = I/s$.

Third, there is a choice within models of this sort to allow for all sorts of more or less arbitrary assumptions, thereby incorporating particular features. Models can be based on adaptive or rational expectations. Some markets might be taken to be perfectly competitive as opposed to monopolistic (just as some might clear or not). And the state is understood to command various instruments for shifting supply and demand curves.

There would appear, then, to be a huge variety of potential models on offer, with relatively limited deviation in substance from the traditional IS/LM Keynesian framework. However, the framing of these models has conceptually shifted towards microfoundations, not least as a way of consolidating a vision in which it is appropriate both to separate the short run from the long run and to deny the systemic (let alone the role of power, conflict and distribution). The NCM, and its variants, are increasingly inappropriately claiming the label of 'Keynesian' whilst also continuing the longstanding trajectory of mainstream macroeconomics' divergence from attributes that warrant affinities to the economics of Keynes. This is so not only because of how the economy is conceptualised and modelled, but also because of how Keynesian policies are conceived and put to work.

For critical presentation of the NCM, see Nachane (2013), Fontana (2009), Sawyer (2009), and Angeriz and Arestis (2009). For discussions on the more or less 'moneyless' nature of many DSGE models of the NCM, see Rogers (2006) and Tobon and Barbaroux (2015). In the case of an open economy, see Arestis (2009). From within its own terms, Borio (2014) stresses the importance of incorporating financial cycles, and questions whether this can be done within the individualistic framework of DSGE models.

Appendix B: Surveying the Fundamentals in the Three-Equation NCM

Behind the apparently neat reduced-form equations of the NCM lies a (range of) fully articulated DSGE model(s), much in the spirit of the RBC modelling, albeit with two important points of departure in its simplest form – monopolistic competition and sticky prices.

A representative agent is optimally choosing consumption and leisure, maximising lifetime utility intertemporally subject to its budget constraint. This gives rise to the Euler equation in consumption that relates current and future consumption (via intertemporal substitution) to the subjective discount factor, and in the log-linearised solution to the model that corresponds to the IS-like curve. The inverse relationship between expected future real interest rate and output gap resembles the old IS curve, but it is worth noting that it derives solely through consumption in the canonical NCM model. (Indeed, it was only later that attempts to include capital and investment in the new Keynesian DSGE emerged.)

Postponed consumption (savings) can be stored in the form of an interest-bearing portfolio of bonds and then be transformed into potentially more consumption in the future. So, a reduction in today's expected real interest rate will induce the representative agent to save less and consume more today, and this is how aggregate demand (i.e. consumption) is boosted. It should be noted that the availability of a portfolio of bonds (so-called Arrow–Debreu securities) is the device by which the assumption can be made of perfect and complete financial markets that gives rise to the representative agent paradigm (i.e. why are we allowed to assume away both heterogeneous individuals and presence of financial markets distinct from money?). In other words, while there can be many different households, it is assumed that they can trade these state-of-the-world-contingent securities amongst themselves, and essentially achieve perfect risk-sharing in response to all possible idiosyncratic shocks (like promissory notes of the sort: 'if I get poor, you help me out', and vice versa). If, therefore, all households can insure themselves against each other, then this is equivalent to thinking of the economy as one representative household that holds this portfolio of bonds. In the equilibrium, the net quantity of this portfolio will have to be zero (as for each asset there is a corresponding liability) although its price (the interest rate) will continue to play a fundamental role in intertemporal optimising.

A unit mass of identical intermediate goods firms operates under monopolistic competition (thus they are price makers), an assumption made to open the space for price rigidities (otherwise, if everyone is a price taker, how would it be possible to have prices not clearing the market instantaneously?). For some time, the new Keynesian school contemplated different underlying justifications for why prices might be sticky, with the most prominent boiling down to menu costs or, in general, costs in continuously reoptimising and adjusting prices. Whatever the motivation, price stickiness is conventionally modelled following what is known as the Calvo mechanism, not least as it simplifies and makes the aggregation problem tractable.

The Calvo staggering mechanism simply assumes that in each period there is a constant and exogenously given probability that a firm might not be able to change its price. Intermediate goods firms are identical, facing the same marginal cost and demand for their differentiated goods, although only a random fraction of firms is allowed to change prices optimally, while the rest keep prices intact. On this basis, the period-by-period profit maximisation problem, when the whole system is solved, derives the new Keynesian Phillips curve.

The rational expectations equilibrium results in purely 'forward-looking' dynamics, whereby the current output gap (in the IS curve) and current inflation (in the Phillips curve) are solely determined by their future optimised values. However, as with the RBC models covered in Chapters 8 and 9, this specification (and essentially the rational expectations assumption) fails to account for observed inertia in the variables in question. Lagged terms can be made to arise with the inclusion of additional (less microfounded?) assumptions. For instance, in the case of the new Keynesian IS curve, some form of habit formation in consumption (or leisure) can link the representative's current utility to both current and past consumption. This will result in the lagged output gap term showing up. For the new Keynesian Phillips curve, the lagged inflation term can emerge by assuming that those firms, that do not reoptimise, index their prices to past inflation. This assumption, however, has two tacit implications. First, and depending on the modelling of price indexation, a non-vertical long-run relationship between inflation and output may be reinstated. Second, such a lever is inconsistent with the price stickiness motivation in the first place (if firms do not change their prices continuously due to some menu costs, why would they still decide to do so through indexation and in a non-optimal way?).

Fiscal policy is not modelled in this approach. This is to be expected, as the NCM is the progeny of the monetarist branch of macroeconomics, although attempts to include it have taken place. But, in the canonical three-equations model of the NCM, fiscal policy is completely excluded or assumed to be neutral. Thus, only monetary policy plays a role, albeit a very narrow one, in stabilising the economy around its 'natural' position, see Section 10.2 for further discussion.

Money supply is supposedly endogenised. This is reflected in the replacement of the old LM curve with the Taylor rule. That is, now the central bank controls the interest rate, but not the money supply other than to adjust it accordingly to set the interest rate. In passing, two points are worth making. First, this is only a theory of endogenous money in a token sense. On the one hand, the equilibrium for the economy as a whole is given by the triplet (y, Π, i) derived from the three canonical equations, without any reference to monetary aggregates. Certainly, a fourth LM-like equation could be appended to the system, and that would solely determine the amount of money stock consistent with the three-equations equilibrium. The money stock would still be redundant and play no role for either the determination of the equilibrium or the transition to it. On the other hand, one could replace the Taylor rule with the LM curve and derive the same equilibrium (in terms of y, Π and M). It then seems that money supply is, indeed, fixed as in traditional macroeconomics by the central bank (even if this is implicitly so when the monetary policy's instrument is the nominal interest rate). There is no account of endogeneity of the money supply out of the credit actions of private agents in response to (anticipated) movements in the economy.

Second, despite the suppression of money supply (and money in general) seemingly standing in sharp contrast to monetarism, the NCM retains much, if not all, of the implications of monetarism, not least that monetary policy is the prime determinant of inflation (even if this is in terms of interest rate rather than money supply policy). There is, furthermore, a very limited treatment of money per se (as a unit of account or a means of payment settlements). For more on this see Rogers (2006).

There is little preoccupation with unemployment, let alone involuntary unemployment, in the NCM models. Sticky prices do not obstruct an otherwise perfectly working labour market from clearing. Incorporation of monopolistic competition in the labour market and wage stickiness may generate (voluntary) unemployment in the transition to the long-run equilibrium after a shock. More recently, coordination failures in the labour market, in the sense of suboptimal 'matching' of vacancies to job searches, have been incorporated in new Keynesian DSGE models. Either way, in all those variants, unemployment has a voluntary, frictional and temporary character that deviates considerably from Keynes' concept of involuntary unemployment due to lack of effective demand.

11
International Macro?

11.1 Overview

In this chapter we begin with Section 11.2, which presents a number of elementary models that extend monetarism and Keynesianism to the international arena in various ways. They are the building blocks of international macroeconomics, thereby reflecting the character of macroeconomics in the absence of international relations. They add very little to our understanding of the nature of the macroeconomy nor of the distinctive role of the world economy as an object of study. Significantly, for example, mainstream economics would tend to treat globalisation as the extension of flows of trade, investment and finance to the international arena without understanding it in terms of shifting and changing balances in the exercise of economic and political power around the world. With a limited understanding of the global economy goes an equally limited understanding of the states that comprise it.

Section 11.3 has a slightly different purpose – to present a model that performs the role of introducing a technique for studying dynamics of the (international) economy. The technique is that of phase diagrams and will be of importance in Chapter 12.

11.2 Monetarism and Keynesianism Go International

So far, the macroeconomics covered has been what is called closed, either for a single economy with no international economic component or, equivalently, the world economy treated as if it were a single economy. To introduce an international element to macroeconomics, three steps are necessary. The first, potentially already undertaken in the context of closed macroeconomics, is to make use of economic theory. Second is to offer, at least implicitly, some notion of what constitutes the nation or the national so that the international can be taken into account. And third is how these two elements interact with one another.

Most (international) (macro)economics both inevitably incorporates these three elements and only does so implicitly, without any discussion at all let alone any critical debate. This is hardly surprising because, whatever the merits of the (closed) macroeconomics making up the first element, the treatment of the nation is generally superficial for the second and, hence, third elements. By way of a particularly revealing example, consider the Heckscher–Ohlin theory of international trade. It is fundamentally based on an economic theory derived from given production and utility functions and resources. Nations are simply treated as if they are individuals trading with one another. What distinguishes them is that factors (such as capital and labour) are completely mobile within countries but completely immobile between them. The outcome of the theory and the notion of a nation is a simple general equilibrium model as if of trading individuals. It is symbolic that Edgeworth boxes should be used both for trading between individuals and for trading between nations!

Interestingly, radical theories of unequal exchange (and dependency of the developing on the developed world) deploy an entirely different theory, such as exploitation of one by the other, respectively, through surplus transfer that undermines potential for development. For what is called the theory of unequal exchange in particular, capital is seen to be mobile between countries, tending to establish a uniform, international rate of profit, but rewards to labour are not seen as tending to be equalised. The surplus transfer mechanism comes through wage differentials between developing and developed worlds, with the latter benefitting from the low wages and prices of exports from the former (and vice versa, with the high wages and prices of the developed economies' exports). More generally, dependency theory draws upon a possible range of surplus transfer mechanisms, such as deteriorating terms of trade for primary commodities, interest and other payments, and technology transfer. The point here is not to suggest that these offer better theories (for lower wages, for example, dependency begs the question of why, if costs are cheaper in the developing world, all production does not take place there), but to show how different economic theories and concepts of the national are combined in the making of international macroeconomic analysis for which it is appropriate to be clear of the three constituent elements of theory, nation and their combination.

Within mainstream international macroeconomics, as already apparent from Heckscher–Ohlin trade theory, the notion of the nation is extremely reduced, in parallel with the reduced notion of the state within macroeconomic theory more generally (as an individual agent with special powers directly in relation to supply and demand through fiscal policy and indirectly through monetary policy). Further, as far as international macroeconomic theory is concerned, it primarily depends upon simple extensions of the Keynesian/monetarism divide from the closed to the international economy. As a result, developments within closed macroeconomics have tended to drive developments within its international counterpart, at least until the era of flexible exchange rates, for reasons that will become apparent.

Thus, just as elementary trade theory, derived from general equilibrium theory, underpins the mainstream understanding of the international real economy, so what is known as the species-flow mechanism plays the monetary counterpart. In simplest form, recall for monetarism that the quantity of money in the economy determines expenditure, $M = kY$, where Y is expenditure and k is the inverse of the velocity of circulation of money, so the lower k is the more expenditure we get for what is taken to be a given money supply. Suppose the economy is at full employment at all times, so that $Y = pX$ where X is full employment output and p is the price level. Clearly, $M = kpX$ and, as k and X are taken as fixed, so p increases as M increases.

However, suppose that there is the option of added expenditure being made abroad, and that there is excess demand in the economy because of an excess of money for the prevailing price level and available output. With fixed exchange rates with the rest of the world, or a commodity money such as gold, as domestic prices rise so (with zero transport costs and single prices for goods across the world) the excess demand will be made up by imports, with money flowing abroad to pay for the balance of trade deficit. As a result, the initial excess demand, deriving from the excess of money, will in part be corrected through a redistribution of money to the source of the imports (and also through some increase in the domestic price level).

This can all be laid out formally as follows. Using the same notation as before but adding the superscript, $i = 1$ or 2, for the two countries that make up the world, and subscript t for time, then:

$$M_t^i = k^i Y_t^i = k^i p_t^i X^i + BT_t^i$$

where BT is the balance of trade deficit, since expenditure is what you produce plus what you import.

However, with money flowing to pay for imports, next year's money is this year's minus the trade deficit, so that:

$$M_{t+1}^i = M_t^i - BT_t^i \quad \text{or} \quad BT_t^i = M_t^i - M_{t+1}^i$$

and so:

$$M_t^i = k^i Y_t^i = k^i p_t^i X^i + BT_t^i = k^i p_t^i X^i + M_t^i - M_{t+1}^i.$$

This is equivalent to $k^i p_t^i X^i = M_{t+1}^i$, or that money in the next period corresponds to expenditure in the previous period, with the adjustment having come through the trade deficit. Now, looking at the two countries together:

$$M_t^1 / M_t^2 = (k^1 p_t^1 X^1 + M_t^1 - M_{t+1}^1)/(k^2 p_t^2 X^2 + M_t^2 - M_{t+1}^2).$$

First, note that equilibrium is given where there are no money flows and imbalances of trade for which $M^1_t - M^1_{t+1} = M^2_t - M^2_{t+1} = 0$. Then:

$$M^1/M^2 = k^1 p^1 X^1 / k^2 p^2 X^2.$$

With a fixed exchange rate, e say, so that $p^1_t = e p^2_t$ at all times, meaning that with e denoting the value of foreign currency in terms of domestic money, the price levels in the two countries are equal. Thus, also at the equilibrium:

$$M^1/M^2 = k^1 e X^1 / k^2 X^2.$$

This tells us that, for equilibrium, money should be distributed between the countries in proportion to their full employment outputs, the inverse of their velocities of circulation of money (how efficient exchange is in the use of money) and relative to the fixed exchange rate.

Out of equilibrium, note that $M^1_t - M^1_{t+1}$ is equal and opposite to $M^2_t - M^2_{t+1}$, since one's trade deficit and money outflow is the other's surplus and money inflow. This means that if, say: $M^1_t/M^2_t > k^1 e X^1/k^2 X^2$, then $M^1_t - M^1_{t+1} > 0$ and, equal and opposite, $M^2_t - M^2_{t+1} < 0$. So if one money supply is too big (small), it flows out (in), thereby tending to correct the disequilibrium.

In terms of what is to come, this model is extremely simple. It does not allow for changing levels of output, and the presumption is that shifts in the composition of output are accomplished instantaneously to serve either domestic or foreign markets. There are no private capital flows, the exchange rate is fixed and no interest is paid, or foregone, for holding money. Essentially, the model is one of the redistribution of money stocks around the world to allow for equilibrium. As such, it is known as the species-flow mechanism (with species being gold reserves), although it is also the most elementary form of monetarism applied to the balance of payments, and known as the monetary approach to the balance of payments. In effect, it is a theory of the optimal, or equilibrium, holding of financial assets (real balances in this simple case) according to transactions to be undertaken.

Consider what would happen if one country increases its money supply. Then there would be an adjustment towards the new equilibrium in which the ratio of money supplies between the two countries would adjust back to $k^1 e X^1/k^2 X^2$, and there would have been a proportionate increase in the price level across the world.

If the exchange rate is not fixed, then there is no need for money to flow between countries to settle imbalances of trade, since currencies would have been purchased to buy goods at the going exchange rate. The equilibrium exchange rate will be given by the relative requirements in circulating income:

$e = M^1k^2X^2/M^2k^1X^1$.

If one country increases its money supply, this will immediately be chasing the same amount of goods in the domestic market, raising the price and lowering the exchange rate in proportion, an instantaneous adjustment to the new equilibrium not least because both goods markets and exchange markets work perfectly.

At the opposite extreme to the monetary approach to the balance of payments is the Keynesian import multiplier. Here, effective demand comes to the fore in determining the level of domestic income and, in its simplest form, money is entirely absent as are the price level and capital flows. Suppose exports are given by T, an element of exogenous demand like investment, I. But suppose that imports, Z, are proportional to income, Y, so that $Z = mY$. Then, with a standard consumption function, $C = cY = (1 - s)Y$:

$$Y = C + I + T - Z = cY + I + X - mY.$$

It follows that:

$$Y = (I + T)/(1 - s + m).$$

The multiplier is reduced by the marginal propensity to import as this is a leakage from demand for the domestic economy, as are savings.

Suppose, though, that there is a need to deal with a balance of trade deficit. One way of attempting to do so is by devaluing the exchange rate to improve competitiveness, thereby increasing exports and reducing imports. But the lower (higher) prices of exports (imports) will only contribute to an improvement in the balance of payments if the percentage increase (decrease) in the quantity sold (bought) is greater than the percentage change in price. This is the same as the elasticity of supply (demand) being greater than one. Taking the two effects together, the condition becomes that the sum of the elasticities should exceed one.

This is known as the Marshall–Lerner condition for improvement of balance of payments with devaluation of an otherwise fixed exchange rate. If account is also taken of the time needed to shift into exports in supply and out of imports in demand, then the condition might be satisfied in the longer but not the short run. This gives rise to what is known as the J-curve in response to a devaluation, where improvement only occurs after a lag (see Diagram 11.1). Such an improvement in the balance of payments arises out of expenditure switching, and it might be complemented by expenditure reduction where the overall level of demand is targeted through deflationary policy to improve the balance of payments.

Balance of Payment

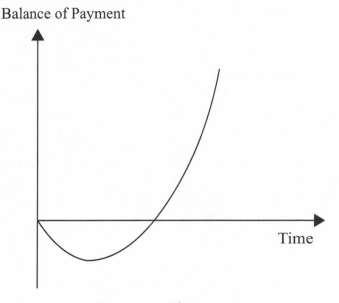

Diagram 11.1   The J-curve

So far, account has been taken of money flows and quantity and price shifts as impacting upon the balance of trade. The fuller Keynesian model also allows for private capital flows by adding a so-called BP curve to the IS/LM framework. Here the idea is that there will be balance of payments equilibrium according to a further relationship between the rate of interest, r, and national income, Y. The higher r is, the more capital flows are attracted into the economy; the higher Y is, the worse the balance of trade. Consequently, r and Y are positively related to one another for balance of payments equilibrium (see Diagram 11.2).

It is, however, only by chance that the three curves IS/LM/BP intersect at the same point. If they do not, equilibrium in the domestic economy will occur at the intersection of the IS and LM curves. If the BP curve lies below this, by dropping down to the BP curve from the domestic equilibrium, it is easy to see that from a position of equilibrium on the BP curve the interest rate has been raised (see Diagram 11.3). It follows that the domestic economy equilibrium is in balance of payments surplus. As a result, money will flow into the economy, shifting the LM curve to the right until all three curves intersect at the same point (much the same procedure follows for the LM curve shifting to the left should the BP curve initially be above the IS/LM intersection, see Diagram 11.3).

A special case of the IS/LM/BP framework, known as Mundell–Fleming, is where there is perfect competition in capital markets, so that a single world rate of interest prevails. Effectively, the BP curve is horizontal at that world rate of interest. From a position of equilibrium with fixed exchange rates, fiscal policy would shift the IS curve to the right, raise the rate of interest and lead

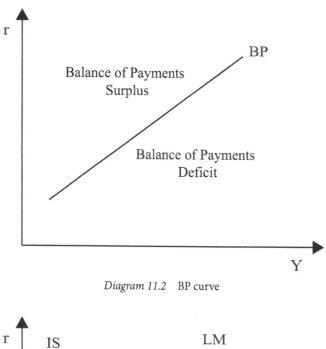

Diagram 11.2 BP curve

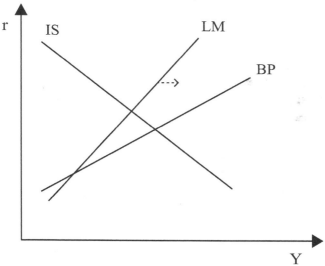

Diagram 11.3 IS/LM/BP curves

to an accommodating inflow of capital, shifting the LM curve to the right and leading to an increase in employment and output. Monetary policy raising the money supply, on the other hand, would shift the LM curve to the right, reduce the rate of interest and lead to an outflow of money until back to the starting position. In other words, for fixed exchange rates, fiscal policy is very effective and monetary policy is totally ineffective.

It is exactly the opposite for a flexible exchange rate. In this case, shifting the IS curve to the right increases the rate of interest, but the exchange rate rises as capital flows in, reducing competitiveness until the IS curve returns to its original position and the interest rate is restored to its equilibrium level. In contrast, monetary policy shifts the LM curve to the right, reducing the rate of interest and leading to a devaluation of the currency, increased competitiveness and a matching rightward shift of the IS curve to a higher level of employment.

What all of these models have in common are two features. First, each narrowly focuses on one or more elementary phenomenon. Second, each does so in a way that is not liable to be consistent in its treatment of the macroeconomy. Thus, for example, there appear to be unlimited quantities of foreign reserves to cover balance of payment deficits, until such reserves provide for the passage to equilibrium, with no consequences for the performance of the economy; or, as with the IS/LM/BP model, little or no account is taken of Walrasian requirements and the difficulties implied by the breakdown of the classical dichotomy (see Chapter 3).

The reason for this apparent carelessness is probably a consequence of the presumed stability of exchange rates and the international payments system prior to the breakdown of the Bretton Woods system in the early 1970s. Prior to this, international macroeconomics primarily consisted in adding foreign sectors – for trade and finance, and for public and private capital flows – to models constructed for the closed economy, with the presumption that national economies had sufficient currency reserves to tide over any disequilibrium without regard for the consequences (e.g. what is happening to flows of interest or profits on capital held in other countries, leading to potential for debt crises – even before consideration of speculation on currency markets once exchange rates are flexible). As will be seen in Chapter 12, the content of international macroeconomics and its relationship to closed economy macroeconomics would change dramatically. Further, notably absent in the models is any account of expectations in contrast to the prominence these were to achieve in the wake of the monetarist counter-revolution.

11.3 Phase Diagrams and Stability Analysis

For the moment, and bearing in mind that macroeconomics has always had the potential to construct models in as many ways as the closed economy – in terms of structural disaggregation into sectors, and whether each of these is perfectly competitive or market clearing or not – consider the following model. It consists of just two sectors explicitly: one for employment and one for trade. It also uses the exchange rate, e, in both of the two ways in which e operates, as an element in both the relative price of financial assets and the relative price of goods. First, e can stand as the relative value of currencies. If e is how much of one currency is to be paid for another, then the higher e is the lower the value of the currency (and assets held in that currency as opposed to another). Somewhat perversely, raising (lowering) e means lowering (raising) the value of the currency. Second, e is a marker of price competitiveness. The higher (lower) e is, the cheaper (more expensive) are domestic goods relative to imports both for the domestic market and for exports. As such, e acts as an equal and opposite factor to price in the cost of goods.

In the model, the demand for labour is simply written as $N(w/e, M/e)$ where w is the money wage rate and M the money supply, with e as the exchange rate taken as fixed. The rationale is that, with e effectively serving as the price level (imported consumption goods cost more the higher e is), the real wage can be represented by w/e. By the same token, the higher M/e is, the higher are real balances. Because the demand for labour is higher, the real wage is lower (on cost of production grounds), $N_1 < 0$; and higher real balances mean higher expenditure, $N_2 > 0$. Suppose, for simplicity, the supply of labour is fixed at some constant level, N, then equilibrium in the labour market is given by $N(w/e, M/e)$ = N, with a positive slope (to compensate for the negative effect of an increase in the real wage on employment demand, there would have to be a corresponding increase in M/e), see NN in Diagram 11.4.

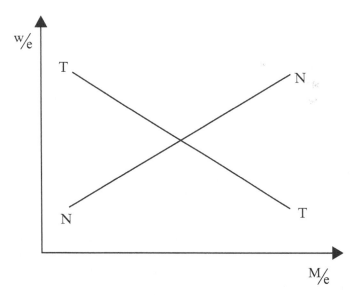

Diagram 11.4   Trade and employment equilibrium

The point at which the trade balance is in equilibrium is also taken to depend upon the same two variables, with $T(w/e, M/e) = 0$. In this case, $T_1 < 0$, as higher real wages increase the level of imports, and $T_2 < 0$, as increased demand with higher real balances also sucks in more imports. As a result, to maintain trade balance, w/e and M/e will need to move in opposite directions to compensate the trade balance effects of one another, as shown by TT in Diagram 11.4.

Equilibrium will be given where the two curves intersect. But what happens out of equilibrium? Consider first being at some point above the NN curve. Dropping down to the NN curve implies that w/e is higher than would allow for labour market equilibrium, suggesting that demand for labour would be lower than required and that there would be an excess supply of labour. It is a small but distinct step to deduce that this would lead to a fall in the money wage, w. Hence, if in short-run disequilibrium the economy is above NN, it is to be expected that w/e will fall and, similarly, that it would rise if the economy were situated below the NN curve, as indicated in Diagram 11.5.

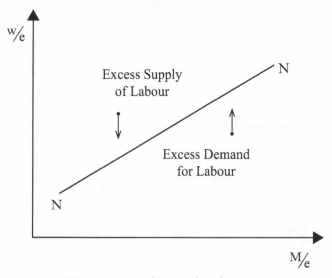

Diagram 11.5   Labour market adjustment

Now consider the TT curve and again a point above it. Dropping down to equilibrium, it follows that w/e is higher than is required for trade balance, suggesting that there will be a trade deficit. As this would have to be paid for by an outflow of money, it follows that M/e will tend to fall with lower M. Again, the opposite occurs on the other side of the TT curve (see Diagram 11.6).

In qualitative terms at least, the analysis has offered a simple account of how the economy adjusts. Further, the two curves divide the space of outcomes for the economy into four quadrants, known as phases, depending upon whether each of the two markets are in excess supply or excess demand. The movement of the economy out of equilibrium will be in the direction of the combination of the two movements. The motion will be a spiral and stabilising (since when adjustment hits each of the curves, it will be moving either horizontally or vertically and then skew inwards, see Diagram 11.7).

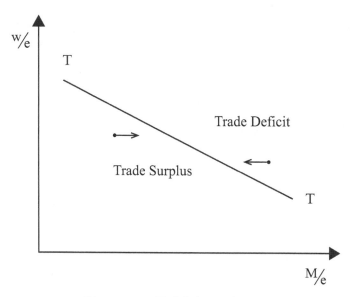

Diagram 11.6   Trade balance adjustment

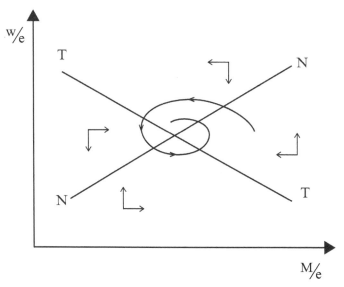

Diagram 11.7   Phase diagram and stability

The purpose of this model lies less in its intrinsic merits than with allowing the apparatus of phase diagrams to be introduced (as these will be used in Chapter 12). But there is also a simple policy exercise that can be undertaken with the model. Is it possible to do better than nothing as far as stabilising the economy is concerned? The answer is yes. Suppose that whenever there is unemployment, the money supply is increased over and above any movement from the trade balance, and decreased if there is excess demand for labour. Then the adjustment for some λ becomes (where otherwise λ would be zero):

$$M'/e = T(w/e, M/e) + \lambda(N - N(w/e, M/e)).$$

This will boost demand whenever there is unemployment and reduce it otherwise. The effect is to strengthen the forces for stability, as indicated by the dotted lines in Diagram 11.8, reinforcing the stabilising changes in the money supply that arise out of the trade imbalance.

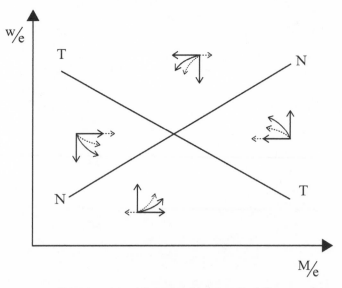

Diagram 11.8   Adjusted and enhanced stability

11.4 Further Thoughts and Readings

As should be apparent from the models presented, international macro-economics appears to be little more than the extension of models of the closed economy to a relatively simply conceived global economy. In this respect, international macroeconomics has, at least until the 1970s, been heavily influenced, even determined, by whatever was going on in closed economy macroeconomics. This began to change with the breakdown of Bretton Woods and the move to an era of flexible exchange rates, as the changes were accompanied by much closer attention to private international capital flows and speculation around movements in exchange rates. Such concerns also dovetailed with the preoccu-pation concerning expectations within macroeconomic theory that arose out of stagflation and the vertical Phillips curve. As a result, in some respects interna-tional macroeconomics was thrust into the theoretical vanguard, given its focus upon how to model private capital flows in the context of highly fluid, or rapidly adjusting, markets in which expectations about future levels of the exchange rate (as opposed to the price level as such) became of paramount importance.

This is taken up in Chapter 12. The models described there and those presented in this chapter are highly standardised but draw upon Dornbusch (1980). See also Obstfeld (2001) for a broad overview of international macroeconomics in the post-war era.

12

The Enigmas of Overshooting

12.1 Overview

As suggested in Chapter 11, international macroeconomics was a parasite on its closed economy counterpart, at least until flexible exchange rates placed it at the forefront of analysing the implications of rapidly adjusting markets for which foreign currencies and financial markets more generally are perceived to be exemplars, not least with electronic trading. This chapter is devoted to Dornbusch's overshooting model in which it is found that, if all markets do not work as rapidly as financial markets, then there can be peculiar outcomes, not least in which the exchange rate overshoots its equilibrium level. There are two versions of the model, covered in Sections 12.2 and 12.3, one with fixed output at full employment levels, and one in which output varies in Keynesian fashion with the level of effective demand. Each offers the possibility that the exchange rate will shoot from below to above its equilibrium level (or vice versa) before converging to it, although the extent to which this occurs is moderated by Keynesian output adjustment.

The Dornbusch model is more remarkable for its results than for its realism (just two financial markets and only one goods market). As discussed in Section 12.4, it demonstrates how perverse dynamics can be generated by the simplest model with a modicum of deviation from a perfectly working economy. As such, it offers salutary lessons to those who proceed as if economies are automatically self-stabilising and that the price system is an appropriate guide for decision making.

12.2 Inflexible Output and Overshooting

In Dornbusch's model of overshooting, the model of the economy is disaggregated into a single real sector and a pair of financial sectors, one for domestic money and one for foreign exchange. The two financial sectors always work perfectly in the sense of price adjustment bringing supply into equality with demand. In the domestic money market, the variable that adjusts to do this is the rate of interest, r. If supply exceeds demand for domestic money, the rate of interest moves instantaneously downwards to adjust to equilibrium (with demand increasing to match what is presumed to be a fixed supply of money since the cost of holding money will fall). Supposing variables are written in log terms and economic relations are log-linear, then:

$$m - p = -\lambda r + \varphi y$$

where m is money supply, p the price level, y domestic income and λ and φ are parameters. This is essentially an LM curve with the demand for money depending upon the price level and the level of income positively and negatively on the rate of interest.

On the other hand, the market for foreign currency adjusts through the exchange rate, e, taken to be how much of the domestic currency is needed to buy foreign currency. If e goes up, the domestic currency is devalued (somewhat unfortunate terminologically since if e goes up it means the currency goes down in value). If there is an excess demand for domestic currency, then e will fall (the currency will appreciate), again assumed to happen instantaneously until supply and demand are equal.

Agents are supposed to take into account the cost of holding the domestic currency, including the possibility that it might depreciate or appreciate, over which rational expectations are formed (i.e. ones that are confirmed by the model). If the exchange rate is expected to depreciate, then those who hold assets in the domestic currency will have to expect effectively to receive a lower real rate of interest than otherwise, equal to the expected rate of depreciation. Otherwise, it would be better to hold your money in some other currency that gets a rate of interest without depreciation. In other words:

$$r = r^* + d$$

where d is the expected rate of depreciation of the currency and r^* is the equilibrium global rate of interest that prevails elsewhere. For the moment, assume:

$$d = \theta(e^* - e)$$

or that the exchange rate is expected to move towards its equilibrium value (e^*) at the rate θ. As it stands this is simply a behavioural assumption, but later it will be shown that this is what happens and so such behavioural expectations are, indeed, rational in the formal sense of being borne out. This cannot be shown now because it is a property of the model that is yet to be fully laid out. In other words, it is not possible at this point to show that these expectations reflect what happens (in the model itself) for a judiciously chosen value of θ.

Putting these two equations together gives:

$$r = r^* + \theta(e^* - e).$$

This equation and the LM curve hold at all times, in the short run since it is assumed that the money markets clear instantaneously. In addition, they define long-run equilibrium, when $y = y^*$, $r = r^*$ and $e = e^*$. This is immediate from the foreign market (expected change is zero when the exchange rate is at its equilibrium value). From the LM curve, though, long-run equilibrium gives:

$$m - p^* = -\lambda r^* + \varphi y^*.$$

Subtracting the short run LM from this curve gives:

$$p - p^* = -\lambda(r^* - r) + \varphi(y^* - y),$$

and then substituting for $r - r^*$ yields:

$$p - p^* = -\lambda\theta(e - e^*) + \varphi(y^* - y).$$

This is the short-run relationship between p, e and y, which simultaneously gives equilibrium in the two financial markets. Attention can now turn to the goods market. In this case, Dornbusch considers two different models. For one, if there is excess demand, prices do not adjust to clear it instantaneously but take time. In the interim, output remains at its fixed equilibrium value, y^*. But prices will gradually increase (or decrease if there is excess supply). So there is a sticky price adjustment in the goods market. If it too cleared instantaneously, then the economy would always be in equilibrium, as would each and every market. For the other model (see Section 12.3), output adjusts to clear the goods market at the level of demand being experienced, but this leads to price increases as with the non-adjusting model just considered. For the model in this section, though, $y = y^*$ in the short as well as the long run. And this means that the previous equation simply becomes:

$$p - p^* = -\lambda\theta(e - e^*).$$

This can be interpreted as follows (with the argument able to run in the opposite direction too). For $e > e^*$ ($e < e^*$), the exchange rate is under (over) valued and so there must be an expected appreciation (depreciation) of the currency. To compensate for this in currency markets, the rate of interest, r, must be lower (higher) than its equilibrium value. This means that the demand for money would be too high (low) unless the price level were above (below) its equilibrium value. In other words, as the equation testifies, p is above (below) its equilibrium value, p^*, as e is above (below) its equilibrium value, e^*.

Now consider the overall demand for domestic goods. It will equal:

$$(A + \gamma y) + \delta(e - p) + (B - \sigma r) + C$$

where the first term is a consumption function. The second term is a trade balance effect on aggregate demand, since the higher e and the lower p are, the more competitive are our exports and the less competitive are imports ((log) prices of foreign goods are normalised to zero). The third term is an investment term related to the cost of capital, r, and C is some exogenous demand from abroad. Excess demand will equal:

$$(A + \gamma y) + \delta(e - p) + (B - \sigma r) + C - y.$$

In addition, by definition this must equal zero for equilibrium values of the variables:

$$(A + \gamma y^{*}) + \delta(e^{*} - p^{*}) + (B - \sigma r^{*}) + C - y^{*} = 0.$$

In subtracting this from the previous equation, the measure of excess demand (expressed in deviations from the long-run equilibrium) becomes:

$$\gamma(y - y^{*}) + \delta(e - e^{*}) - \delta(p - p^{*}) - \sigma(r - r^{*}) - (y - y^{*}).$$

If excess demand leads to inflation, at the rate Π, then:

$$p' = \Pi\{\gamma(y - y^{*}) + \delta(e - e^{*}) - \delta(p - p^{*}) - \sigma(r - r^{*}) - (y - y^{*})\}.$$

That is, inflation is assumed to be proportional (by Π) to excess demand.

For the model in this section, $y = y^{*}$ by assumption, so the goods market will be in equilibrium when excess demand, and consequently inflation, are zero:

$$p' = \Pi\{\delta(e - e^{*}) - \delta(p - p^{*}) - \sigma(r - r^{*})\} = 0.$$

But from the LM equation, allowing for $y = y^{*}$, it follows that $p - p^{*} = -\lambda(r^{*} - r)$. Putting this together with the previous equation, it follows that short-run equilibrium on the two domestic markets together (goods and money) requires:

$$p' = \Pi\{\delta(e - e^{*}) - \delta(p - p^{*}) - \sigma(p - p^{*})/\lambda\} = 0$$

where the expression in {} measures overall excess demand. Simplifying gives:

$$p' = \Pi\{\delta(e - e^{*}) - (\delta + \sigma/\lambda)(p - p^{*})\} = 0.$$

This means equilibrium in the domestic goods and money markets is given by:

$$(e - e^*) = (1 + \sigma/\lambda\delta)(p - p^*).$$

This is a positive relationship between e and p that ensures zero overall excess demand (and zero inflation) in the short run. For there to be equilibrium in the domestic markets, if p is higher than its equilibrium value then so must e, but by a little bit more ($\sigma/\lambda\delta$). Why this is so can be seen by walking around the markets concerned (and going in the opposite direction if preferred). Suppose p is too high, then there will be two effects. The first is direct: domestic production will be less competitive and e will have to be equally higher (currency devalued to compensate). In addition, there will be excess demand for money for transaction purposes at the higher prices, which will raise the interest rate to restore the domestic money market equilibrium at the rate $1/\lambda$. This will reduce demand for investment at the rate σ, and so reduced demand for goods at the rate σ/λ will need to be compensated for in order to retain equilibrium in the goods market through a further devaluation at rate $1/\delta$ to boost competitiveness. All these interacting effects mean that e has to adjust by an extra $\sigma/\lambda\delta$ to compensate for a price increase to retain equilibrium in the goods market.

With equilibrium in domestic markets and equilibrium in financial markets each giving a relationship between e and p (or their deviations from their equilibrium values), the short run can be represented by the Diagram 12.1, with equilibrium unsurprisingly given by $e = e^*$ and $p = p^*$. With e along the x-axis, the slope of the money markets curve, AA, is $-\lambda\theta$, and the intercept on the y-axis is $p^* + \lambda\theta e^*$. The slope of the curve for equilibrium in the domestic markets, GG, is $1/(1 + \sigma/\lambda\delta)$, i.e. positive but less than one, and the intercept is:

$$p^* - e^*/(1 + \sigma/\lambda\delta).$$

Now consider the phase diagram for this set of curves. Below the goods market equilibrium, dropping vertically for example to a lower price level, the demand for goods will be higher, both directly because of the lower prices and increasing competitive demand, and because this will mean deficient demand for money, a lower interest rate and increased demand for investment goods. This frustrated excess demand (since y is fixed) will translate into higher prices. As a result, prices will tend to increase from below the GG curve and to decrease from above (see Diagram 12.1).

For the AA curve, suppose a hypothetical positioning of the economy on a point to the right of the curve. In a vertical comparison to the short-run equilibrium on the AA curve, p can be considered to be higher than its short-run equilibrium value. With the assumption of sticky prices, there will be an excess demand for money for transaction purposes, with a correspond-

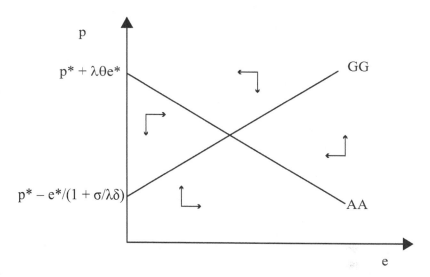

Diagram 12.1   Phase diagram

ingly immediately adjustment to a higher interest rate. This will lead to capital inflows and a resulting increase in demand for the currency, shifting e down (appreciation and vice versa, depreciation, should we be on the other side of the AA curve). However, once again by assumption, both financial markets work instantaneously so that e will adjust immediately back to the AA curve if it is temporarily driven off (see Diagram 12.2). From the hypothetical starting point, agents will also expect this appreciation (depreciation) and buy up (sell)

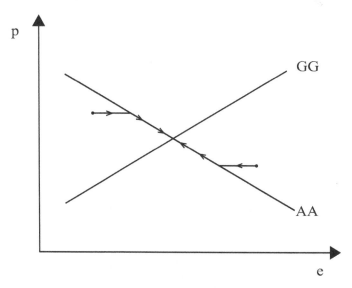

Diagram 12.2   Adjustment

the currency instantaneously until short-run equilibrium is restored on the AA curve.

As a result, the phase diagram, with both adjustments taken together, is as in Diagram 12.3 with two examples showing. As soon as the price falls from above (below) the GG curve, it is immediately driven back horizontally to the right (left) through the e adjustment to the AA curve. This means that the model's adjustment is stable, moving along the AA curve to the equilibrium, either from above or below. The pace at which the economy moves to equilibrium depends upon how quickly prices adjust to excess demand. Note also that, informally at least, rational expectations are borne out. The exchange rate is expected to move towards its equilibrium value, and it does so according to the model itself. See Appendix C for formal details (and to test your understanding at a technical level if you care to do so – but bear in mind it will be an exercise in the agent choosing a value of θ so that the model's and their own expectations coincide with one another).

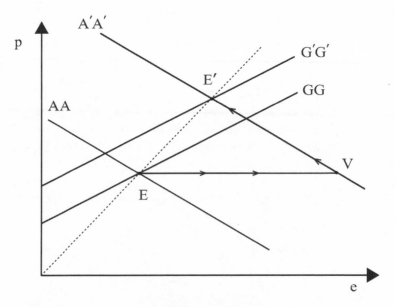

Diagram 12.3   Overshooting

Now consider a shock increase in the money supply. There is a new long-run equilibrium, with prices increasing in proportion, and shifts in the AA and GG curves to A'A' and G'G', respectively, as indicated. With an excess supply of money, the exchange rate immediately jumps to the new A'A' curve at point V (as financial markets adjust fully instantaneously) whilst sticky prices of goods in the domestic market remain temporarily fixed. After this, prices adjust slowly upwards along the A'A' curve until the new equilibrium is reached, but the exchange rate is appreciating in this adjustment after an initial overdepreciation (Diagram 12.3). The exchange rate takes the route from old equilibrium E, jumping up instantaneously to V before declining gradually from V to the new equilibrium E'.

In other words, there is a shock overshooting in the depreciation of the exchange rate before an appreciation to the new equilibrium. The reason is relatively simple. With too much money around at existing prices, and these prices remaining sticky, the domestic interest rate is driven down so that the currency is sold in disproportionately large quantities until e is driven up so high that it is expected that there will be an appreciation of the currency to compensate for the low interest rate.

The implications of this model will be discussed later, after coverage of the second model. For the moment, observe that there appears to be this perverse behaviour in the adjustment of the exchange rate even though only the slightest deviation has been made from a perfectly working economy. All markets clear instantaneously, except the one for goods that is sticky, there is full employment at all times and expectations are rational.

12.3 Overshooting with Keynesian Features

The second Dornbusch model is exactly the same as the first except in the way in which the goods market adjusts. Specifically, instead of always being at full employment and fixed output, the economy is presumed exactly to meet any excess demand over equilibrium with some temporary overheating of the economy and expansion of output. The result, though, is to cause inflation. Exactly the same applies in case of deficient demand, with a lower level of output but a deflation of prices. Now y is allowed to diverge from its equilibrium value y^*.

The equation for the domestic money market is as before:

$$p - p^* = -\lambda(r^* - r) + \varphi(y^* - y).$$

As is the equation for the exchange rate:

$$r = r^* + \theta(e^* - e).$$

The level of excess demand is now also given by the general case derived before, but this will, by assumption, immediately adjust to zero by change in the level of output, y, so that:

$$\gamma(y - y^*) + \delta(e - e^*) - \delta(p - p^*) - \sigma(r - r^*) - (y - y^*) = 0.$$

This leads to inflation during the short-run adjustment process, at the rate Π if $y > y^*$:

$$p' = \Pi(y - y^*).$$

Note that demand and supply are equal in the short run as the goods market clears. Nevertheless, inflationary pressure comes purely and simply from the difference in (short-run) output from its long-run equilibrium level (e.g. overheating of the economy) whereas, in the previous model, the inflationary pressure came from the unsatisfied excess demand that depended on a variety of variables (prices, exchange rates and the interest rate). Clearly, equilibrium is given by variables taking on their long-term * values. In the short term, though, the first three equations, shown above, can be used to find a relationship between p and y, which ensures equilibrium in all three markets simultaneously. This is represented in Diagram 12.4 by YY, by eliminating r and e across the three equations for them given above.

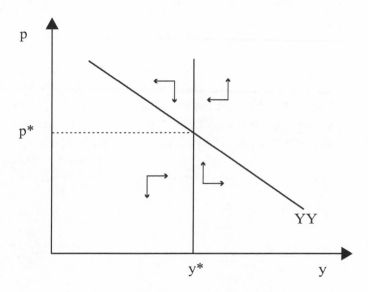

Diagram 12.4   Keynesian adjustment

It turns out that:

$$y - y^* = - X(p - p^*)$$

for a complicated constant X made up out of the various parameters as follows:

$$X = (\delta\lambda\theta + \delta + \sigma\theta)/\{(1 - \gamma)\theta\lambda + \varphi(\delta + \sigma\theta)\}.$$

This looks very complicated but two points stand out. The first is that X is unambiguously positive (so that p is negatively related to y). Second, this is because X represents a set of negative multipliers, a triple whammy, that connects y and p to one another as one market knocks onto the next. Thus, suppose p is too big, then there is an immediate loss of demand for goods because of competitiveness for domestic production. There is also an excess demand for money for transactions, and this means there needs to be a higher interest rate. This reduces demand for investment goods. The higher interest rate must correspond to an expected devaluation of the currency, which means that it must be too high (e is too low). This also means reduced competitiveness for domestic goods.

The relationship between p and y can be represented in the phase diagram (Diagram 12.4). The curve YY represents equilibrium across all three markets, each of which is realised instantaneously as y always adjusts to the level of demand for the domestic goods markets and e always adjusts to demand for currencies. Otherwise, p' = 0 only when y = y*. To the left of the vertical line where y = y* there will be excess supply and prices adjust downwards, and to the right there is excess demand and prices adjust up. But adjustment is always immediately to the YY curve, as all the markets it incorporates always clear instantaneously. So, from out of equilibrium, the economy jumps horizontally to the YY curve, and then moves along it to equilibrium as sticky prices adjust.

What happens now in case of a surprise increase in the money supply? The new equilibrium and adjustment is illustrated in Diagram 12.5. The immediate impact is an increase in output that falls as inflation takes hold. Will there be overshooting? The phase diagram does not inform of movements in e. It might be thought that the extra money would have to be sold until the rate of interest

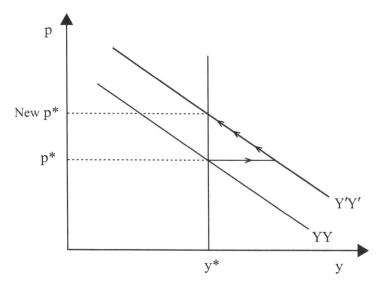

Diagram 12.5 Keynesian overshooting?

fell sufficiently to expect an appreciating currency as before. This may well be so, but there is a moderating influence that did not previously prevail. This is the increase in output from the increase in demand. Should this be so great and/or the demand for money to circulate it turn out to be so strong that it more than absorbs the increase in the money supply, then there will be no overshooting. In other words, if the increase in output more than absorbs the money that has been fed into the domestic money market, there is no need for the rate of interest to fall and for the devaluation of the exchange rate to overshoot. This might be thought to be highly unlikely and perverse – that a stimulus to demand and output from an increase in the money supply leaves it unable to circulate the extra output induced. On this, see the end of Appendix C for details of the formal conditions under which overshooting does or does not occur.

12.4 Further Thoughts and Readings

Dornbusch's model of overshooting was first put forward in 1976, and it remains a major part of international macroeconomics, not least drawing its popularity from the neat and simple elegance with which potential instability, at least in the path to a stable equilibrium, is presented in the form of overshooting of the exchange rate. This itself seems to correspond to the instability attached to a world of flexible exchange rates. Indeed, much of the subsequent literature has focused on two issues. First, is there overshooting in the real world? Second, if so, is it a consequence of the factors identified by Dornbusch or due to something else?

Such concerns are both too narrow and misplaced. The Dornbusch model is so stylised and simplified that it is not going to make much sense to try and track movements in exchange rates on the basis of so few, highly aggregated variables. Rather than being used to estimate exchange rate movements, the significance of the Dornbusch model is primarily theoretical. It offers the following result after all. In the simplest model, with all markets but one working perfectly, it is possible for the outcome to be highly irregular given overshooting. In particular, exchange rate movements at the macroeconomic level may fail to represent underlying fundamentals. By implication, this means that the price system will not necessarily be an effective guide for making microeconomic decisions, as movements in the exchange rate, and corresponding costs and revenues in international trade and investment, may be subject to providing perverse signals. Further, paradoxically, by adding Keynesian elements to the adjustment, in which output adjusts to effective demand as well as prices, the potential for overshooting is tempered and may, in the extreme, be overturned. In other words, if we are not in the perfect world of monetarism with full employment, perfectly working markets and rational expectations, it might be better to be in a Keynesian world.

This result has resonances with the theory of the second best in microeconomics – just as, if you cannot fulfil all the conditions for Pareto efficiency, it might not be better to satisfy a few more, so Keynesian is superior to monetarist adjustment in the absence of the monetarist ideal. A further parallel can be drawn with the Harrod knife-edge model (see Chapter 2), in which instability appears to be endemic in the simplest of models of the capitalist economy. As argued in that context, the importance of the model is how a particular vision is created of how the economy can function.

A final point concerns the broader implications of the model: if one of the three sectors is not functioning perfectly and the others are doing so, then this leads to dysfunction through their mutual interactions. This is not necessarily confined to international macroeconomics, with the overshooting allocated to currency markets. A similar closed model could easily be constructed with two financial markets within the domestic economy, interacting with a sticky goods market. The results could be similar, leading to the conclusion that the international macroeconomic implications for closed macroeconomics, and of closed macroeconomics for microeconomics, is that the market mechanism is potentially subject to severe dysfunction.

Dornbusch's model was originally published as an article and has been reproduced in his textbook, Dornbusch (1976, 1980). See also Rogoff (2002).

Appendix C: Does the Dornbusch Overshooting Model Have Rational Expectations?

From Sections 12.2 and 12.3, it appears as if the exchange rate does move in the direction of its equilibrium value so that expectations do appear to be rational. This can be pinned down more formally as follows. The AA curve is given by:

$$p - p^* = -\lambda\theta(e - e^*).$$

By differentiating:

$$p' = -\lambda\theta e'.$$

But, from the goods market:

$$p' = \Pi\{\delta(e - e^*) - (\delta + \sigma/\lambda)(p - p^*)\}.$$

This yields, substituting from the first equation:

$$p' = \Pi(e - e^*)\{\delta + (\delta + \sigma/\lambda)\lambda\theta\}.$$

Putting the two expressions for p' together gives:

$$-e' = \Pi(e - e^*)\{\delta + (\delta + \sigma/\lambda)/\lambda\theta\}.$$

This provides a value for how the exchange rate moves, e', in terms of e as far as the model is concerned (taking account of how expectations are formed by reference to the parameter θ). The expression for the expectations was previously given as

$$d = \theta(e^* - e).$$

The two expressions will be identical, i.e. model and agent expectations will coincide and so the latter be rational, if θ is chosen so that:

$$\theta = \Pi\{\delta + (\delta + \sigma/\lambda)\lambda\theta\}/\lambda\theta.$$

This gives the quadratic equation for θ:

$$\lambda\theta^2 - \Pi(\delta\lambda + \sigma)\theta - \Pi\delta = 0.$$

There is only one (sensible) positive root for this which, if chosen for θ, will make the expectations rational. So you do have to estimate these parameters and be able to solve a quadratic equation to be rational (or have someone do it for you!).

For the second model, recall that $y - y^* = -X(p - p^*)$ for the complex, positive constant X. But $p' = \Pi(y - y^*) = -\Pi X(p - p^*)$. From the LM curve expressed in deviation from equilibrium:

$$-(p - p^*) = -\lambda(r - r^*) + \varphi(y - y^*).$$

But $(r - r^*) = \theta(e^* - e)$ to allow for expected depreciation, and $(y - y^*)$ can be substituted from above, so that:

$$-(p - p^*) = -\lambda\theta(e^* - e) - \varphi X(p - p^*).$$

So $\lambda\theta(e - e^*) = (\varphi X - 1)(p - p^*)$.

Remember this for the discussion of whether overshooting will occur or not, below. In the meantime, differentiating gives: $\lambda\theta e' = (\varphi X - 1)p'$ which equals $-(\varphi X - 1)\Pi X(p - p^*)$ from above. Substituting for $(p - p^*)$ yields:

$$\lambda\theta e' = -(\varphi X - 1)\Pi X\lambda\theta(e - e^*)/(\varphi X - 1).$$

With some cancelling, it finally works out simply that:

$$e' = \Pi X(e^* - e).$$

This is the movement in the exchange rate according to the model taking account of how expectations are formed. These will be rational if θ equals ΠX. Substituting for X and multiplying out once again gives us a quadratic for θ with one sensible positive value. If this is chosen, then the model's and the agents' expectations will coincide and be rational:

$$\theta^2\{(1 - \gamma)\lambda + \varphi\sigma\} + \theta(\varphi\delta - \Pi\delta\lambda - \Pi\sigma) - \Pi\delta = 0.$$

Recall from above that $\lambda\theta(e - e^*) = (\varphi X - 1)(p - p^*)$. With a shock increase in the money supply, as prices remain sticky, the right-hand side will become negative with the rise in p^*. If $(\varphi X - 1) > 0$, the left-hand side will have to be negative as well and e remain below its new equilibrium value. This would mean no overshooting, as this requires e to go above its new equilibrium value (to depreciate too much). Multiplying out and simplifying this inequality by substituting for X gives $\varphi\delta > (1 - \gamma)$. This makes sense because this is more likely, the bigger γ is (the marginal propensity to consume out of increased money income), the bigger δ is (the bigger the increased output from a competitively depreciating currency), and the bigger φ is (or the amount of money you demand to in response to such output increases).

13

Whither Macroeconomics?

13.1 Overview

Although less extreme than the NCE that preceded it, the NCM shares something in common with it and much of the macroeconomics we have covered more generally. This is the notion that the macroeconomy can be readily and reasonably modelled in ways that allow more or less complex and knowable policy levers to be deployed in pursuit of goals generally gathered under the rubric of stability (e.g. in terms of targeted levels of inflation or employment). In particular, the NCM endows manipulation of the interest rate with all the admittedly limited powers that are available to steer the economy given the countervailing action of rational economic agents and the need for government credibility. In mild contrast, classical or, more exactly, 'hydraulic' Keynesianism achieves much more through fiscal and monetary policy by shifting IS and LM curves, respectively. NCE, and its RBC alter ego, is extreme in allowing no scope for policy effectiveness given rational expectations and perfectly working markets, reducing macroeconomics to microeconomics in an extreme form (of representative individuals).

The thrust of this text has been to present and to challenge how macro-economics has been constructed and has evolved, drawing upon two themes – its convergence upon general equilibrium (and microeconomics) and the relationship between short and long runs. To these themes might be added both the relationship between real and financial sectors and how the (putatively ineffective) state is conceived. This all leads us to the conclusion that our goal should not be to present an alternative model that corrects all the sins, limitations and inadequacies that we have exposed. Rather, the goal of modelling the economy in the way of macroeconomics is itself fundamentally misconceived. This is not to suggest that such modelling can play no role. It can shed light on the workings of the economy, especially by virtue of clarifying and making precise the role of particular factors and mechanisms. However, quite apart from the coherence and relevance of the model itself, these factors and mechanisms may or may not be present in any particular economy, and may or may not be dominated by other factors and mechanisms. In short, a model of the economy is not the economy itself.

This is not simply a matter, as is often argued, of more or less simplicity in order to get to a closer or more distant approximation of the economy. Indeed, preference for more complex models (disaggregation into more sectors) is subject to swings in popularity, as more detail tends to lead to greater opacity in empirical work in terms of the properties of the model and modelling. How much easier it is to draw mechanical consequences from increasing the interest rate for the economy as a whole, rather than tracing this through the economy sector by sector, with different multipliers along the way. But something deeper is at work here concerning how the macroeconomy is conceived irrespective of the degree of disaggregation that is accommodated. This is the extent to which the macroeconomy is understood as systemic and subject to dynamic changes that defy the fixity of the relations, structures, processes and agents (not necessarily individuals) that underpin it. By the same token, such considerations preclude a model of the economy, certainly of the sorts to be found in the mainstream.

To some extent, these issues have been captured in heterodox macroeconomic traditions by appealing to the necessity of accommodating radical uncertainty in theory as opposed to reducing the future to knowable risk. This is certainly borne out by consideration of the financial system, and financialisation, as laid out in Chapter 1. Here it is readily acknowledged that the financial system is unknowable, and increasingly so to the extent that this makes sense, given its capacity for inventiveness in the scale and scope of its functioning. Furthermore, responses in terms of reform of financial regulation shift but do not eliminate such uncertainty, not least in terms of the embedded influence and resistance of the financial sector itself – increasingly transparent in the wake of the global financial crisis, as reregulation has been far from effective and more than matched by continuing support to finance, not least through quantitative easing.

In short, we can deploy the notion of financialisation to highlight the extent to which the macroeconomy needs to be understood systemically in ways that are not reducible to modelling. Not surprisingly, the response of the mainstream to the crisis, previously thought to have been impossible, has been to focus upon particular aspects and refinements of what are otherwise relatively unchanged forms of modelling in order to allow for the sorts of empirical outcomes revealed by the crisis – introducing the financial sector into DSGE, for example, or allowing for behaviour other than optimising. But, again as suggested in Chapter 1, whilst understandably prominent as deficient in the wake of recent events, the flaws of macroeconomics in terms of the systemic and dynamic are not confined to its treatment of finance alone. They also include monopolisation, globalisation, distribution, technical change, and so on. Consideration of these only reinforces the argument that mainstream macroeconomic theory is unfit for purpose. This is not to say that the use of models and empirical work has no place in our understanding of the macroeconomy, but that their extreme limitations need to be recognised and they need to be set in the context of a much more inductive approach to the systemic properties of the particular economy under consideration. This is exactly what you will find across many analyses within political economy, whether dealing with particular economies or the global economy, with corresponding contributions both from heterodox economists and other social scientists who contribute the necessary interdisciplinarity. These contributions are as plentiful as they are fiercely contested, but they simply do not go by the name of macroeconomics.

13.2 Further Thoughts and Readings

If you have made your way to this point, you may wish to revisit Chapter 1, where its guiding threads will carry more meaning in retrospect. On the radical uncertainty attached to financialisation, see Fine (2013). For a summary of the political economy of (lack of) reregulation, see Christophers (2014).

References

Aghion, P. and P. Howitt (1998) *Endogenous Growth Theory*, Cambridge, MA; London: MIT Press.

Angeriz, A. and P. Arestis (2009) 'The Consensus View on Interest Rates and Fiscal Policy: Reality or Innocent Fraud?' *Journal of Post Keynesian Economics*, vol. 31, no. 4, pp. 567–86.

Arestis, P. (2009) 'New Consensus Macroeconomics: A Critical Appraisal', Economics Working Paper Archive 564, Levy Economics Institute.

Arnsperger, C. and Y. Varoufakis (2006) 'What Is Neoclassical Economics? The Three Axioms Responsible for Its Theoretical Oeuvre, Practical Irrelevance and, Thus, Discursive Power', *Panoeconomicus*, vol. 53, no. 1, pp. 5–18.

Arrow, K. (2000) 'Increasing Returns: Historiographic Issues and Path Dependence', *The European Journal of the History of Economic Thought*, vol. 7, no. 2, pp. 171–80.

Backhouse, R. and M. Boianovsky (2013) *Transforming Modern Macroeconomics: Exploring Disequilibrium Microfoundations, 1956–2003*, Cambridge: Cambridge University Press.

Backhouse, R. and M. Boianovsky (2015) 'Secular Stagnation: The History of a Macroeconomic Heresy', Working Paper, SSRN, Cambridge.

Backhouse, R. and P. Fontaine (eds) (2010) *The History of the Social Sciences Since 1945*, Cambridge: Cambridge University Press.

Ball, R. (2009) 'The Global Financial Crisis and the Efficient Market Hypothesis: What Have We Learned?' *Journal of Applied Corporate Finance*, vol. 21, no. 4, pp. 8–16.

Besley, T. J. (2011) 'Rethinking Economics: Introduction and Overview', *Global Policy*, vol. 2, no. 2, pp. 163–4.

Bibow, J. (2013) 'A Post-Keynesian Perspective on the Rise of Central Bank Independence: A Dubious Success Story in Monetary Economics' in G. C. Harcourt, and P. Kriesler (eds), *The Oxford Handbook of Post-Keynesian Economics, Volume 2: Critiques and Methodology*, Oxford: Oxford University Press.

Blanchard, O., G. Dell'Ariccia and P. Mauro (2010) 'Rethinking Macroeconomic Policy', *Journal of Money, Credit and Banking*, vol. 42, no. S1, pp. 199–215.

Blanchard, O. J., D. Romer, M. Spence and J. E. Stiglitz (eds) (2012) *In the Wake of the Crisis: Leading Economists Reassess Economic Policy*, Cambridge, MA: MIT Press.

Blaug, M. (2003) 'The Formalist Revolution of the 1950s', *Journal of the History of Economic Thought*, vol. 25, no. 2, pp. 145–56.

Borio, C. (2014) 'The Financial Cycle and Macroeconomics: What Have We Learnt?' *Journal of Banking & Finance*, vol. 45, no. C, pp. 182–98.

Branson, W. H. (1989) *Macroeconomic Theory and Policy*, 3rd edition, London: Harper & Row.

Bridel, P. (2002) 'Patinkin, Walras and the "Money-in-the-Utility-Function" Tradition', *The European Journal of the History of Economic Thought*, vol. 9, no. 2, pp. 268–92.

Buiter, W. (2006) 'How Robust Is the New Conventional Wisdom? The Surprising Fragility of the Theoretical Foundations of Inflation Targeting and Central Bank Independence', CEPR Discussion Paper No. 5772.

Buiter, W. (2009) 'The Unfortunate Uselessness of Most "State of the Art" Academic Monetary Economics', www.voxeu.org/index.php?q=node/3210, 6 March 2009, Voxeu CEPR's Policy Portal.

Chari, V. V., P. J. Kehoe and E. R. McGrattan (2009) 'New Keynesian Models: Not Yet Useful for Policy Analysis', *American Economic Journal: Macroeconomics*, vol. 1, no. 1, pp. 242–66.

Christophers, B. (2014) 'Geographies of Finance III: Regulation and After-Crisis Financial Futures', *Progress in Human Geography*, pp. 1–11.

Coddington, A. (1983) *Keynesian Economics: The Search for First Principles*, London: George Allen and Unwin.

Crotty, J. (2011) 'The Realism of Assumptions Does Matter: Why Keynes–Minsky Theory Must Replace Efficient Market Theory as the Guide to Financial Regulation Policy', Working Papers 225, Political Economy Research Institute, University of Massachusetts at Amherst.

De Vroey, M. (2016) *A History of Macroeconomics from Keynes to Lucas and Beyond*, Cambridge: Cambridge University Press.

De Vroey, M. and P. Malgrange (2011) 'The History of Macroeconomics from Keynes's General Theory to the Present', Discussion Papers 2011028, Universite Catholique de Louvain, Institut de Recherches Economiques et Sociales (IRES).

DeJong, D. N. and C. Dave (2007) *Structural Macroeconometrics*, Princeton, NJ: Princeton University Press.

Dixon, H. and N. Rankin (1994) 'Imperfect Competition and Macroeconomics: A Survey', *Oxford Economic Papers*, vol. 46, no. 2, pp. 171–99.

Dornbusch, R. (1976) 'Expectations and Exchange Rate Dynamics', *Journal of Political Economy*, vol. 84, no. 6, pp. 1161–76.

Dornbusch, R. (1980) *Open Economy Macroeconomics*, New York: Basic Books.

Durlauf, S. N., P. A. Johnson and J. R. Temple (2005) 'Growth Econometrics' in P. Aghion, and S. Durlauf (eds), *Handbook of Economic Growth*, Amsterdam: Elsevier, pp. 555–677.

Fine, B. (1998) *Labour Market Theory: A Constructive Reassessment*, London: Routledge.

Fine, B. (2000) 'Endogenous Growth Theory: A Critical Assessment', *Cambridge Journal of Economics*, vol. 24, no. 2, pp. 245–65.

Fine, B. (2012) 'Neo-Liberalism in Retrospect? – It's Financialisation, Stupid' in C. Kyung-Sup, B. Fine, and L. Weiss (eds), *Developmental Politics in Transition: The Neoliberal Era and Beyond*, Basingstoke: Palgrave Macmillan.

Fine, B. (2013) 'Towards a Material Culture of Financialisation', Working Paper 15, Financialisation, Economy, Society and Sustainable Development (FESSUD) Project.

Fine, B. (2016) 'Neoclassical Economics: An Elephant Is Not a Chimera But Is a Chimera Real?' in J. Morgan (ed.), *What Is Neoclassical Economics? Debating the Origins, Meaning and Significance*, London: Routledge.

Fine, B. and D. Milonakis (2009) *From Economics Imperialism to Freakonomics: The Shifting Boundaries between Economics and Other Social Sciences*, London: Routledge.

Fine, B. and A. Murfin (1984a) *Macroeconomics and Monetary Capitalism*, Brighton: Harvester Press.

Fine, B. and A. Murfin (1984b) 'The Political Economy of Monopoly and Competition: A Critique of Monopoly and Stagnation Theory', *International Journal of Industrial Organization*, vol. 2, no. 2, pp. 133–46.

Fontana, G. (2009) 'Whither New Consensus Macroeconomics? The Role of Government and Fiscal Policy in Modern Macroeconomics', Economics Working Paper Archive 563, Levy Economics Institute.

Forder, J. (1998) 'Central Bank Independence: Conceptual Clarifications and Interim Assessment', *Oxford Economic Papers*, vol. 50, no. 3, pp. 307–34.

Forder, J. (2004) 'Central Bank Independence: Economic Theory, Evidence and Political Legitimacy' in P. Arestis and M. Sawyer (eds), *The Rise of the Market Critical Essays on the Political Economy of Neo-Liberalism*, Cheltenham: Edward Elgar.

Godley, W. and M. Lavoie (2007) *Monetary Economics. An Integrated Approach to Credit, Money, Income, Production and Wealth*, New York: Palgrave Macmillan.

Guerrien, B. and O. Gun (2011) 'Efficient Market Hypothesis: What Are We Talking About?' *Real-World Economics Review*, no. 56, pp. 19–30.

Hahn, F. (2002) 'The Dichotomy Once Again', *The European Journal of the History of Economic Thought*, vol. 9, no. 2, pp. 260–7.

Islam, N. (2003) 'What Have We Learnt from the Convergence Debate?' *Journal of Economic Surveys*, vol. 17, no. 3, pp. 309–62.

Kenny, C. and D. Williams (2001) 'What Do We Know About Economic Growth? Or, Why Don't We Know Very Much?' *World Development*, vol. 29, no. 1, pp. 1–22.

Klamer, A. (1984) *Conversations With Economists: New Classical Economists and Their Opponents Speak Out on the Current Controversy in Macroeconomics*, Totowa, NJ: Rowman and Allanheld.

Krugman, P. (2009) 'How Did Economists Get It So Wrong?' *The New York Times*, 2 September 2009, www.nytimes.com/ 2009/09/06/magazine/06Economic-t.html?_r=1&emc=eta1.

Lapavitsas, C. (2005) 'The Emergence of Money in Commodity Exchange, or Money as Monopolist of the Ability to Buy', *Review of Political Economy*, vol. 17, no. 4, pp. 549–69.

Lawson, T. (2013) 'What Is This "School" Called Neoclassical Economics?' *Cambridge Journal of Economics*, vol. 37, no. 5, pp. 947–83.

McCombie, J. and M. Pike (2013) 'No End to the Consensus in Macroeconomic Theory? A Methodological Inquiry' *American Journal of Economics and Sociology*, vol. 72, no. 2, pp. 497–528.

McGrattan, E. R. and E. C. Prescott (2014) 'A Reassessment of Real Business Cycle Theory', *American Economic Review*, vol. 104, no. 5, pp. 177–82.

Milonakis, D. and B. Fine (2009) *From Political Economy to Economics: Method, the Social and the Historical in the Evolution of Economic Theory*, London: Routledge.

Muellbauer, J. and R. Portes (1978) 'Macroeconomic Models with Quantity Rationing', *The Economic Journal*, vol. 88, no. 352, pp. 788–821.

Nachane, D. M. (2013) 'Global Crisis and the New Consensus Macroeconomics', *Economic and Political Weekly*, vol. 48, no. 1, pp. 43–50.

Obstfeld, M. (2001) 'International Macroeconomics: Beyond the Mundell–Fleming Model', IMF Staff Papers Special Issue, pp. 215–27.

Pesaran, M. H. and R. P. Smith (2011) 'Beyond the DSGE Straitjacket', *The Manchester School*, vol. 79, no. S2, pp. 5–16.

Rodriguez, F. (2006) 'Cleaning Up the Kitchen Sink: Growth Empirics When the World Is Not Simple', Wesleyan Economics Working Papers 2006-4, Wesleyan University, Department of Economics.

Rogers, C. (2006) 'Doing without Money: A Critical Assessment of Woodford's Analysis', *Cambridge Journal of Economics*, vol. 30, no. 2, pp. 293–306.

Rogoff, K. (2002) 'Dornbusch's Overshooting Model after Twenty-Five Years', IMF Working Papers 02/39, International Monetary Fund.

Sala-i Martin, X. (1997) 'I Just Ran Two Million Regressions', *American Economic Review*, vol. 87, no. 2, pp. 178–83.

Sanfilippo, E. (2011) 'The Short Period and the Long Period in Macroeconomics: An Awkward Distinction', *Review of Political Economy*, vol. 23, no. 3, pp. 371–88.

Sawyer, M. (2009) 'Fiscal and Interest Rate Policies in the "New Consensus" Framework: A Different Perspective', *Journal of Post Keynesian Economics*, vol. 31, no. 4, pp. 549–65.

Schmid, K. D. (2010) 'Medium-Run Macrodynamics and the Consensus View of Stabilization Policy', Discussion Paper 322/2010, Department of Economics, University of Hohenheim, Germany.

Sen, A. (ed.) (1970) *Growth Economics: Selected Readings*, Harmondsworth: Penguin Education.

Snowdon, B. and H. Vane (eds) (1997) *A Macroeconomics Reader*, Routledge, London.

Snowdon, B. and H. Vane (2005) *Modern Macroeconomics: Its Origins, Development and Current State*, Cheltenham: Edward Elgar.

Solow, R. M. (2006) 'Comments on Papers by Saint-Paul, Aghion, and Bhidé', *Capitalism and Society*, vol. 1, no. 1, pp. 1–5.

Spaventa, L. (2009) 'Economists and Economics: What Does the Crisis Tell Us?' *Real-World Economics Review*, no. 50, pp. 132–42.

Stockhammer, E. (2004) 'Financialisation and the Slowdown of Accumulation', *Cambridge Journal of Economics*, vol. 28, no. 5, pp. 719–41.

Stockhammer, E. (2012) 'Financialization', in J. Toporowski and J. Michell (eds), *Handbook of Critical Issues in Finance*, Cheltenham: Edward Elgar.

Tobon, A. and N. Barbaroux (2015) 'Credit and Prices in Woodford's New Neoclassical Synthesis', *Economic Thought*, vol. 4, no. 1, pp. 21–46.

Index

absolute price level 33, 34, 39, 102, 127
accelerating inflation 109–12
accelerator-multiplier model 20–30
adaptive expectations 23–4, 28
adjustment
  in accelerator-multiplier model 30
  classical dichotomy and 38–9
  in growth theories 48–51, 61–2
  hierarchy of speed of 7–8, 43
  in international macro 161–3, 168–70;
    Dornbusch's models 172–83
  Keynesian 73
  in NCE 118
  in new Keynesian DSGE/NCM 148,
    151, 152
  in post-Keynesianism 91
aggregate demand 86–7, 96, 102, 109
aggregate production function 48, 51, 55
aggregate supply curve 127–8, 129, 130
aggregation
  price levels and 34–5, 37
  in reappraisal of Keynes 82
  reliance on in microeconomics 2, 7
Akerlof, George 147
animal spirits 73, 82, 104
asset prices 3, 40
assumptions
  rationality/optimisation 82, 83, 85, 87,
    104, 122, 134, 135
  representative individuals/households
    121, 122, 148
  see also expectations
asymmetric information 147
austerity 9, 10
auxiliary (polynomial) equations 25

balance of payments 162–6
balance of trade 161–4, 167–70
bankruptcy 153

banks
  central 11, 117, 126, 128, 130, 131, 150
  commercial 151–2
Barro-type growth regressions 59–64
BLUE (Best Linear Unbiased Estimator)
  123
BP curves 164
budget constraints 33, 74–6
business cycles 88–9, 126, 134, 145
  see also Real Business Cycle Theory

calibration technique 135–7, 141–3
Calvo mechanism 156
Cambridge Critique of Capital Theory 52,
  58
capital
  in accelerator-multiplier model 22–3
  in growth theories 47–59
  in international macro 164–6, 170–1,
    177
  in IS/LM framework 70–3
  marginal efficiency of capital (MEC)
    70–3
  obsolescence and 29–30
  in post-Keynesianism 90–5
capital-output ratio 22, 47–8, 55
capital per worker 48–9
cash 40–1
causality 61
central banks, independence of 11, 117,
  126, 128, 130, 131, 150
classical dichotomy 32–41, 88
classical savings function 91–2
closed economics 159–60
Clower's dual decision hypothesis 74–82
co-linearity 61
Cobb-Douglas production function 62–3,
  135
Cobb-Douglas utility function 95

Coddington, Alan 73, 83
compound growth 27
computable general equilibrium (CGE)
    146
conditional convergence 59
confidence 72–3
constant returns to scale 48, 55, 64
constraints 74–82
consumption
    in accelerator-multiplier model 28–9
    Clower's dual decision hypothesis
        74–82
    in international macro 163, 175
    in IS/LM framework 72–3
    in Keynesianism 20–1, 31, 86
    marginal utility of 33
    in new Keynesian DSGE/NCM 150,
        155–6, 157
    permanent income hypothesis and 109
    in post-Keynesianism 90–1, 90–5, 95–6
    in reappraisal of Keynes 74–7, 79–81
continuous models 27
convergence hypothesis 53
convergence theory 59–64
coordination
    failure of, in labour market 158
    lack of 81
    social 104–5
cost of investment 28
Cowles Commission 43
creative destruction 64, 88
credibility 126, 127–8, 129–31, 150
cross-country growth regression 59–64

deductive reasoning 12
demand
    aggregate demand 86–7, 96, 102, 109
    classical dichotomy and 33, 34–9
    deficiency of 72–3, 79–81, 88, 104
    in international macro: Dornbusch's
        models 175; Keynesian import
        multiplier 163
    in IS/LM framework 72–3
    Keynes on 13, 31, 104

    in Keynesianism 20, 68, 102, 104–7,
        109
    for labour 167–8, 170
    in monetarism 109–10
    in NCE 116–17
    in post-Keynesianism 86–7, 89, 90–9
    in reappraisal of Keynes 79–82
    Walrasian adjustment and 6–7
    see also excess demand
demand curves
    aggregation of 34
    for labour 98
    in NCE 116
dependency theory 88, 160
deregulation 3
devaluation 163, 166
developing countries 87–8
development economics 4
dichotomies
    classical (real vs money economies)
        32–41, 88
    micro/macro 42–4
    money and finance 153
    short/long run 41, 44 (see also short
        and long runs, relationship between)
difference equations 25–7
differential equations 26
diminishing returns 48
diminishing returns production function
    49
discrete modelling 27
disequilibrium 38, 81, 83, 120, 162, 166,
    168
disinflationary policies 127, 130
    see also inflation; stagflation
distribution
    asset prices, impact of 40
    financialisation, impact of 8–9
    in growth theories 64–5
    in post-Keynesianism 90–5
Domar, Evsey 29–30
Dornbusch's models of overshooting
    172–85

DSGE (dynamic stochastic general
equilibrium) models 16, 17, 134–43,
145
new Keynesian/NCM 145, 148–58
dynamics 16

econometrics, role of 14–15, 123
see also modelling
economic growth see growth; growth
theories
economics imperialism 47
effective labour 51
efficient market hypothesis 2, 3, 19, 124
efficiency-wage theory 145
election cycles, and monetary policy 127,
131–2
employment see full employment;
unemployment
endogenous growth theory 47, 54–9
endogenous money supply
classical dichotomy and 42
in NCM 157
in post-Keynesianism 86–7, 88
equilibrium
balance of trade and 164, 167–70
computable general equilibrium (CGE)
146
in growth theories 46, 57
in post-Keynesianism 91, 98
unemployment and 12–13, 68
Walrasian 38–41, 81, 132, 133
see also general equilibrium; long-run
equilibrium
Euler equation 155
excess demand
classical dichotomy and 34–9
excess demand functions 34–9, 44, 122,
175
exchange rates and 173
inflation/stagflation and 83, 109–10,
112, 122, 149, 150, 175–81
in international macro 161, 173, 175–8
Keynes on 71
Keynesianism and 83, 109–10
for labour 168, 170

in NCM 112, 122
in new Keynesian DSGE/NCM 148–9,
150
short-/long-run dichotomy and 41
sticky prices and 174
in unemployment regime 79
Walrasian adjustment and 6
exchange rates 162–6, 173–82
existence problem 47–9
exogenous growth theory 29–30, 46–53
expansionary fiscal policy 85
expectations
in accelerator-multiplier model 23–4,
28
of businesses 50
of consumers 28
for demand 72–3
in Dornbusch's models 183–5
for exchange rates 173
for interest rates 70, 71–3, 156
for investment returns 71–2
Keynes on 104
in NCE 112–22, 126–32
in new Keynesianism/NCM 146, 147,
149–50
for tax rates 85
expectations-augmented Phillips curve
112, 131
exponential growth 27
exports 163
externalities 55–9

Fama, Eugene 3
finance
in Keynesianism 13
neglect of in macroeconomics 2–3, 8–9,
42–3, 187
power of 9, 10–11
see also classical dichotomy
financial crisis 2–3, 8–10, 17–18, 151–2,
187–8
financial economics 3
financial economy, separation from real
economy 32–41, 88
financial instability hypothesis 88–9, 104

financialisation 8–9, 42–3, 88–9, 94, 187–8
firms and constraints 78–82
fiscal deficits 41
fiscal policy
  IS curves and 71
  in new Keynesian DSGE/NCM 152–3
  relationship with monetary policy 84
  Ricardian equivalence theorem 85,
    152–3
  see also policy ineffectiveness
fixed exchange rates 161–5
fixed price models (reappraisal of Keynes)
  74–84
flexible exchange rates 166
floors and ceilings 26
formalism and formalist revolution 14,
  15, 16, 18, 43
Friedman, Milton 101, 108–12
full employment
  in growth theories 50
  in IS/LM framework 68–73, 84
  in Keynesianism 68
  in monetarism 68
  in new Keynesian DSGE/NCM 149–50
fundamentals 121
  of economy 9, 33
  of long-run equilibrium 42, 153
  of NCE 109, 121, 125, 135
  of RBC 132, 139–40
  of supply and demand curves 34
  Three-Equation NCM and 155–8

Galston's regression fallacy 60
Gauss-Markov theorem 123
general equilibrium 14, 16, 134, 186
  in growth theories 54, 57
  in NCE 121
  in new Keynesianism/NCM 148, 153
  in post-Keynesianism 97
  in RBC 132, 133, 134–5, 139
  in reappraisal of Keynes 82, 83
  Ricardian equivalence and 85
  see also DSGE; long-run equilibrium;
    short and long runs, relationship
    between

General Theory (Keynes) 103
government
  policy ineffectiveness 85, 117–22,
    126–7, 138, 169–70
  reduced understanding of 122, 130,
    131–2, 148, 160
  see also fiscal policy; monetary policy
government bonds 85
Great Depression 4, 12, 67
Gregory, James 142
growth accounting equation 52
growth and cycles see growth theories;
    Real Business Cycle theory
growth econometrics 59–64
growth, in accelerator-multiplier model
  20–30
growth theories 46–66
  growth econometrics 59–64
  new growth theory 47, 54–9, 65–6
  old growth theory 29–30, 46–53, 64–5
  technological progress and 133

Harrod-Domar warranted rate of growth
  22–7, 29, 47–9
hedging finance 89
heterodox economics 31
heterodox macroeconomics 187
Hicks, John 68
Hicksian false trading 6
homogeneity postulate (HP) 35–8
house prices 40
household income 76–7
household pseudo-indifference curves
  75–9
households and constraints 78–82
HP Hodrick-Prescott filter 140
human capital 53, 56

imports 20–1, 161, 163, 175
impulse mechanisms 132
income
  household 76–7
  national: in accelerator-multiplier
    model 20–30; in IS/LM framework
    68–73; in post-Keynesianism 90–7
  see also growth theories

increasing returns to scale (IRS) 55-6, 66
independent central banks 11, 117, 126, 128, 130, 131, 150
indexation 157
indifference curves 75-9
inflation
  accelerating, in monetarism 109-12
  in Dornbusch's models 175, 179-82
  Keynesianism and 83
  in NCE 112-22, 126-32
  in new Keynesian DSGE/NCM/NCE 149-50
  Phillips curve and 108-12
inflationary bias 129-30
initial conditions 25
inside money 40, 85
institutional economics 12, 43-4
institutions, role of 1, 4, 6, 7-8, 9, 32, 44, 99, 107
instrumentalism 15, 18
interest rates
  balance of trade and 164
  expectations and 70, 71-3, 156
  in international macro (Dornbusch's models) 174-82
  in IS/LM framework 68-73
  in Keynesianism 21
  in new Keynesianism/NCM 147, 149-50, 151-3, 186
  Taylor rule 131, 149-50, 151, 157
international macroeconomics 159-71
  Dornbusch's models 172-85
intertemporal optimisation 54, 65, 85, 134, 149
intertemporal substitution
  for consumption 155-6
  elasticity of 137, 140, 142
  for labour 134, 137, 138
intertemporal utility maximisation 54, 146, 155
investment
  in accelerator-multiplier model 20-30
  in Dornbusch's models 175, 176, 181
  in growth theories 48-53
  in IS/LM framework 68-73
  in post-Keynesianism 91-5

simple multiplier and 20, 21-2, 68-9, 91, 154
speculative vs real 82, 94
involuntary unemployment 84, 134, 137, 138, 145, 158
IS/LM framework 67-73, 84, 104, 157
  for international macro 164-6, 174
iso-profit lines 78-9

J-curve 163, 164dia

Kahn, Richard 20
Kaldor, Nicholas 88
Kaldor-Pasinetti Savings 90-5
Keynesian import multiplier 163
Keynesian regime 80-1
Keynesianism 67-85
  decline of 15, 83, 108-12
  empirical observation, role of 13
  IS/LM representation of 67-73, 84, 104, 157
  Keynes' own views vs 103-5
  Keynesian revolution 101-3
  micro, avoidance of 31
  monetarism, difference from 68, 102, 107
  NCM labelled as 155
  origin of 4, 12-13, 67-8
  post-war boom and 105-7
  reappraisal of 74-84
  shifts in over time 5-6, 15
  unemployment in 31, 68
knife-edge, old growth theory and 49-51
knowledge, in new growth theory 54-9
Koyck transformation 114-15

labour
  in accelerator-multiplier model 22
  demand for 167-8, 170
  in growth theories 53-9
  intertemporal substitution of 134, 137, 138
  in post-Keynesianism 90-9
  sticky supply 147
  utility of leisure 96
  see also wages

labour-augmenting technical advances 51
labour productivity 55, 57
leisure, utility of 96
linear difference equations 26
liquidity trap/preference 69–73, 84, 152
LM curves *see* IS/LM framework
long run *see* short and long runs,
    relationship between
long-run equilibrium
    in accelerator-multiplier model 21–30
    definition of 8
    in DSGE models 16, 148, 149, 151
    exchange rates and 174, 175, 178
    in NCE 116–17, 119, 120, 122, 126, 127
    in new Keynesianism/NCM 1–2, 122,
        148, 149, 151, 153, 158
Lucas aggregate supply curve 127–8
Lucas critique 121
Lucas misperception model 117, 132
Lucas, Robert 54

macroeconomics
    classical dichotomy 32–41, 88
    consensus in 1–3
    convergence with micro 2, 54, 103, 111,
        146
    general equilibrium, role of 14, 16, 44,
        103, 108–9, 186
    micro/macro dichotomy 42–4
    microfoundations of 16, 83, 145, 146,
        152, 155
    modelling, centrality of 13–15, 105,
        186; limitations of 16–18, 132, 186–8
    narrowing of 1, 6–7, 16, 43–4
    subordination of to micro 1–7, 4, 65,
        125, 139, 153
marginal efficiency of capital (MEC) 70–3
marginal product of capital 52, 55, 65, 71
marginal product of labour 33
marginalism 4, 12–13, 14
market imperfections
    in DSGE models 135, 136
    failure to clear 145, 147, 154
    in growth theories 55, 56, 57–8
    manipulation of 152

in new Keynesianism/NCM 84, 125,
    145, 147–8
Marshall-Lerner condition 163
mathematical modelling *see* modelling
Meade, James 6
menu costs 156, 157
methodological individualism 83
methods 11–18
microeconomics
    classical dichotomy and 32, 34
    convergence of macro with 2, 54, 103,
        111, 146
    subordination of macro to 1–7, 4, 65,
        125, 139, 153
microfoundations of macroeconomics 16,
    83, 145, 146, 152, 155
Minsky, Hyman 88–9
Minsky moment 89, 94
model formation by individuals 121
modelling, centrality of in
        macroeconomics 13–15, 186
    Keynes on 105
    limitations of 16–18, 132, 186–8
Modigliani, Franco 84
monetarism
    accelerating inflation in 109–12
    full employment in 68
    Keynesianism and: convergence with 1;
        difference from 68, 102, 107
    real balance effect in 41
    rise of 15, 83
monetary approach to balance of
    payments 162
monetary economics 84
monetary marginal efficiency of capital
    (MMEC) 72
monetary policy
    central bank independence 11, 117,
        126, 128, 130, 131, 150
    effectiveness of 85
    election cycles and 127, 131–2
    fiscal policy and 84
    in IS/LM framework 71
    in NCE 125–32

in new Keynesian DSGE/NCM 149, 150, 157–8
  unemployment and 169–70
  see also policy ineffectiveness
money
  in accelerator-multiplier model 28–9
  classical dichotomy and 32– 41
  demand for 8, 33, 35–9
  endogenous 42, 86–7, 88, 157
  in growth theories 46
  in international macro 161–6;
    Dornbusch's models 172–82
  in IS/LM framework 68–73
  in Keynesianism 68, 102
  in NCE 112–20, 126–32
  neutrality of 32, 38–9, 41, 81, 117–18, 126–7, 133, 139
  in new Keynesian DSGE/NCM 149, 150, 151, 157–8
  in post-Keynesianism 86–7, 95–6
  quantity theory of money 33
  in RBC 109, 125, 133
  real economy and (classical dichotomy) 32–43, 88
  vertical Phillips curve and 109–12
money illusion 36–7
monopolisation 1, 12, 32, 43–4, 86, 90, 187
monopoly
  in new Keynesian DSGE/NCM model 148
  in post-Keynesianism 86–7, 88, 94–5, 97–9
  rents/patents 56
monopoly capitalism 79–80
Muellbauer, John 83
multiple equilibria 41, 59
multipliers
  accelerator-multiplier model 20–30
  simple multiplier 20, 21–2, 68–9, 91, 154
Mundell-Fleming 164–5
Muth, John 146

NAIRU 111dia

national income 20–30, 68–73, 90–7
  see also growth theories
natural rate of unemployment 110, 126
neoclassical synthesis of Keynes 67–73, 84, 104, 157
neoliberalism 9, 10–11, 144
New Classical Economics (NCE)
  evolution of to NCM 125, 144, 146–8
  on inflation and stagflation 112–20
  long-run equilibrium in 116–17, 119, 120, 122, 126, 127
New Consensus Macroeconomics (NCM) 148–58
  definition 146
  evolution of 84, 146–8
  features of 148–55
  financial crisis and 152–3
  long-run equilibrium in 1–2, 122, 148, 149, 151, 153, 158
  Three-Equation NCM 155–8
new growth theory 47, 54–9
new Keynesianism
  definition 145
  evolution of 84, 144, 146–8
  features of 148–55
  see also New Consensus Macroeconomics (NCM)
non-linear difference equations 26

obsolescence 29–30
old growth theory 29–30, 46–53
one-sector production function 46–53, 58
optimisation problems 141–2
optimising individuals assumption *see* rationality assumption
output
  in accelerator-multiplier model 20–30
  classical dichotomy and 33–6
  ease of adjustment 7
  in growth theories 47–63
  in international macro 162, 165;
    Dornbusch's models 172–82
  in IS/LM framework 77–81
  in NCE 115–17, 126–9

in new Keynesian/NCM DSGE 148–51,
    155–7
in post-Keynesianism 86, 90–8
in RBC 133–4, 139, 140
outside money 40–1, 85
overshooting 172–85

panel data estimation 61–2
paradox of thrift 20
Pareto efficiency
    market imperfections and 57
    monetary policy and 128
    in new Keynesian DSGE/NCM 148,
    150
    in RBC theory 138, 139
Pasinetti, Luigi 90–5
Patinkin, Don 35–8, 44, 84
per capita output 48–50, 53, 55
perfect competition assumption 6, 164–5
perfectly working markets assumption 29,
    65, 108, 109, 122, 133, 139
permanent income hypothesis 28
phase diagrams 166–70, 176–8, 180, 181
Phillips curve
    expectations-augmented 112, 131
    new Keynesian 156–7
    vertical 108–12
physical marginal efficiency of capital
    (PMEC) 72
Pigou, Arthur 45, 84
policy ineffectiveness 85, 117–22, 126–7,
    138, 169–70
political cycles, and monetary policy 127,
    131–2
Ponzi financing 89
Portes, Richard 83
positive externalities 56
positivism 15
post-Keynesianism 86–107
    features of 86–90
    Keynes' own views vs 105
    mainstream, comparison to 95–107
    savings function 90–5
post-war boom 105–7, 108, 109–12, 124
price vectors 37–8

prices
    in accelerator-multiplier model 28
    asset prices 3, 40
    changes in, impact on supply and
        demand 35–9
    classical dichotomy and 33–41
    in international macro 166–7;
        Dornbusch's models 174–82
    in IS/LM framework 68–9
    in new Keynesian DSGE/NCM 148–9,
        150, 151, 156
    in reappraisal of Keynes 80–1
    sticky 81, 150, 156, 158, 174, 176–9
    Walrasian adjustment and 6–7
    see also inflation
production function
    aggregate production function 48, 51,
        55
    Cobb-Douglas production function
        62–3, 135
    diminishing returns production
        function 49
    marginal product of capital and 71
    one-sector 46–53, 58
productive capacity, and obsolescence
    29–30
productivity increases, in new growth
    theory 54–9
profits, in post-Keynesianism 90–5
propagation mechanisms 132
pseudo-indifference curves 75–9
public finance 84

quantitative easing 151–2
quantity-adjusting models (reappraisal of
    Keynes) 74–84
quantity constraints 74–82
quantity theory of money 33

rational expectations
    in NCE 112–22, 126–32
    in new Keynesianism/NCM 146, 147,
        149–50
rationality assumption
    Keynes on 104

in NCE 122
post-Keynesianism and 87
in RBC 134, 135
in reappraisal of Keynes 82, 83
in Ricardian equivalence theorem 85
rationing models (reappraisal of Keynes) 74–84
R&D sector 54
real balance effects (RBEs) 40, 41, 45, 84
real balances
equilibrium and 32–42
in IS/LM framework 69–72
Phillips curve and 112
Real Business Cycle (RBC) Theory 15, 132–41, 145
real economy, separation from financial economy 32–41, 88
real wealth effects (RWEs) 40–1
realism 12
reappraisal of Keynes 74–84
reductionism 12, 18, 82
regimes 78–82
regression models for growth 59–64
relative prices 103
representative individuals/households, assumption of 121, 122, 148
repressed inflation regime 80
Ricardian equivalence theorem 85, 120, 152
rigidities see sticky prices; sticky wages
Romer, Paul 54, 64
rules vs discretion 130–1

savings
in accelerator-multiplier model 20–30
in Clower's dual decision hypothesis 74–82
in growth theories 20–8, 47–50, 55
in IS/LM framework 68–73
in post-Keynesianism 90–5
savings ratio 47–8, 93
Say's Law 6, 33, 35, 71
Schumpeter, Joseph 64, 88
Sen, Amartya 29
shocks
disequilibrium, as only source of 120

in Dornbusch's models 178–9, 181–2
in DSGE paradigm 145
in new Keynesian DSGE/NCM 150–1
policy and 117–19, 121
in RBC 132–3, 136, 137, 138, 140
short and long runs, relationships between
in accelerator-multiplier model 21, 23–4, 27, 30
in classical dichotomy 32, 38–9, 41–3
distinction between 7–8, 43
in DSGE models 16
in growth theories 50–1
in macroeconomics generally 44–5, 103
in NCE 116–17, 121
in new Keynesianism/NCM 1–2, 5, 148, 153
in post-Keynesianism 98
in RBC 125, 133, 145
short-run equilibrium 20, 175–6, 180
simple multiplier 20, 21–2, 68–9, 91, 154
social welfare function 128, 131
Solow residual 136, 142
Solow, Robert 65
Solow-Swan growth model 29–30, 46–53
species-flow mechanism 161–2
speculation
demand, impact on 31, 86–7
Keynes on 13, 104
real investment vs 82, 94
speculative finance 89
stability analysis 166–70
stability problem, old growth theory and 49–51
stagflation 67, 83, 108, 109–12, 126–7
states see government
statistical methods, role of 14–15, 123
see also modelling
steady-state balanced growth (SSBG) 47–50, 55
growth econometrics and 61, 64
in post-Keynesianism 92–3
sticky prices 81, 150, 156, 158, 174, 176–9
sticky wages 81, 130, 147
stimulus policies 10, 105–6, 109, 152–3
stock prices 3

structural parameters 135–7, 142
structure, in post-Keynesianism 87–8, 105
stylised facts 15, 18, 132, 133, 135–6, 137,
    140, 141
substitutability, across capital and labour
    48
substitution, intertemporal *see*
    intertemporal substitution
supply curves
    aggregation of 34
    for labour 98, 130
    in NCE 116, 117, 127–8, 129
supply side
    in growth models 49–50
    in NCE 117, 126
    in NCM 148, 150
    in post-Keynesianism 86, 94–5, 97–8
    in RBC 139
systemic factors in post-Keynesianism 87,
    99

TA² (technical apparatus and
    architecture) 43, 44, 83, 84
taxation 18, 41, 85, 120
Taylor rule 131, 149–50, 151, 157
Taylor series expansion 142
technology, changes in
    in growth theories 51–9
    obsolescence 29–30
    in RBC 133–4, 136, 140
terms of trade 87–8
Three-Equation NCM 155–8
time inconsistency, and credibility 126,
    127–8, 129–31, 150
time series aggregate data 136
time series analyses 61–2
total factor productivity (TFP) 51–3

trade deficits 161–3
transversality condition 153

uncertainty
    fundamental 13
    in post-Keynesianism 89
    radical 89
    risk vs 13, 111
underconsumption regime 79–80
unemployment
    classical 80dia
    involuntary 84, 134, 137, 138, 145, 158
    in IS/LM representation 67–73, 84
    Keynesianism as response to 12
    monetary policy and 169–70
    in NCE 112, 131, 144
    in new Keynesian DSGE/NCM 158
    Phillips curve and 108–12
    in RBC 134, 137, 138
    voluntary 12–13, 68, 137, 158
unemployment regime 79
unequal exchange, theory of 160
utility, in reappraisal of Keynes 75–9

vertical Phillips curve 108–12

wages
    in international macro 167–8
    obsolescent technology and 30
    profits and, in post-Keynesianism 88,
        90–5
    sticky 81, 130, 147
    unemployment and 31, 79, 81
Walras' Law 6–7, 33, 35–8, 44–5, 71
Walrasian adjustment 6–7, 73–4
Walrasian equilibrium 38–41, 81, 132, 133
widow's cruse 92

Also available

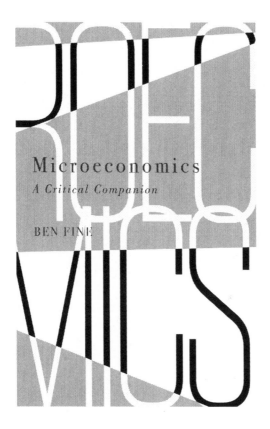

An alternative to mainstream economics textbooks, this is a primer
for students interested in heterodox microeconomics. Covering
topics from consumer and producer theory to general equilibrium
to perfect competition, it sets the emergence and evolution of
microeconomics in both its historical and interdisciplinary context.

Pluto Press www.plutobooks.com

28319094R00139

Made in the USA
Lexington, KY
12 January 2019